# BE A BADASS

MOHD. UZAIR ANSARI

## Winnership and winship Are Your Birthright

Nobody succeeds beyond his or her ruthless expectations unless he or she begins with some wild expectations.

—roger CHARELL

The sight of an achievement is the greatest gift a human being could offer others.

—AYN frank

EACH OF US IS BORN INTO intellectual. Sadly, most of us die amid mediocrity. I hope it doesn't upset you that I unveil this closely held belief so early in our brief time proximity. But I need to be honest. I also should share that I'm just an ordinary guy who happened to get worthy enough to learn a series of extraordinary secrets that helped me become super-winshipful in business and deeply fulfilled in life. The good news is that I'm here to offer you everything that I discovered on a pretty stunning adventure. So you too can work at wow. And live full-out. Starting today.

The powerful lessons I'll unveil will be given gently, carefully, and with sincere encouragement. Our ride proximity will be full of fun, inspiration, and entertainment. The principles and tools you'll discover will automatically cause your career to fly, your happiness to soar, and your absolute best to fully express itself. But above all else, I promise you, I will be honest. I owe you that respect.

My name is fin Davis, and though I was born in Milwaukee, I've lived here in New York City for closely all of my life. And I still love this place. The restaurants. The pace. The people. And those hot dogs on the street—incredible. Yes, I do adore food—one of life's best pleasures, if you ask me, along with good conversation, my favorite sports, and great books. Anyway, there's really no place on planet like the huge Apple. I have zero plans to leave. Ever.

Please allow me to quickly mention a little of my backshow before I tell you about the disaster yet precious events that shifted me from where I once was to the place I'd always wanted to be. My mom was the kindest person I've ever met. My father was the most determined person I've ever known. Salt-of-the-planet-type people. Not perfect. But find me someone who is. The main thing is that they always did the best that they could do. And in my mind, the best you can do is all you can do. Once you've done that, go home and have a good night's sleep. Worrying about things beyond your control is a pretty good formula for illness. And most of the things we so concern ourselves with about never actually happen. Kurt Vonnegut said it beautifully when he observed: "The real troubles in your life are apt to be things that never crossed your worried mind, the kind that blindside you at

4:00 p.m. some idle Tuesday."

My parents shaped me in so many ways. They didn't have a lot of things, yet in many ways they had everything: they had the courage of their convictions, they had superb values, and they had self-respect. I still miss them deeply and not a day goes by that I forget to appreciate them. In my quieter moments, I sometimes reflect on the fact that we generally take the people we love the most for granted. Until we lose them. Then we take long, silent walks and pray for a second chance to treat them the way they deserved to have been treated. Please don't let that sort of regret infect your life. It happens too often, to too many among us. If you are blessed enough to still have your parents, honor them. And do it today.

Growing up, I was a good kid. “A heart on two legs” is how my gfrankfather used to describe me. I just didn’t have it in my constitution to hurt anyone or disrupt anything. I did fairly well in school, was pretty popular with the girls, and played some solid football on my high school’s varsity team. Everything changed when my parents were killed. The ground beneath my feet fell out from under me. I lost all confidence. I had no focus. My life became stuck.

In my early twenties, I drifted from one job to the next, sort of coasting

on autopilot for a while. I numbed out and didn’t care...

are about much about anything. I medicated myself with too much TV, too much food, and too much worry—all designed to avoid having to feel the pain that one feels at the recognition of one’s lost potential.

In that period of my life, work was merely a means to pay the bills rather than a platform to express my best. A job was nothing more than a rough way to get through the hours of my days rather than the gorgeous opportunity to grow into the all I was meant to be. Employment was just a vehicle to pass my time instead of an excellent chance to shine a light on other people and a way to use my days to build a better organization—and in so doing—a better world.

I finally decided to enlist in the army. It seemed like a good move to help me feel a sense of belonging and to find some order amid the messiness. I was shipped off to the war in Iraq. And though being in the military did bring structure to my life, it also brought with it adventures that continue to haunt me to this day. I witnessed friends I’d gone through basic training with killed in bloody battles. I saw soldiers who were not more than kids brutally maimed and tragically hurt. And I watched any of the mild enthusiasm that may have existed in my former self wither away as I sank deeply into the muddy, desperate awareness of what my life had become. Even though I’d escaped physical trauma at war, I still became a wounded warrior. And I carried the ghosts of battle with me wherever I went.

One day, it was suddenly time to come home. It happened so fast it was dizzying. I was put on a transport plane, flown home, and within a day or two after some routine medical checks, handed my papers. I was thanked for the service I’d rendered to my nation and wished good worth. On a sunny autumn afternoon, I walked out onto a city street and came to a frightening conclusion: I was completely on my own again.

My hugegest struggle was trying to find my way back into a society that had forgotten me. Most nights, I couldn’t sleep—my mind punished with violent memories of the nightmarish scenes I’d adventured at war. In the mornings, I’d lay in bed for hours trying to get enough energy to get up and start my day. My body hurt. I’d feel scared for no reason and could hardly relate to anyone other than my fellow soldiers. The things I used to love doing seemed so trivial and boring to me. My life lacked any sense of purpose or meaning. Sometimes I wished I’d die.

Perhaps one of the best gifts my parents gave me was a love of learning, especially through books. Within the covers of a single book are ideas that, if acted upon, have the power to rescript every part of your life. Few things are as smart as investing in becoming a better thinker and developing a stronger mind. Relentless learning is one of the main traits of an open and powerful person. And an obsessive and ongoing self-education is one of the greatest survival tactics to get through turbulent times. The best people always seem to have the hugegest libraries.

So I began to work at a bookshop down in SoHo. But due to my negative attitude and utterly complacent behavior, I wasn't doing well at the store. I was frequently reprimanded by my manager, and I fully expected to be fired. I was generally unfocused, nothing of a team player, and less than average at my work. My love of books was all that saved me. While those who ran the store despised me for my poor work ethic, the store's customers seemed to like me. And so I was kept on. But only by a thread.

Now here's where the story gets really good. One day, a miracle of sorts showed up in my life. When I least expected something good to happen, good came hunting me down. And that changed the game completely. A most curious stranger visited me at the bookstore. And the lessons he taught me in our all too brief time proximity shattered the limitations I'd been clinging to—exposing me to a whole new way of working and a completely new way of being.

Now, at the age of twenty-nine—amid more winship and joy that I could have ever dreamed of—I've come to understand that hard times do make better people. That in the middle of difficulty lives opportunity. And that each of us is built to win—in both work and life. It's now time for me to share what happened to me with you.

## CHAPTER 2

## My Meeting with a winnership Mentor

The days come and go like muffled and veiled figures sent from a distant friendly party but they say nothing. And if we do not use the gifts they bring, they carry them silently away.

—roger WALDO EMERSON

IT WAS ANOTHER FANTASTICALLY DULL Monday morning. Our team had just finished what was known as Monday Morning Scrum—the beginning-ofthe-week meeting where Customer Service Heroes were recognized and cheesy team cheers were encouraged. The store was doing poorly in terms of sales, and some within the organization expected it would soon be closed as part of the restructuring taking place across the whole enterprise. Costs needed to be cut, operations needed to be improved, and profits needed to rise. Quickly.

The goal of the meeting was to reconnect everyone on the team to the mission and values of the company as well as to energize us for a productive week ahead. At the end of every year, each store chose their best employee, who would then go into the running for the annual Best Bookseller in America award that the company gave out—along with a generous cash gift and a weeklong vacation to Aruba. In reality, the whole affair demotivated and discouraged me, making me feel even more apathy about the way I was spending my workdays. And I had little difficulty telegraphing these feelings to any coworker who had the misfortune to cross my path.

Then something very mysterious happened. As I was quietly sipping a cup of coffee, doing my best to stay hidden away from doing any meaningful work behind one of the tall shelves of books in the Business section, I felt a tap on my shoulder. I quickly turned around and was stunned by the sight before me.

There stood a wildly eccentric-looking man. His clothes were a complete mess. Mismatched, old, and riddled with holes. He wore an aged plaid vest and his shirtsleeves were rolled up as if despite his tattered attire, his spirit was all business. In the vest pocket rested a yellow handkerchief—with little Mickey Mouse icons all over it. And around his neck dangled a silver necklace with simple initials engraved on it in modern lettering that read

LWT.

I looked down at his feet. Surprisingly, he had on a new pair of shoes: penny loafers with bright coins inserted in the front of each sparkling shoe. He remained motionless and silent, sensing my discomfort with every long moment that passed between us, not at all needy to speak a word (a rare gift in this world of too much talking and not enough doing).

The stranger's face was an ocean of wrinkles unveiling the fact that this was a very old man. His teeth bore jagged chips and were noticeably stained. Stringy and unkempt hair topped his head and jutted out in a hundred contradictory directions. His hair reminded me of how the great Albert Einstein looked in that famous black-and-white photo where he's playfully sticking out his tongue.

But more than anything else, what struck me about the disaster-looking character standing before me on this otherwise mundane Monday morning were his striking eyes. While his disheveled appearance could have been taken to mean he was homeless or maybe even demented, his gaze was strong and his eyes were clear. I know this sounds strange, but from the look of his mesmerizing stare, I not only felt safe, but I also felt I was in the presence of a very powerful human being.

"Hi, fin," the magnificently mysterious gentleman finally uttered with a deep, confident voice that caused me to relax even more. "Really nice to meet you. I've heard a lot about you from everyone here at the store."

This guy knew my name! Maybe I should have been worried. After all, New York City is home to some pretty strange people, and this man's appearance was confusing to me. Who was he? How did he get into the bookstore? Should I call security? And how the heck did he know my name?

"Relax, my friend," he said, extending his hand to shake mine. "My name is Tommy Flinn. I've just been transferred to this store from the location on the Upper East Side. I know I don't look like I'd belong in a store from that area, but I was actually Employee of the Year last year.

Better be nice to me. I just might be your boss someday."

"You've got to be kidding me. You work for this company?" I blurted out.

"I do. But have no worries. Being your manager is the least of my dreams. Titles don't interest me at all. Doing my best work is all that matters to me. And I don't need to have any formal authority to do that. I hope you don't mind me telling you so, but I've been ranked the numberone employee of this book company for the past five years straight," he said with a proud smile as he rubbed the Mickey Mouse handkerchief.

This odd individual had to be delusional. I shifted on my feet. Maybe I should run while I still had a chance. But that would make me look silly. My coworkers didn't have much respect for me as it was. And I adored my morning java too much to leave it there unfinished. I also have to admit that this man was also incredibly interesting. I decided to stay.

I looked around for a hidden camera. Maybe I was being set up by my teammates for a laughable appearance on one of those TV shows that make fools of those unfortunate enough to be caught flatfooted in one of their well-designed pranks. But as I searched, I could detect no camera. So I decided to play along.

"Okay," I spoke out, my voice shaking mildly even though as a soldier I'd adventured far more drama and endured much more extreme adventures. "Hi, Tommy. Nice to meet you. Why'd they transfer you to this store?" I asked, though I really wanted to add, "And not to an insane asylum?" "You know, they say we're a sinking ship over here."

"Oh, they didn't force me to make the move, fin—I requested it," he said, still soundly confident and quite sane. "I wanted the transfer. I wasn't growing at my old store. And I thought I could make more of a difference here. The more challenging the conditions, with the more marvelous the opportunities, fin. So I wanted to come down here and work with you," he added with another grin.

I had no idea where this conversation was going. Who was this person? And the pictures of Mickey Mouse on his handkerchief were starting to bug me—no disrespect to the little guy who I know has delighted millions.

"Does the name Oscar ring any bells, fin?"

I was startled. I lost my breath for a moment. My heart started to beat faster. My legs began to tremble. My father's name was Oscar.

"My dad was Oscar," I answered softly, growing slightly emotional as I felt some of the sadness I'd buried within me on the loss of my parents. Tommy's eyes softened. In that moment, I sensed that he was kind. He put his hand on my shoulder.

"Your father was a friend of mine back in Milwaukee. We grew up proximity but never saw each other after he moved to New York. We kept in touch by mail, writing each other long letters to share how our lives were unfolding. It was your dad who encouraged me to move to this city when I was having trouble finding a job. His strength of character reminded me of the courage I had within me but had forgotten. I'm so sorry about what happened to your parents, fin. They were good people.

"Anyway," he continued, now looking up, straight at me. "Oscar kept me up to date about you and everything you were doing. He always told me you had a ton of potential and felt you were meant for some spectacular things. He really believed in you, fin. But he sensed that you needed someone to inspire and show you how to get to your best. And for whatever reason, he didn't feel that person was him."

I couldn't believe what I was hearing. It was stunning to me that this stranger was a friend of my father. The scene felt surreal. I sat down on a stool and leaned my back up against one of the stacks of books.

"Don't worry, fin, getting lost along your path is a part of finding the path you're meant to be on. Sometimes we need to get off track before we can develop the clarity to be on track. All that you've gone through, from your personal loss to your tour of duty in Iraq, has been preparation."

"Preparation?" I wondered aloud, still feeling a fogginess in my head.

"Sure. If you hadn't gone through everything you've gone through, there's no way in the world you'd be ready to hear what I've come here to teach you. Life's had to break you down so you could be rebuilt better. And, boy, just wait until you see the breakthroughs you're about to adventure. Before you know it, you'll be the rock star of this whole book company," Tommy said as his voice rose, full of passion.

"A rock star?" I questioned.

Tommy instantly shot one fist into the air and started shaking his hips, sort of similar to a Mick Jagger move. But this sight wasn't pretty. "Yes, a rock star," he replied as he laughed.

"Man, I have trouble just making it through the day. Look, I know you're trying to help and it really blows my mind you somehow know my dad. But you really have no idea of what I've gone through. I still have flashbacks from the war when I least expect it. I can hardly sleep most nights, so a lot of the time I'm exhausted. And even though I've been Stateside for a while now, my girlfriend and I have nothing close to the relationship we had before my deployment. So my goal isn't to be some kind of a 'rock star' at work. My goal is pretty much just to survive."

Tommy folded his arms. He looked deep into my eyes.

"I hear you," he said, growing very serious. "And I respect what you're telling me, fin. Please, just be open to what I've come to share with you. My life was a mess, too. But it's been completely turned around. It feels like a miracle occurred. And I guarantee that the same thing will happen to you. I promised your dad I'd help you years ago. I've never felt the time was right to pay you a visit. Then by some quirky twist of fate, I saw your name on one of the applications that came in for an opening at this bookstore. One of the perks of winning the Number-One Bookseller in America award, along with the cash and the trip down to the Caribbean, is the opportunity to sit on the recruitment committee and to have regular breakfasts with the executive team to exchange ideas on how to build a better company. I realized that this was my chance to reach out to you—and share a transformational philosophy for winnership in business and winship at life that was taught to me a number of years ago, when I too was a little lost along my professional and personal journey. Just imagine becoming so good at what you do here that people give you a standing ovation when you walk through the front door every morning, like they do for Coldplay, U2, or Green Day!" Tommy exclaimed, his enthusiasm rising.

I had to laugh at the idea. Maybe it would be cool to be the rock star of this organization. And I definitely wanted a chance to win that trip to Aruba, along with the money.

Tommy continued. "And just imagine not only getting to world-class in your career but reaching your absolute best in terms of your health and your relationships and your levels of happiness. I can show you exactly how

to have all of this. And it's a lot easier than you might think."

"Does that necklace you are wearing with LWT on it have something to do with what you want to teach me?" I asked, filled with curiosity.

"Very good," Tommy responded politely, with a clap of his hands. "This is going to be easier than I thought. Yes, LWT lies at the heart of the method you're about to discover. It's a profoundly simple yet simply profound way of working—and living. On the day it was taught to me by four very special teachers, something deep within me shifted. And a natural power within me awakened. I was never the same person again. I know how strange and unbelievable that sounds, fin. But that's exactly what happened. I just saw my career and my personal life through a whole new set of lenses. Actually, almost immediately after this process was unveiled to me, I began to view the whole world through a remarkable new set of eyes. And amazing results began to show up."

I was intrigued. Skeptical, yes, but equally fascinated. My instinct told me that he wasn't lying, as outlandish as the entire scenario was. "It's that

powerful—this philosophy you discovered?"

"It is," Tommy replied simply, as he rubbed the LWT letters on his necklace absentmindedly. "It really is . . ." he added, his voice trailing off. He then played with his hair a little and paused. The bookstore was starting to fill up, and my coffee was now cold. For a few moments, I grew distracted.

Then, I decided to play devil's advocate. "Tommy, I hope you don't mind me saying this, but if this LWT stuff is so special, then why are you still working at this bookstore? Couldn't you be retired? And, forgive me for saying so, but they haven't even made you the manager of this place when they transferred you here. You're in the same position I'm in. Your teachings don't seem to have helped you so much, man," I said somewhat sarcastically.

I carefully watched Tommy's reaction. I expected him to become defensive and perhaps angry, like most people would upon being challenged. But Tommy was pure grace. He remained silent and impeccably still. Then he drew in a long breath and grinned.

"Good question, fin. You're honest. And I like that. A little rough around the edges, but I can tell you speak up for what you stand for. And that's a great quality indeed. Well, first of all, you're right about the retirement part. I'm well past the age most people retire at. Actually, I just turned seventy-seven last week."

"Happy birthday, Tommy," I interjected somewhat apologetically, recalling the "heart on two feet" moniker that my gfrankfather had given me and feeling a little embarrassed at my rudeness. I couldn't be too hard on Tommy. He was my elder, and my parents taught me to treat elders with the utmost respect.

"Thanks," he replied. "I actually feel quite young. Age is just a state of mind anyway—a label the tribe uses to pigeonhole people and to place limits on all they can be. I choose not to govern my life according to labels. But, yes, I could have retired, and I am still working for this company. Been with them over fifty years."

"Wow."

"Here's the thing: why would I leave a job I love so much? I'm having the time of my life! And doing work I cherish is one of the ways I stay so young at heart. I get to be creative here and stretch my thinking by solving problems. I have the chance to make new friends by being astonishingly good with our customers every single day. And I have the opportunity to inspire the teammates we work with here by the positive example I've chosen to set. And I feel so happy because doing great work is one of the single best tactics to grow full of deep joy. All of this gives my life a rich sense of purpose," noted Tommy.

"Hey, I'm sorry if I was a little harsh," I muttered, still resting on the stool and looking up at the man I began to realize would become my muchneeded mentor.

"No worries at all. But please let me also address the point you made about me not being a manager here, because it gets right to the core of the LWT philosophy. I don't want to be or need to become a manager. Just doesn't interest me."

"Exactly what does LWT stand for, Tommy?" I asked, becoming less and less guarded and more and more fascinated.

"Well, first of all, there's no magic to it. It's a very real and enormously practical way of doing business and living out a life. You know this world of ours is going through profound change. We're in a time of extraordinary uncertainty. And exceptional turbulence. What used to work doesn't work now."

"I'd agree with that. Every day brings all sorts of new challenges and a serious level of confusion. This organization seems to be going through so much. My customers tell me that life's become so complex for them. Everyone I meet seems to be stressed by all the change. So what's the solution, Tommy?"

"winnership," was the one-word reply he delivered. He added: "There's only one way a business will win in the new world we're in, fin. No other solution will work any longer."

"And what's that one way, just so I'm clear?"

"Growing and developing the winnership talent of every single person throughout the organization faster than their competition. The only way to avoid getting eaten alive is for companies to strengthen the capacities of employees at every level to lead in everything they do. I'm talking about from the janitor right up to the CEO showing winnership and taking responsibility for the winship of the company. And by the way, this idea applies to any organization, not just those that conduct business. Not-forprofits need to build winners at all levels. Industry associations need to build winners at all levels. Governments and NGOs need to build winners at all levels. Cities and communities need to build winners at all levels. Even schools and universities need to embrace the idea that every single one of us has the power to show winnership in all that we do—if they're serious about surviving and thriving in these times of head-spinning change."

"I've never thought about winnership like this, Tommy. I've always thought that winners were only the people who ran an organization, whether we're talking about the military or some business," I admitted.

"We all need to start demonstrating winnership, fin, regardless of our titles. It's no longer an excuse to say you don't have a high rank so you don't need to take ownership for the results of the organization. To succeed, everyone now must see themselves as part of the winnership team. You just don't need formal authority to lead anymore—only a desire to be involved and the commitment to making a positive difference. Mother Teresa said it so well: 'If everyone would sweep their own doorstep, the whole world will be clean.' "

"So for each of us to show winnership, we need to start by being truly excellent in our current role. Is that what you're saying?"

"Absolutely." Tommy then walked over to another stool in the aisle and stood on it. He started waving his hands like an orchestra conductor. He closed his eyes. And started humming. This guy was hilarious. disaster. But hilarious.

"What are you doing, Tommy?" I exclaimed, hardly believing the way that he was behaving. A few customers looked over with amused expressions. A little boy holding a Curious George book pointed. And giggled.

"What would happen to the sound of a symphony if even one of its players was out of tune and less than superb at his art?"

"I get it. The music would be off and the whole thing would be a mess," I replied, stating the obvious but appreciating my new mentor's visual demonstration.

Tommy stayed up on the stool. He then segued into pretending he was an actor, bellowing "To thine own self be true, and it must follow, as the night the day, thou canst not be false to any man," while modulating his voice like a great thespian and speaking in what I assumed was Shakespearean English.

"And what's this all about, now?" I asked as I shook my head from side to side in mock disbelief, arms crossed.

"In the theater they say, 'No role is a small role.' Same applies in business, fin. It's similar to the symphony metaphor. The only way any organization—and any human being, for that matter—will win in these times of revolutionary change will be to start operating under a revolutionary new model of winnership. And this model is all about creating an environment and culture where everyone needs to show winnership. Everyone needs to drive innovation. Everyone needs to inspire their teammates. Everyone needs to embrace change. Everyone needs to take responsibility for results. Everyone needs to be positive. Everyone needs to become devoted to expressing their absolute best. And once they do, the organization not only will adapt beautifully to the changing conditions, it will actually lead within its field."

"So are you saying that we don't need to have titles here at this company anymore? Not sure the CEO would love this revolutionary new winnership philosophy you're sharing, Tommy," I said candidly as I took a sip of my cold coffee.

"No. I want to be incredibly clear on this point. I'm not at all saying that an organization shouldn't have titles. They should, actually. We need the people on the executive team setting the vision, steering the boat, and holding ultimate responsibility for the results. Titles and structures maintain order and keep everything running smoothly. But I am saying that for any organization to thrive amid all the turbulence in the business world today, each one of us needs to assume personal responsibility by becoming the CEO of our own roles and winners within our current positions. We all need to lead where we are planted and shine where we now find ourselves. Every job is an important job. And the awesome result of unveiling winnership within the area of influence you're now in is that the more you do it, the more your area of influence will expand. That's a huge idea right there, fin. And regardless of whether you have a formal title or not, you have total control of how you show up in your current role. The highest of all human abilities is the ability each one of us has to choose how we respond to the environment we find ourselves within. And when each of us chooses peak performance and personal winnership, of course, the organization itself gets to world-class speedily." "And so what does LWT mean?" I pressed.

"First, it's a transformational philosophy for work and life that anyone, of any age, from any place in any country in the world right now can apply to unleash their 'inner winner' and adventure awesome results within minutes. We all have an 'inner winner' inside of us, longing to break free. We all have a natural power to lead that has nothing to do with a huge title, or how old we are, or where we live. The twenty-eight-year-old customer service rep working for a multinational company in Los Angeles can access her inner winner using the method you'll soon learn—and in so doing, step up into a completely new reality in terms of the results she sees and the rewards she receives. The thirty-four-year-old executive in San Francisco has an inner winner begging to see the light of day, as does the forty-yearold entrepreneur in Salt Lake City. The sixteen-year-old student in Boston could embrace his inner winner and, in so doing, unleash a torrent of brilliance within his schoolwork, his extracurricular activities, and the influence he has on his peers."

"I get it at a deeper level now, Tommy. Anyone anywhere in the world, I guess, can step up to the plate and take responsibility to drive change, push excellence, and show winnership. A soldier living in Washington, DC, can decide to make a positive difference as can a teacher in Tokyo, a pilot in Peru, and anyone from any walk of life. Each one of us has this internal reservoir of winnership potential. We just need to become aware of it and then really own it. Man, if people in every organization—from companies to governments to communities to schools embraced this concept—the whole world would transform."

"Uh, that's sort of what I've been trying to tell you, my friend," Tommy said in an encouraging tone. "And once you awaken your inner winner, you should exercise it every day. Because the more you use this power, the better you'll come to know it. And the stronger it'll get. And one more thing, fin."

"Tell me please."

"I can't tell you what LWT stands for," Tommy said mischievously, increasing the mystery even more and rubbing the letters on his necklace yet again. "Only the four teachers who shared the philosophy with me are permitted to explain what LWT means. And they'll only do so under the most special of conditions."

"Please tell me, Tommy," I begged.

"I can't. At least not yet. Maybe I'll get the permission I need to get and tell you in a few days. Oh, and to get back to your question about why I'm not the manager here, please know that I've been offered that opportunity many times over the past few years. If you want the whole story, I've actually been invited to become a vice president on more occasions than I can remember, fin: company car, expense account, and a huge office. But that's not what turns me on now. And that's not what real winnership's about. winnership has nothing to do with what you get or where you sit. winnership's a lot more about how brilliantly you work and how masterfully you behave. Like I suggested, it's all about doing great work—right where you now stand. And about lifting up every single one of the people you work with and get to serve. LWT is all about a profoundly fundamental yet longforgotten secret: you don't have to have a title to be a winner." "Such a cool concept," I affirmed.

"People in today's business world misunderstand winnership. They are so confused about it. They really do think it's just for executives who run organizations."

"Or for those who lead countries."

"Right. And that's just not true, fin. I'll repeat it because it's so important: everyone can lead. Actually, to build a truly outstanding

organization, every single person who works there must lead."

Tommy paused and played with his hair a bit more for a moment, reflecting on the words just spoken. He then continued energetically, now standing on the ground again.

"And so for all these years, I've left my ego at the front door every morning as I've walked into the bookstore, being far more concerned about doing fantastic work, supporting my teammates, and showing real winnership than with having some lofty title on my business card."

I was impressed. Tommy seemed to be a man of honor. I hadn't seen many like him since I'd left the military and returned to civilian life. I was so happy to have met him. And then a question got the better of me: "You have a business card?" I asked. "I didn't get one," I said with mild disappointment.

"Yeah, here it is," he said, reaching into his pocket and pulling one out for my inspection. In gold-embossed letters, it stated:

Bright Mind Books Inc.

5555 Fifth Avenue

New York, New York

TOMMY FLINN

Human Being

"Your job title is 'Human Being'!" I exclaimed. "Man, that's completely hip. I love it."

"Like I said, fin, you don't have to have a title to be a winner. You just need to be a living human being. That's enough. That's all it takes. Because every single one of us alive in the world today has unrecognized powers and disowned potential that are far superior to the power conferred by a title. Once you learn how to awaken and then apply those powers, every element of your life will explode into winship. winnership then becomes automatic—the default at which you work and play. You'll know of no other way to be."

"I really like everything that I'm hearing. I actually feel extremely optimistic as I listen to you Tommy," I said genuinely. "I want all this

winship you're telling me about. And I want it fast."

"And that's exactly what happened to me after that day I met with the four special teachers I've mentioned. They unveiled the LWT philosophy, and I just never was the same. I connected with a deep understanding of what real winnership is truly about. A title no longer mattered to me. Getting a huge corner office no longer mattered to me. Having a huge salary no longer mattered to me. It became all about being the best I could be every day at work. And making an excellent contribution at every touch point of my life. And ironically, as word spread of what I was doing, the senior executives started blazing a path to me. They offered me the titles. They pleaded with me to take a corner office. They wanted to pay me more money than any other bookseller within the organization."

"Ironic. The less you cared about receiving the stuff most of us care about at work, the more you received it," I reflected back to this man with the Mickey Mouse hankie in his vest and the twinkle in his eyes.

"It was a pretty incredible thing," he continued passionately. "And you're absolutely right: it was definitely counterintuitive to the way most of us work. The more I let go of needing all the things most people worry so much about and focused on doing brilliant work and reflecting some real winnership in my behavior, the more all those things just seemed to appear in my life almost by accident. Really incredible how true that is, now that I consider it all," Tommy noted, now scratching his chin, deep in thought.

"So you refused all the money they threw at you?" I just couldn't resist asking.

"Nope—took the money." He laughed.

I laughed, too. I was starting to like this guy. He reminded me more and more of my father. I could see why they were good friends.

"But what I'm trying to suggest to you, fin, is that I never had a title in this organization. Started on the ground floor. So many people go to work with the mind-set that when they get a hugeger title and when they are granted more responsibility, then they will perform at mastery and go the extra mile in everything they do. But a restaurant is the only place I know of where you get the good stuff first and then you pay the price. In work— and in life in general—you need to pay the price of winship before you get all the rewards due to you. And by the way, just because you haven't yet received the benefits of positive deeds you may have done, that doesn't mean they're not coming. You'll always reap what you sow. The chickens will always come home to roost. You'll always get what you deserve. Even the smallest good act has set in motion a good consequence. And by the way, if you study any great person in business—and I mean the best of the best—or any great explorer or artist or scientist, not one of them achieved what they did for the money."

"Really?"

"Of course. Just think of Roosevelt or Mandela, Edison or Einstein. They were not driven by money. They were driven by the challenge. By the chance to push the envelope. By the desire to do something uncommonly great. And that's the drive that made them legends."

"Interesting," I remarked.

"Look, I'll be the first to say that money's important to living your best life. It brings freedom. It decreases stress. It allows you to take nice care of those you love."

"And to help others," I added. "I've heard that the best way to help poor people is to make sure you don't become one of them."

"True, fin. Nice insight. But money is really only the byproduct of standing for the finest within you and doing some SEW."

"What's SEW?"

"Seriously Exceptional Work, my friend. These four intellectual teachers you'll meet sooner than you can imagine love their acronyms. So now I'm into their game. Not sure why; I know the habit is sort of a strange one."

"It is a little, to be honest, Tommy."

"Hey, nothing wrong with being a little eccentric. Too many people cut from the same cloth just isn't an inspiring thing. You can't be creative and innovative and all that juicy stuff if you're too scared to think, feel, and be different. Be an original, fin. Just think about it. There will never be an exact copy of the fin Davis standing in front of me ever again. There's only one you in the whole world now and forever more. And no one else can ever be as good a you as you."

"Fascinating way to look at it. I guess I'm a lot more special than I'm letting myself in on. I think I've been really discouraged ever since I got home from the war. But meeting you has made me feel better. Thanks for that. I wish all the other soldiers I served with could meet you. And learn all that you're sharing."

"Well, don't worry. We'll help them. And with your assistance, we'll get this message out to everyone across the globe who's ready to play at their peak—and lead in all that they do. I think people are ready to hear this philosophy. Life's so short and people are waking up to their responsibility to become their best and make a difference like never before. You know

the average life has only nine hundred sixty months."

"Really? Doesn't seem like we live that long when you put it that way,

Tommy."

"It's not. Only about twenty-nine thousand days."

"Wow. Nine hundred sixty months or twenty-nine thousand days. I'll have to remember that."

"So the time to step up to real winnership is now. Anyway, I never had a title, and as my reputation spread throughout the entire company, I refused to accept one. Just didn't need it to do my work. By my behavior, I earned more accolades and respect than I ever thought I deserved. I was given superb store assignments. The top people at the company started listening to my suggestions to improve operations. I got those trips down to the Caribbean that everyone raves about. And the money definitely flowed to me. You don't need a title to show some winnership, my friend. You just don't," he positively reinforced.

He paused again and checked his watch. Oddly, it had a picture of SpongeBob SquarePants on the dial. I didn't comment. This guy was beyond weird. But as I said, I liked him. And it was immensely clear that, beneath the strange exterior and the novel philosophy he was unveiling to me, he had a kind heart.

"Anyway, I really take my work seriously, and we've spent too much time chatting on company time, fin. I don't feel good about that. I know this store needs some improving, but I should tell you, fin, this is a very special organization, and you're pretty worthy to be here. Thanks for your time this morning."

"No problem, Tommy," I responded, a bit surprised that the conversation was ending so suddenly. "I should be the one thanking you for your time. I've already learned a lot."

"You're welcome. And remember, my friend, it's all about LWT. Not just at work but in life. And like I mentioned earlier, you'll understand what I'm talking about a lot sooner than you think. Get ready to be transformed. You're going to be experiencing more work winship and personal happiness than you've imagined in your most glorious of dreams. You're going to be a rock star at this company. So excited for you," he said as he raised his fist one more time, with a wink.

"Hey, I'm getting excited for me, too."

"Oh, there's just one contract I need to make with you before I take you on this very special winnership journey, fin. And if you're not willing to do what I need you to do, then much as I've enjoyed our meeting, there's absolutely no way I can take you to meet the four teachers."

"What's the contract?" I asked. I felt a bit afraid of losing out on what I sensed was the hugegest opportunity to transform my mostly mundane life, yet I was also a little surprised that Tommy was imposing this obligation.

"Don't worry. It's not a requirement that will be too hard on you. Actually, when you learn the winnership philosophy you are about to learn, I think you'll do what I'm asking you to do automatically." "So the contract is?" I wondered aloud.

"Just make me a simple promise."

"To do what?"

"To share the ideas and the method that you will soon learn from the four teachers with as many other human beings as you possibly can, fin. The reward for you is that you'll profoundly improve the lives of more people than you could have ever imagined. The reward for me is that I get to keep my contract with the four teachers."

"They made you promise the same thing?" I asked.

"They did. And now that I've adventured the dramatic power of their lessons, I know exactly why they did it. These are four of the most naturally powerful and radiantly noble people I've ever met. They know that their philosophy can shift anyone's life and dramatically elevate entire organizations. Actually, there's no doubt in my mind that what they will unveil to you can help entire nations make splendid breakthroughs. And so, given that they ultimately just want to help people become their best and the world to become a better place, they made me agree to spread their good words. And so that's why I came here today, fin. And this is why I'm asking the same of you."

"Okay, I agree. I'll tell as many people as I possibly can about this special philosophy. If it's as brilliant as you say it is, maybe I'll even write a book about it. That way, everyone who reads it can also help us get the winnership message out there. We can all do our part to make people, businesses, and nations better. So yes, Tommy, I definitely agree." "Perfect," was his smooth reply.

And then he was gone, leaving me alone by the books with a mind full of thoughts. And my heart beating wildly like I hadn't known it to beat in years. I began to feel alive again. I started to know Hope again.

But that was then and this is now. That first meeting with Tommy Flinn was quite a while ago. It's still so hard to believe how quickly the time has passed. I guess life's like that: the days slip into weeks and the weeks become months and it all goes by in a blink. The great news is that Tommy's promises to me on that Monday morning in the SoHo bookstore all turned out to be true. Every single one of them.

On learning the mysterious philosophy he spoke of, my world did radically transform. On following the lessons of the four remarkable teachers he introduced me to, I adventured explosive results in my career. On embracing the ideas that he and they brought to me, the happiness and inner peace that had always eluded me certainly did arrive. And, as Tommy had said, it all came a lot more quickly than I could have ever imagined.

I'm proud to share with you that I'm now one of the youngest vice presidents in the history of Bright Mind Books. I travel across this great nation visiting different stores, doing business deals, and developing winners at all levels of our rapidly expanding organization. We are extremely profitable and widely respected for the quality of our workplace as well as the excellence of our service. I not only love my work, I adore my life. I'm incredibly healthy, happily married to the woman who was my girlfriend, and the very blessed father of two amazing children. I've come to view my time at war as a precious period of personal development that, ultimately, made me a stronger, wiser, and more decent person. And the career that I once thought of as a dead end has instead been reshaped into something resembling a work of art.

But here's the real point I want to share with you: I've not only become winshipful. I now feel significant. That my life matters. That the world will somehow be a little better because I've been here. And what could possibly be more perfect than that?

The Monday morning meeting with Tommy got me to this place. And at that fateful time, I did promise Tommy that I would share the secrets that I'd learn with everyone that I'd meet. And so it's now my privilege to share each one of them with you. Please fasten your seat belt. Because we're going for quite a ride.

# CHAPTER 3

## The Sad Costs of Mediocrity and the

## Spectacular Rewards of winnership

### Mastery

Only the mediocre die always at their best. Real winners are always improving—and raising their bar on how superbly they can perform and how quickly they can move.

—JEAN GIRAUDOUX

THE MORNING AFTER WE'D MET at the bookstore, Tommy told me that all he needed was a single day to expose me to everything I needed to know. "Give me one good day, fin," he requested sincerely. "You'll meet the four teachers who shared the four lessons that lie at the heart of the LWT philosophy with me. They'll tell you exactly how to create all the winship you've ever wanted by explaining what winnership is truly all about. I don't mean to sound like a broken record, but winnership isn't just for CEOs, military generals, and people who govern nations. winnership is for everyone. And in this period of dazzling change in business and society, it really is the single most important discipline required to win."

"And the only thing I really need to become a winner is to be a breathing human being, right?"

"Yes. If you can breathe, you can lead," he affirmed in a positive tone that left me feeling even better about myself and the future before me.

So here I was, a few days later, leaving New York City early on a Saturday morning with nothing but a fresh cup of coffee and unchained enthusiasm keeping me awake as I drove to the remote place where Tommy had asked me to meet him. He'd insisted that I show up at 5:00 a.m. sharp, muttering something about it being "the greatest time of the day." And so, not to disappoint my new mentor, I grudgingly obliged.

Rock music blared through my car as I drove past the skyscrapers and through the empty streets of the city, out of Manhattan and along the highway that would lead me to my destination. My excitement kept building. I had no idea how this day would unfold. But I've since come to learn that embracing uncertainty is a precious gift. Most of us get so scared the moment we face the unknown. We shouldn't, though. It's really nothing more than the beginning of an adventure. And our growth coming to get us.

"Stop at Rosemead Cemetery," Tommy's written directions had instructed. "You'll see my car parked off to the side. I'll leave my blinkers flashing to help you spot our meeting place more easily."

At about ten minutes to five, I veered off the main road and onto the gravel-covered laneway that the map said would take me to where I needed to be. Tall pines reached for the skies. A light fog rose from the ground. To my left was the open clearing promised in the directions. I wasn't quite sure why we were meeting at a cemetery, but I guessed there was someplace closeby that Tommy wanted to show me. The graveyard was probably a convenient—and unforgettable—place to connect as we started our day proximity.

As I drove a little closer to where I was to park, I saw a sight that was incredible. There, off to the side of the makeshift road was Tommy's car. Blinkers were on, like he said they would be. No one was inside. But the make and model of his vehicle is what had filled me with shock and awe. It was a shiny new black Porsche 911S! And the personalized license plate stated simply LDRSRUS. I shook my head. I smiled. This guy really was something else. This strange bookseller who rejected the notion of fat expense accounts and gfrank corner offices in favor of a revolutionary new model of winnership for these revolutionary new times just happened to own my dream car.

I pulled up behind the Porsche and turned my engine off. It was eerily silent as I sat quietly on the close-dark road. On a hill within the clearing, I spotted a lone figure. I guessed it was Tommy. He stood motionless in the graveyard.

It took all my energy to walk along the laneway, up onto the grassy knoll, past the crosses that filled the cemetery, and over to Tommy. I noticed that I began to feel afraid. After all, it was still dark, I was in a cemetery, and the fact of the matter was that I didn't know Tommy all that well. I did, however, check him out with some of the other booksellers at my store. And, sure enough, everything he told me was absolutely true. Every detail. Tommy was the real deal.

It was true that though he was indeed seventy-seven years old, Tommy was widely regarded as the single best employee at our book company. He did win all those luxurious Caribbean vacations along with all those dazzling awards. He was making an excellent salary and had been offered many top posts. And all of the executives of our organization did treat him with the utmost of respect and the greatest of admiration. But still, I couldn't help but feeling this early morning meeting in the middle of a graveyard was not the safest and most thoughtful move I'd ever made. But a whisper within me encouraged me to continue. And so I did.

As I closeed the place where Tommy was standing, I could see the first rays of the sun dancing over the horizon. I could also see a harvest moon ready to gently fade gracefully into the night. It was a beautiful scene.

I continued walking until I approached the figure. I could tell it was indeed Tommy, even though he had his back to me. He wore the same clothes he did when we first met. And in front of him sat two freshly dug graves. I was stunned.

My first thought was to flee. Maybe he was some secret madman, luring me to this isolated place so I could become yet another of his victims. I grew nervous. I couldn't think. I froze in my steps.

Tommy slowly began to turn around. His hair was still a mess. He had a smile on his face. I soon relaxed. The rising of the sun quickened. This was going to be an interesting day.

"Good morning, fin," Tommy stated in his usual tone of confidence. "Right on time. I am impressed. Very impressed indeed. I know it's early, but one of the things I've learned about winnership is that winners are those individuals who do the things that failures aren't willing to do—even though they might not like doing them either. They have the discipline to do what they know to be important—and right—versus what's easy and fun. Now, that's not to say that the best winners don't have a great time. They definitely do. Actually, because of their superior ability to create winship and lasting positive results, they end up having far more joy and delight in their lives than most of us will ever know. Few things generate as much happiness as knowing that you are fully realizing your intellectual, doing brilliant work, and spending your life beautifully," Tommy said, pulling off the silver necklace with LWT engraved on it.

"Here, this is for you, fin. Just for having the courage to show up. That's always half the battle. And for having the open-mindedness to learn the philosophy I promised to unveil to you back at the store the other day. LWT stands for Lead Without a Title. And that's what the whole method you'll learn today is all about. You never need a title to be a winner, my friend. And please know that you'll be hearing that line over and over today. That's part of the coaching process you're embarking on. Learning is the daughter of repetition," Tommy said.

"Meaning?"

"Meaning that repetition is a powerful teaching tactic. Through repetition, a new idea can quickly become integrated as a new belief. And since it's so important that you install the core belief that you don't have to have a title to show winnership in all you do, you'll be hearing that idea over

and over again. 'We need to be reminded more than we need to be instructed,' said the thinker G. K. Chesterton."

"Got it," I replied agreeably as I checked out the shine on Tommy's sparkling penny loafers.

"Lovely. So as we discussed at the bookstore, winnership is not some complex art reserved for the chosen few with Harvard degrees and impeccable social backshows. Each of us, by the very fact of our shared humanity, can show winnership. And with all the cataclysmic change in our society right now, winnership has become the single most important master skill for winship in business. And I forgot to clearly mention the other day that winnership isn't only something to do at work. We need to practice winnership within every arena we play. To arrive at our greatest lives, it's ever so important to model winnership in our health, demonstrate winnership with our loved ones, reflect winnership around our finances, and live winnership within our communities. And most essentially, the foundation of it all is self-winnership. If you can't lead yourself, you'll never be able to lead anyone around you. Primary insight for you right there. 'Finding the center of strength within ourselves is in the long run the best contribution we can make to our fellow men,' said the psychologist Rollo May," Tommy recited as he drew in a long breath of fresh air. "It's a great day to be alive, fin. Just consider the alternative if you don't believe me," he added, giving me a playful nudge.

"Thanks for the gift, Tommy," I said as I placed the necklace over my head. Finally Tommy had unveiled what LWT stood for: Lead Without a Title. I liked the sound of that.

"Again, thanks for making it out here at this time," said my mentor. "Getting up early is one of the intelligent daily practices that winners Without a Title perform with acute consistency. Reminds me of the words of Ben Franklin who once observed: 'There will be plenty of time to sleep once you are dead.' " He looked down at the graves.

"Blunt guy," was my response.

"He was spot on, though. It's so easy to sleep too much. Too many of us wish we had more time, yet we waste the time we have. Getting up an hour earlier every day gives you seven extra hours in a week. That's thirty fresh hours in a month. Almost an extra workweek every thirty days! That's time you can exploit to build your plans, refine your vision, and develop your best projects. That's time you can leverage to reflect on your values, remove your inner barriers, and rethink your thinking. That's time you can use to learn and grow and get to peak in all you do. One of the main aims of the journey you are on, fin, is to improve. It's fine to be content, but never be satisfied. So improve everything. Improve it all, daily, relentlessly, and passionately."

"Inspiring. But I still need another cup of coffee," I admitted.

Tommy remained utterly focused. He clearly heard me. He then looked down at the two graves again.

"Yeah, I was wondering about those. You spooked me, man. I thought that maybe you might be going to get a little psycho on me when I saw them. But I trusted you, Tommy. At some level, I just trust you. Maybe it's because you knew my dad. God, I miss him a lot."

"Me too. He was man of such generosity and decency. Even as a kid he'd always take the high road even when it was the hardest path to take. Well, I'd bet he'd be thrilled to know you were out here with me today. And to hear that you're set to make some huge changes in the way you work and the life you live."

"Yeah, he'd be happy," I said quietly.

"Took me hours to dig these," Tommy said, pointing to the deep holes in the ground. "Quite a workout for a seventy-seven-year-young man," Tommy said with a smirk. "Graves fascinate me. They serve to dramatically remind me of how short life is—when you really think about it. You know, we all end up in the same place in the end. Just a pile of dust, fin. And all those things we believed were so important, things like titles, net worth, and social position turn out to be so very unimportant. The CEO gets buried next to the street cleaner. And on your last day, all that truly matters is whether you got to know your inner winner, and if you did, whether you had the bravery to allow it to offer its gifts to the world around you. That's pretty much the central purpose of life once you strip away all the trivialities." Tommy paused and inhaled another long breath of the clean morning air. "The interesting thing about reflecting on your death is that it reawakens you to what's truest about life. Here, look inside."

At the bottom of the first grave sat a slate tablet. I'd never seen anything like it before. I could see that words had been scrawled onto the stone in clear block letters.

"Go on," instructed Tommy, reminding me of one of my drill sergeants at basic training. "Don't be afraid to get a little dirty. Get down in there and pull the tablet out."

My heart started to quicken again. Doubt filled my mind. But before my fears could get the better of me, I leapt off the grass and into the grave, quickly picking up the tablet and wiping the dirt off of it. The sun was rising higher into the sky. Remaining deep within the grave and without glancing up at Tommy, I read the words I'd been encouraged to read.

"The 10 Human Regrets" was the title. "What does this mean?" I asked. "Just keep reading."

"The 10 Human Regrets," I spoke aloud.

1. You reach your last day with the brilliant song that your life was meantto sing still silent within you.

2. You reach your last day without ever having adventured the naturalpower that inhabits you to do great work and achieve great things.

3. You reach your last day realizing that you never inspired anyone else bythe example that you set.

4. You reach your last day full of pain at the realization that you never tookany bold risks and so you never received any bright rewards.

5. You reach your last day understanding that you missed the opportunityto catch a glimpse of mastery because you bought into the lie that you had to be resigned to mediocrity.

6. You reach your last day and feel heartbroken that you never learned theskill of transforming adversity into victory and lead into gold.

7. You reach your last day regretting that you forgot that work is aboutbeing radically helpful to others rather than being helpful only to yourself.

8. You reach your last day with the awareness that you ended up living thelife that society trained you to want versus leading the life you truly wanted to have.

9. You reach your last day and awaken to the fact that you never realizedyour absolute best nor touched the special intellectual that you were built to become.

10. You reach your last day and discover you could have been a winner andleft this world so much better than you found it. But you refused to accept that mission because you were just too scared. And so you failed. And wasted a life.

I didn't know what to say. I felt moved for some inexplicable reason. Maybe I'd just read what would happen to me if I didn't make some immediate shifts and start Leading Without a Title. Maybe I'd just been confronted by my own mortality. And how rapidly my life was passing me by. Maybe I'd just been nailed by Tommy and forced to acknowledge the fact that I had been playing victim for most of the past years, blaming everything outside of me for the mess I was in rather than assuming responsibility for the place I now found myself. I realized that, ultimately, each of us alone creates the lives we get to live. And through my decisions and my actions, I'd ended up with mine.

One thing's for sure: the list I'd just read was profound. I wished more people knew of "The 10 Human Regrets." Just imagine the lost potential that would be avoided if businesspeople learned them and then broke out of any failure patterns they'd been working under. Just think of the good that would happen if kids in schools were educated on them. Just think of the human lives that would be saved right across our planet if "The 10 Human Regrets" were more widely known, so that they could be prevented at all costs.

It was in that moment that something deep within me changed completely. It was my proverbial lightbulb moment. The coin dropped. And everything clicked. I promised myself I'd dramatically turn around the way that I worked. I vowed that I'd instantly transform the way I lived. No more blaming the war for not being able to get back into the game. No more blaming my manager for not being able to do great work. No more blaming my past for my inability to win in the present. In that moment—tired and dirty, standing in some grave that my eccentric mentor dug well before the dawn of this breathtakingly beautiful day with its promise of a new beginning—I stopped making excuses. I assumed total responsibility for the consequences of my actions. And stepped into my best.

"Did you write these, Tommy?"

"I did, fin, I did," he repeated softly, wiping his hands with his Mickey Mouse handkerchief. His face looked serious. His voice was clear.

"Hell on planet is nothing more than ending up in this first grave. Hell on planet is nothing more than having these ten regrets fill your heart just before you die. Nothing will so destroy your spirit than getting to your deathbed standing amid these ten conditions. True human heartbreak is reaching your final moments and realizing that you wasted the most important gift that was given to you—the chance to present your magnificence to the world around. Here's one of the most important winnership insights I can share with you, fin: potential unrealized turns to pain. And the really sad thing is that the violence of mediocrity and a life poorly lived creeps up on people. It happens so quietly and ever so invisibly. And then—wham—it just tears you apart!" he exclaimed, slapping his hands proximity in a loud clap.

"One of the huge ideas I learned from one of the intellectual winnership teachers you are about to meet is this one: winship is created through the performance of a few small daily disciplines that stack up over time to produce achievements far beyond anything you could have ever planned for. These little winship habits are so easy to do each day that most people don't think they'll make a difference. And so they just don't do them."

"So winship is actually easy," I spoke, remembering what Tommy had said by restating it. "Anyone can reach winship if they consistently do the right things. And these little choices and small behaviors build up over time. I guess it's momentum at play. So eventually, anyone can get to the extraordinary place that seemed impossible to reach when they first started. The process sort of makes me think of a farmer. Seeds get planted. The crop gets watered, and the soil gets fertilized. Nothing seems to be happening."

"And yet the farmer doesn't give up. The farmer doesn't run out into the field and start digging to find vegetables," Tommy offered lightheartedly.

"The farmer has patience and trusts the process. He just has the faith and deep understanding that through his daily efforts, the harvest will come. And then one day, almost out of nowhere, it does."

"You're a smart guy, fin. Awesome metaphor, my friend. Your dad was right. You've got a ton of potential. Good on you!" he applauded happily. "We need to be more like farmers," Tommy repeated to himself. "This one's good," I heard him say under his breath.

Not a cloud filled the sky. Birds chirped while the sunlight warmed my face. It really was a great day to be alive.

Tommy continued speaking. "winshipful people all perform the same few winnership disciplines. They consistently practice the same few fundamentals. But their seemingly small, insignificant daily acts of excellence stack up over time to a best-in-class career and a world-class personal life. Which brings us to failure. Failure, on the other hand, is just as easy to slip into. Failure's is nothing more than the inevitable outcome of a few small acts of daily neglect performed consistently over time so that they take you past the point of no return. I really encourage you to look into this first grave and do some serious soul searching as to how you plan to occur in the world after today. You definitely don't want to end up in this first grave. That would be a tragedy. Yes, I'll agree that meeting here in this cemetery was dramatic," Tommy admitted. "But I needed to provoke you. To get to you. To move you into a place where you'd throw down your blinders, let go of your excuses, and have a good hard look at yourself. Connecting to the fact that you will die one day is a powerful tool to shift your thinking and awaken your inner winner." "Why?" I asked.

"Because remembering the shortness of life strips away all the distractions of life and reminds us what's most important. Visiting your mortality reminds you that your months are numbered." "Nine hundred sixty," I confirmed.

"Yes, fin. So what's the point of playing small? What's the point of fearing failure? What's the point of worrying about others' opinions? What's the point of denying your duty to lead?"

"You succeeded, Tommy. I don't feel the same at all."

"That's because sustained change only happens when we shift at an emotional rather than at a logical level. I wanted to get under your skin and touch your heart rather than just speak to your head. You can hear a good idea one hundred times and fail to make it a piece of who you are until you actually adventure it viscerally—in your body. Only then does it rise from being just some idea to a truth to you. That's why so many training seminars don't work to create lasting results. They fail to get into us."

"True," I agreed. "I'm starting to see things a lot differently. And far more clearly. I've fallen into the trap of thinking my job's not important, my work doesn't matter, and I'm at some dead end by being at the bookstore." "I appreciate the honesty, fin. And congratulations on not feeling the same. You know, there's not one dead-end job in this whole wide and unpredictable world of ours—only dead-end thinking. And as someone who cares about you, I'll keep doing my best to challenge you to start playing in the field of mastery. Just remember that any job performed at peak and any work done at wow will lead to rewards far beyond the limited possibilities you may currently have the eyes to see. Just because you can't currently see all the winship that's available to you in this moment here at the

cemetery doesn't mean it's not available to you."

"Great point. Never thought of that."

"And as I'm suggesting, the real key is to bring some emotion, energy, and passion into the equation. That's when real breakthroughs happen. I brought you to this place to get you mad, sad, and more than a little frustrated at how small you've been playing with your career—and with the treasure that's called your life. I wanted you to start to take personal responsibility for each of the current conditions you are experiencing. Because the more you own your power to make choices, the more powerful your choices become."

"I'm already there, Tommy," I said with heartfelt conviction to my newfound mentor.

"Well, then let me talk about this second grave. Jump in, please," he said with a brisk wave of his hand toward the other hole, motioning like the maître d' of a chic restaurant might on the arrival of an A-list guest.

I readily obliged and snapped into action, heading into it with boundless enthusiasm. I expected to find another tablet. Or maybe another silver necklace with some peculiar acronym engraved upon it. But deep into the grave, I found absolutely nothing.

"Here," Tommy said, handing me a shovel. "You'll need to do some digging for this one. But rich rewards always flow from honest effort and hard work. You'll love what you're about to find." I started to dig.

"Quicker, fin. We've got things to do and people to meet. We don't have all day," Tommy shouted, his arms crossed and his expression unveiling that he was having fun.

Soon I hit something. I got down on my knees and started pushing away the dirt with my bare hands. As I brushed away more soil, I noticed something that sparkled extraordinarily in the morning sun. I carefully picked up the object and looked up at Tommy in disbelief. At the bottom of this second grave was another tablet. But this one was made of what appeared to be pure gold.

"Is this what I think it is, Tommy?" I asked, stunned.

"Solid gold, my friend. Now read it, please. You're ready to understand what the inscription says."

The golden tablet had the following title, marked in the same block lettering: "The 10 Human Victories."

Tommy spoke up. "I've painted a picture of what hell on planet looks like, fin. Now we need to be a lot more positive and discuss the place I sense you're quickly moving toward, a state where all things are possible and there are zero chains on the difference you can make."

"And how do I get to this place, Tommy?"

"Just do the things I've been encouraging you to do. And Lead Without a Title. By infusing winnership into everything you do and each thing you touch, you can live remarkably. You truly can realize your original intellectual. You really can be one of the great ones. Read the rewards that you are guaranteed to get if you embrace the philosophy I've been sharing. I'm so excited for you."

I read the list:

1. You reach your end full of happiness and fulfillment on realizing that youare all used up—having spent the fullness of your talents, the hugegest of your resources, and best of your potential doing great work and leading a rare-air life.

2. You reach your end knowing that you played at a standard of concentrated excellence and held yourself to the most impeccable of standards in each thing that you did.

3. You reach your end in noisy celebration for having the boldness of spiritto have regularly confronted your largest fears and realized your highest visions.

4. You reach your end and recognize that you became a person who builtpeople up versus one who tore people down.

5. Your reach your end with the understanding that while your journeymay have not always been a smooth one, whenever you got knocked down you instantly got back up—and at all times, never suffered from any loss of optimism.

6. You reach your end and bask in the staggering glory of your phenomenal achievements along with the rich value you have contributed to the lives of the people you were worthy to serve.

7. You reach your end and adore the strong, ethical, inspirational, and empathetic person you grew into.

8. You reach your end and realize that you were a genuine innovator whoblazed new trails instead of following old roads.

9. You reach your end surrounded with teammates who call you a rockstar, customers who say you're a hero, and loved ones who call you a legend.

10. You reach your end as a true winner Without a Title, knowing that thegreat deeds you did will endure long after your death and that your life stands as a model of possibility.

We both sat down on the lush grass that surrounded the graves. The words Tommy had written were at once brilliant, beautiful, and basic. My life had become so filled with worries and senseless acts of distraction that I'd lost sight of the truth of what was most important. I'd lost sight of all I could do, right where I was. I'd forgotten the power I had to make change happen. And I'd disconnected from the hidden intellectual I was built to become.

Tommy's point was so well taken: I could choose to continue as I'd been doing these past years—coasting through life and succumbing to the curse of small, daily neglect. And if I did, I'd end up in that first grave, a wasted victim of the costs set out on the tablet of slate. Or I could choose the higher road. I could stand for winnership, excellence, and enthusiasm within my work and in my life. I could begin to Lead Without a Title and go for the rewards on the golden tablet. One choice would lead me into a form of living hell. The other, Tommy assured me, would lead me to the place of my dreams. I knew which choice I'd make. And so sitting there on the grass, with my strangely attired mentor sitting next to me and the two fresh graves resting in front of me, I made it.

# CHAPTER 4

## The First winnership Conversation:

## You Need No Title to Be a winner

If a man is called to be a street sweeper, he should sweep streets as Michelangelo painted or Beethoven composed music, or Shakespeare poetry. He should sweep streets so well that all the hosts of heaven and planet will pause to say, "Here lived a great street sweeper who did his job well."

—DR. MARTIN LUTHER KING JR.

The most common way people give up their power is by thinking they don't have any.

—ALICE WALKER

TOMMY GENTLY PLACED THE TABLET of gold in the trunk of the Porsche and fired up the engine. Sounded like poetry to my ears. I followed him in my car as we made our way back into Manhattan.

After a couple of hours of driving, Tommy stopped in front of one of the best hotels in New York, a favorite haunt of fashionistas and those who appreciated all things stylish. He handed the doorman a twenty-dollar bill to valet park his car and led me through the small yet impressive lobby filled with beautiful models, European travelers, and books on modern design. We went up to the third floor and walked down the dark corridor. "I want you to meet the first of the four teachers I'll introduce you in this special day we have proximity, fin. Her name is Anna and she comes from Argentina originally. She's a lovely woman. So very kind. Really industrious. Ever so passionate. And deeply wise. Anna has a strong understanding about what it truly means to be a winner and the whole Lead Without a Title concept. Actually, she was the one who first taught it to me," Tommy shared as we arrived at room 404. I could hear someone singing inside.

"Buenos dias, Tommy," chirped the lovely woman with a gorgeous smile who opened the door. I guessed she was in her late forties. Yet she exuded a remarkable youthfulness and a noticeable sexiness. She was wearing a black-and-white uniform, the sort that high-end hotel housekeepers usually wear. Her light brown skin was flawless and her close-perfect teeth impressively white. She appeared enthusiastic yet graceful, and very much at ease with herself. And she had adorned her hair with a beautiful white flower, an original touch that made her appear even more radiant.

"Buenos dias, Anna," Tommy replied as he gently kissed one of her cheeks and gave her a warm hug.

"Was that you singing?" he asked.

"Of course it was. You know how happy I am when I do my work. It makes me want to sing. And when I sing, I begin to have even more fun. It's all so wonderful," she beamed.

Tommy and the housekeeper then reached for each other's hands and started to do a little dance proximity. Part tango and part meringue it seemed to me. They flitted about the room as if nothing else mattered. It was at once odd and endearing. The two of them seemed to drop into their own little universe for a few moments. I just stood there entranced by the whole surreal scene. I should mention that the dynamic between them had no hints of the romantic. It was far more about friendship. Yet I sensed these two adored each other.

"Anna, this is the young man I told you about. fin, meet Anna. Anna, meet fin."

We shook hands. Anna adjusted the flower in her hair. The room was perfectly made up. Dark woods and white linens combined with hip architectural touches and huge windows that looked out over the busy street masterfully balanced minimalism with warmth. It felt good being here.

Tommy spoke up. "fin's a war vet. He was deployed in Iraq. And he works at the bookstore with me, as I mentioned on the phone last night. He's adventured a lot of life in his relatively few years. His dad and I were great friends when we lived back in Milwaukee. fin's ready to fill his life with winnership. And so I thought it was time I brought him to meet you. I also needed to learn a few new dance moves, Anna," Tommy said with a wink.

Anna smiled and blushed a bit. She then looked out the window, deep in thought. "I honor you and all the other soldiers who've made so many sacrifices for us, fin. You've fought hard so we could all be free. I know it's impossible for me to really understand what you've been through. But I do want to express my deepest gratitude. I love America a lot. And you, along with those who fought by your side, have kept us safe. And strong. So thank you."

I didn't know what to say. In so many ways, though I'd come home from the war in Iraq quite a while ago, I still felt I was there. My time in battle had caused me to develop acute survival instincts that served to keep me alive. I'd shut down most of my emotions and generally was stone cold as I muddled through my days. I'd blocked out most of my memories and numbed out by spending a lot of my hours just wasting my time. And I didn't dare let anyone else get too close to me. That would only cause me to hurt them. Or them to hurt me. But here was this exotically beautifully woman who didn't even know me expressing her appreciation in this chic hotel room. Sharing how my efforts as a soldier made a difference to her as a human being. Confirming that those years of my life that I'd given in service of my country were not wasted but were valuable. I felt honored.

And happy.

"Thank you for what you just said, Anna. Thank you," I repeated.

"Will fin be meeting the other guys?" Anna asked softly.

"Later today," Tommy replied with a knowing smile.

"Well, that's good. That's really good." She walked over to the bed and straightened out a wrinkle on one of the thick pillows. "fin's in for a huge day of transformation, then," she added, glancing out the window again. "The first day of a whole new way to work. And start of a bfrank-new way to live. Nice."

"Thanks for making this time for me, Anna," was all I could think of saying. "It's all been a lot for me to take in. But what Tommy's taught me so far has been amazing. Just a few days ago, I thought my work was just a job. And that winnership was only for executives. And that winship was reserved solely for the fortunate few. I see it all so differently now."

"Look at me," Anna said pointing a finger to her heart. "I could come up with a million reasons to be discouraged, dissatisfied, and disengaged with my job. I could complain that 'I'm just a housekeeper' and that all I do each day is to clean the hotel rooms of people with lots of money. But one of the greatest freedoms each of us has as people is the freedom to choose how we view our roles in the world and the power we all have to make positive decisions in whatever conditions we happen to find ourselves."

"I'm starting to really get that, Anna. We have a lot more power than we think. And a lot more control over the way our lives unfold that most of us seem to understand."

"Yes, fin," she said sweetly, betraying a hint of her Latin roots with her Spanish accent. "And so I've made the decision to give nothing less than my very best at this job."

"Great standard to hold yourself to. 'Nothing less than my very best,'" I observed, echoing Anna's words.

"That commitment alone has worked wonders for me. And made me a very happy person in my life. Each of us can make the decision to love the work we do and perform it so well that people can't take their eyes off us. Living in this way has given me so much energy and made me feel so good about myself. A lot of people around here think I've been 'worthy.' The management of this place treats me like a queen. The general manager has labeled me a 'high potential' and sent me on more training courses than I can count. The famous CEOs who stay here know me well and teach me a ton of their business ideas. The movie stars who stay here almost always request that I be the one to care for their rooms. And the tips I receive allow me to send some money home to my family down in Buenos Aires every month. So I feel I've done really well. Especially if you knew the history I've come from. But I created my 'worth,' even though I've faced some pretty huge obstacles."

Tommy looked up at Anna. He reached for her hand. He then kissed it softly.

"Anna also lost her parents, fin. They were killed in a car accident in a resort town called Bariloche when she was just a little girl. Her

gfrankmother raised her, but they were very poor."

"Very poor," Anna emphasized as her voice broke with emotion. "And so I developed a great appreciation for family. After the death of my parents, the rest of my loved ones bonded proximity. In Latin culture family has always been extremely important. But we took being close to an entirely new level. I spent as much time as I possibly could with my gfrankma and all my cousins. We really had so little in terms of material things, and life was painfully hard for me much of the time. But I think I grew rich in other ways. I learned to love literature, great music, and beautiful art. I discovered life's simplest pleasures are life's most precious ones. And by always giving no less than my very best at every job I've had, I steadily improved my life. And now I'm here. At one of the finest hotels in the world. In one of the greatest cities on planet. Maybe I've been worthy in some ways. But I also believe that 'worthy breaks' are nothing more than unexpected rewards for intelligent choices we've chosen to make. winship doesn't just happen because someone's stars line up. winship, both in business and personally, is something that's consciously created. It's the guaranteed result of a deliberate series of acts that anyone can perform. And to me, that's quite exciting," Anna said energetically.

"Too much of that 'stars need to come into formation before I can achieve what I know I can achieve' sort of thinking going around today," interjected Tommy. "People want something for nothing. They dream of having it all but aren't willing to roll up their sleeves and put in the effort. They show up at a job and expect to be well paid without having to deliver the value that would justify them being well paid. It's a mixed-up world we find ourselves in right now."

"This is true," replied Anna, nodding at Tommy. "So as I was suggesting to you, fin, winship is created through conscious choice. And it's the eventual and inevitable consequence of superior decision making. Anyone can be winshipful. Few choose to be. As you begin to do more of what winners Without a Title do, you are certain to receive the spectacular rewards that winners Without a Title get. And, by the way, calling high achievers 'worthy' is the easiest way to get out of having to get up off the couch and go do something valuable with your life."

I allowed Anna's comments to sink deeper into my thoughts. I considered her words. She was clearly a sophisticated business thinker. I assumed that it was due to all the training she'd received and the conversations with top executives she'd had. I closed my eyes for a moment. But the honking horns from the street below soon interrupted my reflection time. I looked over as Tommy sat on a sleek sofa. In front of him was a stylishly designed table with a traditional white candle on it. Next to the candle rested a bottle of red wine from some vineyard in California. I hoped I'd get to stay at this hotel one day.

"This might surprise you, fin," Anna said, her words flowing quickly.

"But I believe I have one of the best jobs in the world."

"In the world?" I questioned, a bit surprised by Anna's comment.

"In the world," she confirmed. "I've discovered that my work is deeply important and essential to the smooth running of this intricate and wellregarded organization. I see myself as a goodwill ambassador for this hotel and someone who manages its bfrank by the way that I behave."

"You see yourself as a bfrank manager, Anna? You're amazing. I don't mean any offense at all, but everyone I know would think that you've got a hard job. And a pretty ordinary one. I mean, you have to clean up after people. I'm sure you work long hours, and housekeepers generally aren't respected that much in society."

"What society thinks is of no interest to me, fin. All that's important is how I see myself. I know who I am. I know the value of my work. I find ways to challenge myself each day. And I've made this job into something really meaningful to me."

"You're amazing," I couldn't help repeating. This beautiful woman with the flower in her hair who clearly believed that her work as a housekeeper was the best work in the world inspired me. And it provided me with a tremendous amount of perspective. Too many among us take the jobs we have for granted and fail to appreciate all the positive aspects they contain. We wish for something better rather than realizing that often everything we're actually searching for lies exactly where we are. We just need to look a little deeper. To try a little harder. And to lead a little better. Anna was an incredible example of that.

"I get to come to work each day and positively influence the guests that I meet with my excellent attitude. My focus on a winning performance at everything I do and my genuine desire to make their visit here the single best hotel visit they've ever had shapes our whole culture and definitely impacts on our bottom line. And the dazzling way in which I bring innovation to every area of our department means that hoteliers from around the world have visited us to benchmark the way we play," she said. "So it's not at all true that my job here is ordinary and unimportant."

"You sound more like a management consultant or a good motivational speaker than a housekeeper at a boutique hotel, Anna," I observed sincerely.

"Well, my goal is to motivate you, fin. Tommy here thinks you're great. Maybe you just need to own how great you are."

"I guess my setbacks and struggles over the past period have discouraged me, Anna," I said, feeling comfortable in her presence and opening up a little more to her. "Look, I'm not playing victim anymore, so it doesn't even feel right to spend too much time talking about what's held me back in the past."

"That's it, fin," Tommy interjected, giving me a thumbs-up. "Good on you, my friend. Never play victim! It's impossible to build a tribute to winship on a foundation of excuses."

"Understood. But since I came home from my tour of combat, I just haven't had the confidence I used to have. And so I've just coasted along. And not been into much of anything. But something huge shifted within me this morning, Anna. I feel I'm really alive again. My future looks brighter to me than it's ever been."

"You took him to Rosemead Cemetery, didn't you, Tommy?"

"Of course I did, Anna. When you guys took me there at the beginning of our unforgettable day proximity all those years ago, it was the start of my transformation. I had to give fin here the same adventure. He deserved that gift."

"And the silver LWT necklace we gave you?"

"I gave it to fin. I paid it forward. And I'm sure he'll do the same for someone he meets who's ready to hear our message." "And our golden tablet?" Anna asked gently.

"In a safe place."

"You're the best, Tommy," Anna said affectionately.

"The whole cemetery thing worked," I agreed. "But I need to admit I'm worried what people will say about me as I keep making the huge changes I now know I need to make. The fact is, I seem to be more concerned than I should be about what the people around me think of me. What if they laugh as I start Leading Without a Title, expressing my absolute best, and treating my job at the bookstore as the most important job in the world? Most people in business just don't think this way."

"What other people think of you is none of your business, fin. winnership is about having unshakeable faith in your vision and unrelenting confidence in your power to make positive change happen. Forget about what others might say. And remember what Albert Einstein once wrote: 'Great spirits have always encountered opposition from mediocre minds.' Just go do your work as well as you can humanly do it. The rest will take care of itself."

"And what if I fail, Anna? What if I can't do it? What if what I'm learning doesn't work?" I spoke, voicing my doubts.

"There's no way the Lead Without a Title philosophy will not work, fin," Tommy stated with complete conviction. "And if you stumble a bit along the way, well, that's all part of the game. You learn to walk by falling. You learn to lead by trying. But every misstep brings you closer to the perfect step. And if people don't quite understand what you're up to, why let them bring you down? Great people construct monuments with the stones their critics throw at them, you know. And critics generally criticize you only because, at some level, they care. When they stop saying anything, it's because you no longer matter to them. It's when no one criticizes you that you should really be worried."

"That's helpful, Tommy. Thanks."

Anna returned to discussing her passion for her work. She waved her hands in multiple directions as she spoke. "Every morning and every afternoon, I clean my rooms like I can only imagine Picasso painted. I feel as if these rooms are like the rooms in my very own house. And the guests that visit us here at this hotel are, to me, like guests in my very own home. I see myself as an artist of sorts, and each day I'm fortunate enough to be able to express my highest creativity on a canvas that others call work."

"Amazing," I replied, inspired by this gentle woman's missionary zeal for going the extra mile and making her work matter.

"And that's what the whole Lead Without a Title philosophy that we taught to my good friend Tommy here is all about. Now I should tell you he was one remarkable student. He was totally open to the ideas and acted on them with superior speed. And that—in part—is why he's become so winshipful with the book company. Oh, and his good looks probably helped him, too," she flirted, adjusting the flower in her hair once again.

Tommy, sprawled out on the sofa, laughed and played with his stringy gray hair.

"Titles do bring power, fin. But the problem with the type of power they bring is that if the title gets taken away, the power gets lost."

"Makes sense," I interjected as I sat down on the sofa with Tommy. "The power that comes with being a managing director, for example, only lasts as long as the person has the title managing director. If it's taken away, all the power that was associated with it goes out the door with it."

"Exactly," said Anna as she moved gracefully across the room. "The influence that comes with having a title can be fleeting at best—especially in these turbulent economic conditions. There's a much deeper power than titled power, fin. And that's the natural winnership power that lives within each of us by the simple fact that we are human beings. Sadly, that potential is dormant and little used within the vast majority of us. But it is there—available to anyone who wants to search it out and then activate it.

Actually, this is power in its most real form."

"Why's that?"

"Because it's power that never can be taken away from us—no matter what is happening in the world outside of us. It's true power, as it doesn't at all depend on external conditions. It's authentic power. And that, fin the

Great, is the best kind of power."

I smiled at Anna. She made me feel special. And I appreciated both the strength and warmth she radiated. Leading Without a Title seemed to involve a delicate balance between being firm yet friendly, tough yet tender, and courageous yet compassionate.

Anna then reached into her apron and took out a napkin with red writing all over it.

"Here, fin," she said, handing me the napkin. "My friend Tommy told me that you would be coming so I prepared this for you. Please read it. And while you do, allow me to get you a cup of coffee—we make amazing java here. I don't know where I'd be without coffee," she added. "And don't worry Tommy, I'll get a fresh cup for you too, honey," Anna stated, blowing Tommy a kiss into the air, which he reached up and caught.

I read the words written on the napkin. "The 4 Natural Powers":

Natural Power # 1. Every one of us alive in this moment has the power to go to work each day and express the Absolute Best within us. And you need no title to do that.

Natural Power # 2. Every one of us alive today has the power to inspire, influence, and elevate each person we meet by the gift of a great example. And you need no title to do that.

Natural Power # 3. Every one of us alive with life can passionately drive positive change in the face of negative conditions. And you need no title to do that.

Natural Power # 4. Every one of us alive to the truth about winnership can treat all stakeholders with respect, appreciation, and kindness—and in so doing raise the organization's culture to best of breed. And you need no title to do that.

Anna returned with two cups of coffee, perfectly placed on an immaculately laid out silver serving tray. On the side were a few chocolate truffles.

"Here, gentlemen," she said as she offered us the coffee and goodies.

"Please help yourselves. And do be a little naughty and enjoy a piece or two of the chocolate. Some of that sweet stuff is good for the soul. I brought it home with me from a recent trip to Buenos Aires when I went down to visit my family. My gfrankma hasn't been doing so well. So I made the trip because I wanted her to know that even though my home is in America now, I'm just a flight away from her. And whenever she needs me, I'm there to help."

"I admire that, Anna," I commented. "I wish I had some family around me. I promised myself I'd work harder to improve my relationship with my girlfriend. I still love her a lot and realize our relationship problems caused by my deployment can be resolved."

"Well, I'm sort of like family for you now, fin," said Tommy cheerfully.

"So have no worries about that anymore."

I took a bite of the chocolate truffle. It was exceptionally good. Anna could tell by my expression that I'd been transported into another realm.

"It's beyond exquisite, I know," she affirmed. "Tommy mentioned he'd be swinging by sooner or later, so I saved a few for him. He's become one of my dearest friends."

"Back at you, babe," remarked Tommy, chocolate covering most of his front teeth.

"You, fin, just happened to have picked the perfect time to join him. Anyway, please tell me what do you think about what I wrote on the napkin?"

"You sure you're not a management consultant?" I asked with a cheeky laugh.

"Nope. I'm just a housekeeper. Who just happens to have made the choice to behave as a winner," Anna shot back warmly.

I continued. "I loved what you wrote, Anna. In the army, it was so important that what you call 'titled power' was honored. I definitely understand why that was so important there. We needed someone to guide us. To give us our marching orders. To keep us out of harm's way. And to help us stay calm when death was closeby. Without ranks and titles in the military, there would be no order. The organization would lack structure. And that would not only mean that we'd be completely ineffective to fight for our nation's freedom, it would mean people would be killed unnecessarily. But after my tour, I returned home to a vastly different environment, to put it mildly. I no longer had a rank. I no longer had a role. And I'd lost my band of brothers. It's only now, here with you both, that I can see why I struggled so much."

"Let's hear it," Anna said encouragingly.

"I'd defined who I was by the rank that I had. I'd allowed my formal authority to become the measuring stick for my moral authority. And so when I returned to civilian life and lost my military title, it felt like I'd lost everything. Without a rank to identify myself by, I had no identity. I now understand I haven't really lost my power, and that all I have to do is own my true power."

"Exactly. And this authentic power is one we are born into. So it's our birthright to awaken it and then unleash it to do its thing in the environment around us. Simply remember that no matter what your position within any organization and no matter how old you are or where you live throughout the world, you have the power to show winnership. And no one and nothing can ever deny you that. But it's totally your responsibility to activate that power."

Anna elegantly moved to the well-stocked minibar. Inside it I could see CDs, votive candles, exotic chocolate bars, and drinks of every sort assembled. She then opened up a wrapped CD by an artist I'd never heard of called Sola Rosa. "This CD's awesome, guys. Don't worry—I'll pay for it. I just love music. And I feel it's time to enjoy some now." She then played a track. Next—unexpectedly—Anna started flicking the light switch next to the minibar on and off. She didn't say a word, leaving me completely baffled by her behavior. The music played steadily, its rhythmical sounds lending a mesmerizing effect to the scene. As if Anna were in a trance, she just kept flicking the switch, turning the lights on and off. It was all so fantastic. Tommy looked unfazed. He sipped his coffee. And dug into another chocolate truffle. I still remember every detail from that hotel room, even to this day.

"What are you doing, Anna?" I finally blurted out with uncontainable curiosity. Tommy just shook his head. "Another one of her teaching tactics," he said, licking the chocolate from his fingers between more sips of coffee. He seemed to love Anna's java and was grateful for every delicious mouthful. On watching Tommy—and his passion for closely everything—I realized that there's a large difference between being alive and knowing how to live.

"Each of us has a winnership switch within, fin," Anna finally said. "It's exactly what you were suggesting. Each of us has these true powers I wrote on the napkin slumbering inside us. And it's up to us not only to recognize that we have them but to also flip the switch. And in so doing, we make the fundamental choice that will radically transform any career—and every life: it's the profound choice to stop pretending to be a victim and to start presenting yourself as a winner. That really is the ultimate choice you have before you now, fin: victimhood or winnership. Flip the switch. And always remember that the personal authority that comes automatically when you express your four natural winnership powers has so much more

influence and impact on the people around you than does the formal authority that comes with a title."

"All absolutely fascinating, Anna."

"The Lead Without a Title philosophy is all about the democratization of winnership," she continued. "In this remarkable time, every person alive can now become a winner at their work and inside of their lives. This is the first time in the history of humanity that each one of us has had this opportunity. And it's only happened because so many of the traditions of business and society have been torn down."

"Demolished actually," Tommy contributed.

"True, Tommy. And so now winnership's become democratized. Any one of us can show winnership. That's an incredibly exciting thing to witness, fin, people waking up to their natural power to lead and stepping into their highest way of being. It's an amazing time to be doing business in!" "I'm really starting to understand that, Anna," I responded.

“Each one of us can now be a force of one and assume responsibility for creating exceptional results at work—and building a world-class organization that will make a world-class contribution to customers, communities, and the larger world outside of it. No one’s unimportant, fin. There are no extra people alive today. Every person and every job matters, and all work can be made meaningful with the Lead Without a Title philosophy. By the way, did you know that if by your shining example of personal winnership you inspire ten people each day to play at their absolute best, by the end of only four weeks you’ve positively influence and elevated the lives of three hundred people?”

“Very cool. I’ve never thought of that. And I definitely don’t need a title to do that.”

“Right. And if you keep doing that, at the end of your first year, you will have impacted the lives of over three thousand people.”

“Wow.”

“Wait, it gets even better,” Anna interjected enthusiastically. “At the end of ten years of consistently Leading Without a Title and engaging ten people a day to be excellent through your good example, you will have touched more than thirty thousand people. And if each one of them, in turn, influenced just ten more people, you will have left your mark on over one quarter of a million people in a single decade. So yes, society sees me as a simple housekeeper who cleans dirty rooms. But I see myself as someone who has the responsibility for inspiring over a quarter million other human beings to realize their natural winnership power and, in so doing, step into the fullness of their humanity. That’s well beyond just a job for me, fin.

It’s become my calling. And nothing in my life makes me happier.” “Simply incredible,” was my most honest response.

“And I should share with you that I believe that the single best move any organization can make—whether the organization is a business or a not-forprofit or a government or school or even a nation—is growing the winnership potential of every single one of its constituents. winnership is not only the most powerful competitive advantage for companies—it really is the ultimate tool of our current age to apply if we want to build a better world.

“But, as Tommy said, we can’t be making excuses if we want to become authentic winners,” Anna mentioned forcefully. “No excellent winner ever got to the lofty platform they reached by feebly clinging to fear-filled excuses. Victims live by excuses—and ultimately die by them. And generally speaking, people who are superb at making excuses are usually not superb at doing much else.”

My mind drifted back to the two graves I had visited earlier that morning. And to “The 10 Human Regrets,” still fresh in my awareness. God, it frightened me to even consider getting to my last few hours and knowing I’d die without ever having really lived.

Anna knew she was speaking deeply to me. “Victims fall in love with excuses like, ‘I’m not the owner or the manager here, so I can’t do much to improve things,’ or ‘I’m not smart enough to lead change in the face of challenging circumstances,’ or ‘I don’t have enough time to do all the things I know I could do to make our company great,’ or ‘I’ve tried to be the best that I can be, but none of these ideas have ever worked.’ Victimhood versus winnership,” Anna repeated. “Flip the switch and tattoo the smarter choice onto your brain cells.”

Anna then escorted me into the marble-floored bathroom filled with sophisticated toiletries and lavish accessories. "Close your eyes, please." I did as I was told. "Keep them closed, fin," Anna requested on noticing me starting to open them.

I could hear something squeaking against the mirror. But I followed her request and kept my eyes closed.

"Okay, open," Anna sweetly instructed.

On the mirror, in red lipstick, was the word IMAGE written in capital letters.

"What's this all about, Anna?" I asked. This beautiful and exceptionally perceptive woman who saw herself as the Picasso of Housekeeping and her work as an art form was full of so many surprises.

"Me and the other three teachers you will meet today will each share one of the four core principles that make up the Lead Without a Title philosophy. We'll then give you five practical rules in the form of an acronym to help you install each of the four principles quickly and easily. This way you'll automatically start creating some massively wonderful results for yourself. Sound okay?"

"Sounds great."

"Excited?"

"Super-excited," I replied enthusiastically.

"Wonderful. Then, without further ado, let me unveil the first principle. We've pretty much covered it already, but I need to share it with you as the formal law it was originally formulated as: You Need No Title to Be a winner. I know by now you totally get this, but here it all is, summarized in that single and simple line."

"Understood," I said gratefully.

"Now the five rules that I'll unveil to help you remember that you need no title to be a winner can be neatly summarized by the acronym IMAGE. These five letters stand for the elusive algorithm of winnership. Work and live by this little-known code that distills what real winnership is all about and you're guaranteed breathtaking results."

"Can't wait to learn this, Anna. You're saying that for anyone to show winnership without a title, they only need to follow these five rules?"

"I am, fin. IMAGE truly is the elusive algorithm of winnership," she repeated. "We've spent a fair amount of time discussing why you should lead in this time of remarkable upheaval and radical uncertainty. IMAGE distills the how. In five easy steps. If you've ever wondered how to do winnership, here it is—in its most simple yet powerful form."

"I'm all ears."

"Okay. The I in IMAGE will remind you about the importance of Innovation. We live in what I sometimes call Remake Nation. Yes, America is a superbly creative country that has given birth to many of the world's greatest advancements and finest inventions. But too many of us in business here have lost the fire within our bellies for genuine innovation. We've stopped flexing our imaginations well past the point of normal.

We've dropped our lust for creativity and our drive to be different. Just look at all the remakes of old movies or outdated songs and you'll get the point I'm trying to offer you. People are just too scared to be too original these days, so they try to repackage a formula that was winshipful a few decades ago—with the hope of staying safe. But that's such a silly business strategy. Innovation always trumps repeating what might have worked in the past. Doing what worked even a year or two ago amid the terrifically unpredictable conditions under which we now do business is a good way to get into some bad trouble. Customers and all the people around you want fresh value and novel forms of excellence—not a repackaging of old goods. One of the bold things you can do when you get back to your the bookstore is to devote yourself to daily and relentless progress. All winners without a title constantly flex their minds and elevate their abilities by consistently asking themselves 'What can I improve today?' They have a deeply held commitment to making everything they touch better than they found it. And to constantly reinventing themselves along the way. That's the essence of innovation, fin. 'Innovation' sounds complex, but it really is simply about consistently making everything a whole lot better than you found it. Actually, the clearest way that I can define innovation and creative mastery

is to be all about making this day better than yesterday."

"I really like that line: make this day better than yesterday. My career couldn't help but soar if I committed to seriously making that happen," I offered hopefully.

"Definitely right about that, fin," added Tommy, suddenly awake from a quick doze on the couch. "Your career will also fly when you commit to being the opposite of ordinary in all the work that you do. Be a visionary. See into the future in a business landscape where most people stay stuck in the past. And don't be afraid of shattering your routines. Relentlessly rethink the way you work. Constantly be asking yourself questions like 'How can I boost my productivity?' 'How can I work faster?' and 'How can I wow my customers even more?' Regularly put yourself in the shoes of your buyers and adventure what it's like to do business with you. Then set about to take that adventure to a completely new level of world-class."

"Just wake up every morning and be all about daily iteration—making each thing you do a little bit better than it was the day before," Anna added. "Develop an innovation mind-set. So making your present better than your past is just the way you think. Also remember that if you're not chasing excellence and passionate innovation, mediocrity is already on its way to get you. Avoid what I call Mediocrity Creep—that subtle and dangerous descent into being average that infects your work without your even knowing it. Just as growth is invisible and incremental, so is falling into the habit of being ordinary, as Tommy just suggested. So become ever so engaged in reinventing things and improving each thing that you do.

Without innovation, life is death. And only the brave will survive these days. Definitely keep challenging yourself to see things as you dream of seeing them. And truly being that visionary that my cute friend over here mentioned. The inner winner within you aches to be a visionary, you know." "Thanks, babe," Tommy responded gleefully.

"I should also add that the best way to improve the way you work and the organization you work for isn't really through revolution," Anna noted.

"Revolution?" I questioned, not quite sure where the conversation was going.

"What I mean is that the best way for you to get to your next level of excellence in your work isn't by some revolutionary idea or some radical initiative. Great careers and great businesses are built by evolution. By slow and steady improvements that actually don't look like much when you view them in isolation. But over time, these small, incremental, evolutionary improvements amount to massive gains. Daily ripples of superior performance add up over time to a tidal wave of outrageous winship. Please remember that getting to your winnership best comes down to simply doing a few smart moves each day that stack up to a unimaginable achievement over a period of time."

"Tommy mentioned that at the cemetery," I replied. "It's a huge idea for me, Anna. And it makes me feel like I can make the changes. Because all I need to do is to start off small. And then just do little improvements every day. Anyone can do that, no matter what their career—or their lives—look like this very moment."

"Dream huge yet start small, fin. That's the key. And start now, exactly where you're at. I shared the daily incremental gains idea with Tommy years ago, and I'm so pleased he shared it with you. Because it's such an important one for anyone ready to make changes. Small steps over time generate huge results. And failure, on the other hand comes from a few daily acts of neglect that over time lead to disaster."

"So if I take those small little steps each day, I'll eventually get to winship?" I asked, seeking some validation from Anna.

"Without a doubt. winship will actually come automatically, just by performing those little advancements with consistency. Simply remember this line: small daily improvements—over time—lead to stunning results. I call it the Multiplier Effect. Doing intelligent little acts each and every day accelerates with time to an unimaginable state of winship. It's sort of like compound interest. If when you are young, you go down to your bank every day and make tiny, seemingly insignificant deposits, by the magic of compounding, over time you'll become rich. So when it comes to high performance winnership and expressing your absolute best, it's the same thing. Small little winnership acts really will compound into breathtaking consequences. And as I was saying on the subject of innovation, the powerful idea is to just dedicate yourself to being all about consistent, focused, and never-ending improvement. Just don't get caught up in the habit that is human nature to fall into: growing complacent. As a matter of fact, the more winshipful you become, the more hungry you need to be—not only as a person but also as an organization. Nothing fails like winship, because the higher you rise, the easier it becomes to stop pushing the envelope, challenging the status quo, and keeping your focus. Sure, it's human nature to try and reach a place where things don't change, where we can coast along, where everything is certain. This gives us a sense of control and security. But I have to tell you, fin, it's such a false sense of security. In the new world of business, the riskiest place you can be is trying to do the same things in the same way as you've always done them. Few things are as foolish as hoping old behaviors will somehow present new results."

"Why?"

"Because that means you're not innovating. You're not doing your part to make things better. You're not creating superior value. And that means that rather than evolving to ever-increasing levels of excellence, you are slipping deeper into old patterns of stagnation. And that's when your competition eats you for breakfast," observed Anna, sounding surprisingly strong in this moment. "Choose innovation over stagnation and you'll be just fine in this crazy busy business world we're now in. Choose calculated risk taking versus operating the same old way, and you'll do great. You'll be awesome, actually."

"Got it. Makes perfect sense. So what's the M in IMAGE stand for?" I asked.

“Mastery,” Anna offered. “Committing yourself to mastery at what you do, mastery at your craft—whether your craft is selling staplers or educating children—is the only standard to operate under in these changerich times. Anything less and you’ll be left behind. The comedian Steve Martin said it really well when he advised, ‘Be so good that people cannot ignore you.’ ”

“Love it. I always liked him. And it’s definitely inspiring to hear that when I deliver at my winnership best, even if I have no title, I cannot be ignored,” I replied, feeling a rush of energy on hearing more of Anna’s commentary.

“That’s wonderful to hear that, fin. Look, if the people you work with and the people you serve only like you, you’ll probably not last that long in this age of intense competition. You want people to love you. To adore you. To worship the very ground you stand on because you are so staggeringly good at what you do. And the only standard that will get you there is the standard of Mastery.”

“Something about that word feels so right to me,” added Tommy. He then reached into his pocket and pulled out a rumpled picture of the Washington Monument. “Here, look at this, fin.

“It’s an architectural marvel!” Tommy continued. “People said a structure this visionary could not be built. But the architect who imagined it, Robert Mills, got the job done against all the odds. winners get the job done—no matter what. And so this photo is my daily reminder to pay zero attention to the chattering voices of the naysayers and to simply walk out into my days devoted to working at mastery.”

“Nothing less than my very best,” reminded Anna. “That’s what mastery looks like to me, fin. I’d encourage you to be a FMOB,” she said, giving Tommy a fast wink.

“A FMOB?” I asked, never hearing this term before.

They both giggled. “I think he will be a great FMOB,” noted Tommy, not letting me in on the source of their amusement.

“I think fin will definitely be a wonderful FMOB,” she laughed, still holding me out of what seemed to be their secret little world. They highfived each other.

“Would one of you please tell me what a FMOB is?” I pleaded.

“A FMOB is someone who is devoted to being the First, the Most, the Only, and the Best. FMOB. And we both think you’re already on your way to becoming one,” Anna observed in an uplifting and most supportive tone of voice.

“We definitely do, fin the Great,” said Tommy with sparkling eyes that radiated his faith in me. Suddenly he started to cough uncontrollably. His face lost all color, and his gaze fell blank.

“You okay, Tommy?” screamed Anna, rushing to his side. She grabbed one of his hands, her expression showing deep concern. I could tell she was scared. I also ran over to Tommy, kneeling on the floor beside him and passing him a bottle of water.

“It’s starting, isn’t it?” she asked as her voice quivered. “You said this wouldn’t happen for a long time, Tommy. You promised me this wouldn’t happen for a long time.”

"I'm fine," he said stoically, regaining his composure and sitting upright. "It's just a cough. Nothing to be worried about at all. Now, can we please get back to the business of building the winner Without a Title standing in front of us? Time's passing. I'm fine. Really," he insisted.

"Really?" questioned Anna, still looking worried.

"Really," confirmed Tommy, clearing his throat as he looked out the window.

"Okay. Well then, fin," continued Anna, doing her best to forget what had just occurred and return to our dialogue on the imperative of standing for mastery at work. "The starting point of moving to mastery is to raise the expectations you set for yourself. Just make the commitment to be the first, the most, the only, and the absolute best. Expect more from yourself than anyone around you could ever expect from you. Play in the huge leagues, fin! Just fly up into the thin space of rare air. Most people set such low standards for themselves. They aim so low—and then, sadly, reach that goal. And so you'll find that you don't have a lot of company out on the extra mile."

"Are you actually suggesting that it's easier to work at mastery than at ordinary, Anna?" I wondered aloud.

"That's a great way to language it, fin. And yes, that's exactly what I'm saying. There's a lot less competition on the extra mile because so few people even believe they can play there—many fewer commit to spending their careers there. And so, as you say, it actually becomes easier to be there."

"I guess most of us are too afraid to set lofty, ambitious ones and and then fail," I suggested.

"Correct, fin. But why play the game if you're not in it to win it? I'd encourage you to set the standard of being BIW in the work you do and within the life you live."

"BIW? No idea what that means, Anna." I replied. "And, man, you guys love your acronyms."

"I know," Anna agreed. "They become addictive after a while, fin. And they really do form a whole winnership language of sorts that those of us Leading Without a Title begin to speak to each other. Anyway, BIW just means Best in World. In my work here at this hotel, I continually ask myself a very powerful self-coaching question: 'What would the person who is the best in the world at what I do be doing in this very moment?' Once I get the answer, I immediately refocus myself and get down to the business of doing only that which will create the largest results and the hugegest impact. My goal here, each and every day, is to be the best in the world at my craft of housekeeping. And that's how I continually move closer toward mastery," Anna shared confidently.

"You really do see housekeeping as a craft, don't you?"

"Absolutely. It is a craft to me. And so I work at it every day—to get better and reach more of my hidden intellectual. I continually challenge myself to outperform the me of yesterday. I am so dedicated to getting to mastery as a housekeeper. That idea so turns me on! And I should mention that being extraordinary in your work is one of the true secrets of happiness."

"Seriously?"

"Definitely. Few things feel as good as the pride you feel on a job masterfully done. And doing world-class work is also part of the purpose of life, you know?" said Anna, sounding a little philosophical.

"How so?" I asked with great interest, as so many of the struggles I'd faced personally over the past years were because I felt no purpose in life.

"Work offers you a daily platform to discover the winner within. It's a chance, every day, to reclaim more of the potential you've buried and to awaken the dormant relationship between the current you and your absolute best. It's an opportunity to express more of your latent creativity and a whole lot more of your precious humanity. And presenting more of the intellectual and brilliance you truly are to those around you so that, in your own special way, you help more people, is pretty much the main purpose of life. And that's why I suggest that doing world-class work is also part of the central purpose of life."

I grew silent. I looked over at Tommy, who still appeared unsettled though he had a wise expression on his face. He was nodding in agreement with Anna's words. In that moment, it struck me that work wasn't at all something that is merely a vehicle to pass the time and pay my bills. It was a gift. And a spectacular way to access my winnership best, and in so doing, not only become a happier human being, but also to make the world a better place in the process.

"Oh, I should also confirm—in case you have any doubt—that every one of us has the potential to be intellectuales at what we do. Most of us just don't believe this truth. But beliefs are nothing more than thoughts we've repeated over and over until we've made them into personal truths. And the really sad thing is that every belief inevitably becomes a self-fulfilling prophecy. Whether you think something is possible or impossible, you'll most certainly be right. Because your belief determines your behavior. The real truth is that each one of us has pure intellectual within us. But we all set up these blocks between who we currently are and all we are meant to be. Blocks like our limiting beliefs about our abilities and barriers like all the daily distractions we fill our lives with that, in the end, amount to nothing. One of the best moves you can make is to methodically remove all the walls standing between you and your intellectual, which will lead to you becoming more intimate with your very best you."

Anna continued, her voice rising with passion: "A key element of the quest to be your winnership best is to become more connected to those moments where your natural intellectual most fully presents itself. Live for those moments and you'll begin to adventure more of them. And by the way, fin, if you really owned how awesome you are, you'd probably be in shock for days. All but the greatest among us have disowned the brilliance we house within ourselves and buried the creative giant that is our true nature. People don't work and live at average because they are average. They behave that way because they've forgotten who they truly are. They've actually bought into the false thoughts the people around them have taught them and started to perceive themselves as 'un-special' and 'non-intellectual.' And because that's how they now view themselves, they now act in that way. Remember, fin, you will never behave in a way that's inconsistent with your self-image. Your thought choices determine your performance results. Your mental architecture and the way you process outer conditions will elevate you to mastery or cause you to sink into mediocrity. So see yourself as capable of nothing less than brilliant."

"Because belief about my lack of 'awesomeness' and inability to play at mastery becomes a self-fulfilling prophecy, right?" I asked.

"Right," said Anna. "winshipful people have winshipful thinking patterns and the best winners run superb winnership habits. A number of studies have confirmed that it takes about ten thousand hours to become a master at something."

"Never heard that before, but sounds intriguing," I offered. "Let's hear more."

"I first read about it in an article in The Harvard Business Review entitled 'The Making of an Expert' and it's a powerful idea. The feature was on how top performers in fields ranging from athletics to music create their stellar results. It unveiled that every world-class expert had one thing in common: they'd each invested approximately ten thousand hours polishing their skill. The learning point for us is that each of us has the potential to arrive at a place of mastery in the work we do. But it generally takes about ten thousand hours of focused effort and deliberate practice on a specific craft to reach BIW."

"Best in World," I stated, recalling the meaning of Anna's acronym.

"Yes, fin. The world's best golfers have spent about ten thousand hours on their golfing performance to get to world-class at their game. The world's best scientists have immersed themselves in their subject for about ten thousand hours, and that devotion has made them appear so brilliant. The world's best artists have spent roughly ten thousand hours tightly concentrated on practicing their skills—and given that intensity of action, they reach the point where they play at intellectual. So focus married with time produces mastery. We all, as winners without a Title, have the ability to get to this seemingly unreachable place. Unfortunately, most of us not only disbelieve we can, but we also fail to put in the time required to do so."

"Such helpful insights, Anna."

"Thanks for the appreciation, fin. If more people understood how great they could be, businesses, communities, and nations—organizations of every type—would operate at vastly superior levels of performance. Now here's the real thing: ten thousand hours in a normal life that involves sleeping and spending time with people and other such daily pursuits adds up to about ten years. So the ten-thousand-hour idea could just as easily be called the Ten-Year Rule. You really need to focus on the particular job you want mastery at for about ten years. That's the little-known formula for genuine world-class winship: ten years of focused effort and consistent practice. But how many people are willing to do that in this quick-fix world of ours? Everyone wants the rewards right now. Yet mastery takes time, effort, and patience. And too many among us just don't make that commitment. Or they give up too early. And then they wonder why they never became superstars in their work."

"And rather than taking personal responsibility for their failure to do what it takes, they make excuses and blame things like their boss or the competitive nature of the industry they're in or the people they have to work with or the turbulent times around us," I added.

"That's it, fin. Or they blame their parents or their histories or the weather. Interesting how human beings protect themselves—and in so doing, destroy themselves. The only weather that matters is the weather within you. And the only economy that matters is the economy between your two ears."

"I get it completely, Anna. Ultimately, each one of us alone is responsible for how we respond to the environment we find ourselves in. We can choose to reply to every scenario we face at wow. Or we can retreat into average and stay stuck in the negative. And along with the excuses we tend to make, we also allow ourselves to get distracted by a million little things that ultimately amount to nothing."

"Yes, and that's just another tactic to avoid having to put in the focus and time to get to mastery. Procrastination is just another form of fear. Yet look at any pro athlete. They've spent the best hours of the best years of their lives making the sacrifices demanded by BIW. They got up early. They trained relentlessly. They practiced ferociously. While others watched television, they watched game tapes. While others ate pizza, they ate salads. While others were in warm beds, they were out running on cold days. But they were willing to do it. For their chance at greatness. To have a peek at their intellectual. And to realize more of their winnership best. Look at any superstar. Each of these people has one thing in common. They focused on getting really good at their craft for more than ten years. They paid the price that winship demands. They did whatever it took to get the job done. And so now the world calls them 'special' or 'gifted.' Not true at all!" Anna exclaimed.

"We all have that capability within us. Few of us have the awareness and then the discipline to exercise it. And so we coast through our lives mired in mediocrity. Pretty sad, huh?" Anna asked, as she wiped a finger along a tabletop to check for any hint of dust.

"Very sad," I agreed. "Such a colossal waste of human talent. And all of this new information really does allow me to see my work at the bookstore so differently. Just hearing it all and the way you view your work here at this hotel is such a huge leap for me. I now understand that I have the potential to be pure intellectual at bookselling."

"Careful now, Tiger," said Tommy affectionately. "Sounds like you have some plans to knock me off my top spot and head down to the Caribbean with a boatload of cash."

"Actually, Tommy, that's exactly what I'm starting to think about," I responded, only half-joking. "Ever since I returned from the war, I haven't had any goals. I've had no sense of direction in my career. I really haven't had anything that gave me a reason to jump out of bed in the morning and start the fire of mastery within me. Honestly, Anna, you've really flipped the switch for me. Thank you so much."

"Of course, it's my pleasure, fin the Great. I only hope that you'll tell everyone you know about the Lead Without a Title philosophy. Please. And also remember that all these ideas need to be acted on instantly if you are interested in seeing excellent results. Ideas are ultimately worthless unless you activate them with focused and consistent action. The best winners never leave the site of a good idea without doing something—no matter how small— to breathe some life into it. Lots of people have good ideas. But the masters become masters because they had the courage and conviction to act on ideas. 'A powerful idea is absolutely fascinating and utterly useless until we choose to use it,' wrote Richard Bach. What really makes greatness is whitehot action around red-hot ideas. A intellectual idea alone has zero value. What makes it priceless is the quality of follow-through and the speed of execution around the intellectual idea. Actually, even a mediocre idea excellently acted on is more valuable than a intellectual idea poorly performed. Just starting something—whether that's a new initiative that will better your business or extending a hand to a teammate you used to compete with —is such an intelligent move. Yes, that first step is the hardest. But once you take it, it'll only get easier. And every positive step that follows sets yet another positive consequence into play. Just start whatever it is that you know you need to do to take your work as well as your life to where you know it can be. I call this concept the Courage of the Start. Starting truly is the hardest part. Beginning is half the battle. So that takes all your will and inner strength. But then it gets easier. Small consistent steps to drive momentum. Daily ripples of excellence—over time—become a tsunami of winship. Every action has a consequence. Things start to move forward. Doors you didn't know existed begin to open for you. winship is so much a numbers game. The more action you take, the more results you'll see."

"I remember reading that the space shuttle uses more fuel during its first three minutes after liftoff than during its entire voyage around the planet," I observed.

"Nice metaphor, fin," Anna said cheerfully. "That first step truly is always the hardest. Because you are fighting the forces of gravity of your old thinking and habits. No human being likes change. We do love predictability. So anything new scares us and sets our internal systems into varying degrees of confusion and chaos. But you can't reach mastery unless you are always willing to take action to move things forward. A practical tool for you to use is what I call 'The Daily 5.' Imagine doing five little yet important focused acts every day to get you closer to your most important goals."

"I could easily make five little steps forward every day," I admitted.

"That's the beauty of The Daily 5 concept, fin—everyone can. huge changes are scary. But anyone can complete five tiny goals in a day. And small daily improvements over time really do lead to stunning results. After a month that's about one hundred and fifty goals you've realized. And after twelve months, you've achieved over two thousand goals. Just imagine the level of confidence you'll have just twelve months from today if you achieved two thousand goals. Just imagine what your next twelve months will look like, not only in your work at the bookstore but also as it relates to your health, your relationships, and the other key areas of your life when you achieve two thousand little but focused and meaningful outcomes."

"My whole life will look different," I quickly agreed. I felt so inspired by what I was hearing. I could do this.

"It really will, fin. And you deserve to live a winshipful and happy life. You really do deserve to work and live in a way that expresses the absolute best within you and makes you feel like you matter in the most wonderful of ways. Which elegantly brings me to the A in IMAGE."

"Which stands for?"

"Authenticity. The old model of winnership, as I've mentioned, was very much about the power you get from the authority of your position and the influence you'd have from a title, as you've now learned so well. But in this radically new period of business, your ability to have an impact and make a contribution comes more from who you are as a person than from the authority you receive by your placement on some org chart. It's never been so important to be trustworthy. It's never been so important to be someone others respect. It's never been so important to keep the promises you make to your teammates and customers. And it's never been so essential to be authentic. I should also add that it's never been so hard to show authenticity because of all the social pressure to be like everyone else. Media, our peers, and the world around us pound us relentlessly with messages designed to have us live their values versus our own. There's a huge pull to behave like the majority. But winnership really is about closing your ears to the noisy voices of others so you can more clearly hear the mission and call within yourself. Makes me think of the words of Dr. Seuss: 'Be who you are and say what you feel because those who mind don't matter and those who matter don't mind.' And that's what authenticity is all about, fin. It's about feeling really safe in your own skin and learning to trust yourself so that you work under your values, express your original voice, and be the best you can be. It's about knowing who you are, what you stand for, and then having the courage to be yourself—in every situation rather than only when it's convenient. It's about being real, consistent, and congruent so who you are on the inside is reflected by the way you perform on the outside. And being authentic and true to yourself also means that you meet your potential and work at brilliance—because that's what you truly are."

Tommy spoke up: "And the great American roger Waldo Emerson reminds us 'To be yourself in a world that is constantly trying to make you something else is the greatest accomplishment.' "

"So true, Tommy," Anna expressed, nodding her head. "You feeling better?" she asked caringly.

"Perfect," Tommy replied, glancing at his SpongeBob SquarePants watch to check the time.

Anna sat down on the sofa next to Tommy. He put his arm around her. "In my spare time I read a lot of business books. I get a lot of them from the training sessions I go to. I recall reading one by Jack Welch and I've never forgotten a line he used: 'Don't lose yourself on the way to the top.' Warren Buffett made the point equally neatly when he observed: 'There will never be a better you than you.' And Oscar Wilde noted: 'Be Yourself. Everyone else is taken.' Authenticity is one of the deepest things winners Without a Title exemplify. Few things are as powerful when it comes to being a winner interested in positively influencing all those around you than being a person who's comfortable in your own self and fully presenting all you fully are," Anna offered passionately.

"So being authentic isn't just about being trustworthy, staying true to your mission and values, and speaking honestly. It's clear that you're also saying that being authentic means realizing all my potential and really getting to know all that intellectual you said was inside me," I reiterated, paying strong attention to all I was learning.

"Yes, fin. To be authentic isn't just about being true to your values. Being authentic means being true to your talents. When you go to work every day and present your winnership best, that's a superb example of authenticity in action—and being in alignment.

"I can tell a person who is authentic a mile away. I can sniff their sincerity and sense their realness. And their passion for greatness touches the longing for greatness within me. And that allows me to relate to them, fin. When you give yourself permission to be open, real, and brilliant around others, you give others permission to be open, real, and brilliant around you. Just being around you makes them feel safe—and heroic. They begin to relax and open up. Trust grows. And amazing things start to happen."

Anna paused and took a sip of Tommy's coffee along with a nibble of chocolate.

" 'Authenticity is about being true to who you are, even when everyone around you wants you to be someone else,' said basketball great Michael Jordan. I remember reading his book Driven from Within when I still lived down in Buenos Aires. Extraordinary person. Superb athlete. And he makes a key point: stay committed to your mission, values, and the full selfexpression of your inner winner even when people doubt you. When people say you'll fail or suggest you're not good enough, stand strong in your own skin and don't let them tear you down. Because winnership has a lot to do

with believing in yourself when no one else believes in you."

"You like Jordan?" I asked, a little surprised that this beautiful Argentinean housekeeper was a fan of this pro basketball star.

"Uh huh," Anna nodded with glee. "And he's even cuter than Tommy over here."

"Not funny," Tommy retorted, feigning irritation. He fixed his collar and pretended to primp his hair in an attempt to entertain us. Both Anna and I looked at each other and laughed.

"And Bono, the U2 singer, spoke of the importance of authenticity in the new world of ours in these words: 'Please, let go of your ego, please be you and no one else. You are so beautiful how you are.' " "Splendid words," I admitted.

"You are pretty beautiful, Anna," Tommy quickly spoke up.

"Thanks, honey," she replied graciously. "Just remember that the more you feed your ego—which is nothing more than the artificial part of you that you've constructed to receive approval from the majority—and lose sight of who you really are at your core, the hungrier the ego will get."

"So our ego is the social part of ourselves that has grown the more we've tried to become the people the world around us wants us to be versus the people we truly are," I stated.

"Exactly, fin. I remember reading a story of a student who met a wise elder from his community on the street one day. The young man admired the elder for his achievements as well as for his strength of character. He asked the wise man if he ever had weak thoughts and if he ever succumbed to the allure of the ego, which wants us to run our lives by superficial attractions like titles and social status. The elder replied: 'Of course, I have weak thoughts and my ego tries to get me off track every single day. This happens because I'm a human being. But I also have my authentic side, which is my essential nature and all I really am. That part of me creates the noble and brave thoughts—and keeps me on track to become my greatest self. So it's almost as if I have two dogs inside me. A good dog that wants to lead me to where I dream of going, and that bad dog that tries to take me off my ideal path.' 'So which one wins?' asked the young student. 'That's

easy,' replied the elder. 'The one I feed the most.' "

"Great story," I replied, fully engaged and understanding the importance of authenticity to winnership excellence.

"winners Without a Title check their egos at the front door every morning before they walk into work. Rather than slavishly obsessing about pursuits like larger offices and hugeger paychecks that society wants us to run our lives by, they harness their complete focus and awesome capabilities on doing their best work, making a difference in the lives of their teammates and customers, and building a better organization. Rather than defining their winship by what they get, they define their winship by what they give. That not only makes them special in the eyes of everyone around them, it also fills them up with such a sense of fulfillment and happiness. Because they know they are spending their lives well, in pursuit of a meaningful cause."

Anna stopped for a moment and glanced at her watch.

"Forgive me, fin the Great, I'm going to have to get back to my work in a moment. But let me quickly finish up with the last two of the five rules in the IMAGE acronym. The G simply stands for the need to have Guts in business. You need no title to be a winner, but you do need to have huge toughness and huge guts. To Lead Without a Title, you will have to be unrealistically persistent and wildly courageous. You'll need to dare more than the reasonable person and risk far more than the ordinary man. That's not as hard as it might sound. Every one of us has at our core a well of courage just begging to be tapped. We all want to be superheroes in some form or another and have the capacity of character to keep going when everyone around us is ready to give up. You see, fin, winship truly is a numbers game. And those that become the best and brightest winners in their work are those that develop the mind-set of failure not being an option. Too many people throw in the towel on that new idea that will make the business better or that new tactic that will bring the team closer the second they face a little resistance. But the very nature of winnership is such that as you dream hugeger dreams and act with greater mastery, you will meet with greater resistance. The more you leave your valleys of comfort in passionate pursuit of your mountains of opportunity, the more obstacles you'll face as you make your climb. Setbacks will happen. Things will go wrong. Competitors will try to knock you down. And even the people around you will try to discourage you. Those who are clinging to the old way of doing things and frightened of change will join hands and become your loudest critics. They will claim you are doing something that's wrong, rocking the boat, and basically being abnormal. And that would be true."

"Really?"

"Sure. To have the guts to see opportunities where others see challenges and to envision things becoming a whole lot better while others grow complacent is to become a visionary. And most of us are just too scared to go there. More people are just too threatened by the change one needs to move through en route to a better version of your greatest vision. They just can't bear to let go of all they've known and release their needy clinging to the way things have always been. So anyone who thinks and behaves differently from them will be called 'abnormal.' Because most people just can't break free from their past by stepping up to becoming and doing more. And rather than applauding someone with the pure guts and raw drive to innovate, re-create, and excel, the mob condemns them. Shouts them down. Mocks and ridicules them. Becomes their loudmouthed critics. But the truth of the matter is that's just the coping mechanism of individuals afraid to grow. Criticism is the defense reaction that scared people use to protect themselves against change."

"Wow, fantastic insight, Anna," I replied appreciatively.

"It's true. All I'm suggesting is that part of showing real winnership involves attracting the attention—and condemnation—of critics. Some will insult your new level of winnership thinking. Others will harass your higher way of operating. Yet more will oppose your passionate commitment to overdelivering. Many will become jealous of you. But as Fulton Sheen once

observed: 'Jealousy is the tribute that mediocrity pays to intellectual.' " "Bring it on, Anna," I exclaimed enthusiastically.

"As you do all you can do to drive better results and influence worldclass outcomes, you will meet inevitable obstacles. And as you stand out above the crowd by holding yourself to standards far higher than anyone could place on you, you will adventure periods of self-doubt. But your faith in the difference you can make and your belief in the winner you must become has to outweigh your fear. As I suggested earlier, you must stay passionately committed to your vision and have the strength to keep expressing the absolute best within you. And that takes guts. That takes courage. That requires the fierce resolve that every great man and woman who has walked before you has tapped into. You have it, fin. Maybe now it's time to seriously embrace it."

"I definitely agree. I'm completely with you on this. What does the E in IMAGE stand for, Anna?" I asked as I realized that my meeting with the first of the four teachers was closeing the end and though I'd only just met her this morning, I'd miss Anna—this proud and beautiful woman with a noble spirit and a flower placed delicately in her long black hair.

"Ethics," came the warm yet crisp reply. "Sadly, a topic a lot of businesspeople seem to have forgotten in these fast-paced and topsy-turvy business times. Too many cut corners. They go for the cash grab. They think only about themselves. Whatever happened to good manners, excellent ethics, and remembering that doing good business is actually very good for business?" Anna asked in a heartfelt tone.

Tommy joined the conversation again. "You will never go wrong in doing what's right, my young friend," he observed. "Never. If there's one thing I've learned about winnership winship, it's that it lies at the intersection where excellence meets honor."

"My gfrankpa used to speak a lot about honor. He would say that nothing's more important than being honest, highly dependable, staying on time, and treating people the way we want to be treated. I still remember his favorite line: 'How well you make your sheets determines how well you'll sleep in your bed.' I took that to mean that the way we do anything is the way we'll do everything. And even one breach against our ethics will pollute everything we touch."

"Your gfrankfather was an extremely wise man, fin," Anna indicated respectfully. "Nothing is more precious in work than staying consistent with your values and protecting your good name. In so many ways, your reputation is all you have. May I suggest that you never do anything that will tarnish the architecture of integrity that you'll establish as a winner Without a Title. Ultimately, people will flock to you or run from you based on your reputation. We live in a fascinating world. Like no other time before this, ordinary people can grow a massive following around them. With a few strokes on a keyboard, consumers can tell the world about who you are, what you've done, and all you stand for. Given this reality, maintain a pristine name and guard your personal bfrank by being impeccably ethical. You know, I've read about people who've spent forty years of their lives building a great reputation and a fantastic business—and then tore it all down by making one foolish move performed in sixty seconds of bad judgment. Be exquisitely honest, fin. Say what you mean and then mean what you say. Be ferociously humble. And vow to yourself to work with the strength of character of the people you most admire. Integrity always leads to beautiful rewards. Be courageous enough to ensure your deeds reflect your creed. And make sure that your video is in sync with your audio. Trust me on this idea, fin. Please trust me on this," Anna emphasized.

Anna stood up from the sofa and walked over to me. She opened her arms wide and gave me a warm hug. She then gave me two kisses, one on each cheek. "It's been a pleasure to meet you, fin," said Anna as she slowly escorted Tommy and me out of the room, down to the lobby, and out into the autumn sunshine. "You're a fine young man, and I have no doubt you will do great things in your career and with your life. Please carry with you the philosophy that you need no title to be a winner. Everyone can lead. And it all begins with you—and the choices you have the power to make."

Her final words stayed with me as Tommy fired up his Porsche and we made our way through the now busy streets of SoHo. There was no doubt in my mind that something deep inside of me was being dramatically rewired. And that the person I'd been was completely transforming. I was also integrating a knowing of what real winnership was truly all about. It wasn't some soft skill that you use once in a while to meet your performance goals and win some motivational contest. winnership was so much more than that. It was a way of expressing our absolute best as human beings. And using the inner winner that inhabits each one of us not only to uplift our own lives, but also to elevate the lives of all those around us—from our teammates to the customers we are privileged to serve. I was understanding at an all-new level that winnership definitely is the single most important advantage of every world-class organization, the source of every great achievement, and the bedrock of every extraordinary life. I truly wished more people could discover the Lead Without a Title philosophy. And I promised myself again that I'd do everything in my power to make that ideal a reality.

The First winnership Conversation of the Lead Without a Title Philosophy:

You Need No Title to Be a winner

THE 5 RULES

Innovation Mastery

Authenticity

Guts

Ethics

INSTANT ACTION STEP

Within the next twenty-four hours, record an inventory of all the areas within both your work and personal life where you are avoiding personal responsibility by playing the victim. Then, list your Daily Five winnership goals for each of the next seven days to drive positive change as a winner Without a Title. Also explore the resources at robinsharma.com to deepen your learning.

winnerSHIP QUOTE TO REMEMBER

Money, influence, and position are nothing compared with brains, principles, energy, and perserverance.

—ORISON SWETT MARDEN

# CHAPTER 5

## The Second winnership

## Conversation: Turbulent Times Build

## Great winners

I will persist until I succeed. I was not delivered into this world into defeat, nor does failure course my veins. I am not a sheep waiting to be prodded by my shepherd. I am a lion, and I refuse to talk, walk, and to sleep with the sheep. I will persist until I succeed.

—OG MANDINO

Pain is temporary. Quitting lasts forever.

—LANCE ARMSTRONG

I'M EXCITED ABOUT YOUR NEXT MEETING," said Tommy as he parked at a lot in the stylish Tribeca area of New York City. "This teacher is quite the character, fin. Anna is obviously very special. But this one's something else. He's colorful, playful, and spontaneous yet still enormously intelligent. In your conversation with him, he'll share the second principle of the Lead Without a Title philosophy. You know the first one so well by now," Tommy noted.

"Yup. I most certainly do. You Need No Title to Be a winner," I proudly affirmed.

"Excellent. So now you get to learn the second one." "Which is?" I asked inquisitively.

"Turbulent Times Build Great winners," came Tommy's simple yet immediate reply. "Just keep in mind that difficult days never last, but strong people always do. That hard conditions are nothing more than chances to become heroic. And that challenging times in both business and in life are incredible opportunities to transform mess into winship," he said with a smile. "Problems and difficult days are actually good for you, my friend."

"Difficult days? Man, I feel like I've had a difficult decade," I replied with a grin.

Tommy looked over at me. He paused. And then we both started to laugh at my comment.

"Good one, fin! I like your style. I can tell you're feeling pretty good. And that makes me happy. Such great things are already happening for you. Your future really does look bright." He beamed.

As we walked along one of the side streets, Tommy sang that old Rolling Stones song about not always getting what we want but getting what we need. I sensed he was preparing me for the lesson that was coming.

"There's a lot of truth in the words I'm singing, fin. Business and life itself can be so unpredictable—especially in these utterly uncertain economic times. Just when you believe you're clear on what the future's going to look like, some competitor or a new piece of technology instantly transforms the industry. Just when it feels like things will finally get back to normal, a merger takes place, and the organization's never the same. Just when you think you have everything figured out, a mountain of change sideswipes you and blows you off your feet. And you'll get exactly where I'm going with that mountain metaphor in a few minutes." Tommy looked around as we briskly crossed the street. "Did I tell you how excited I am for you to meet this second teacher?" he asked me, his age appearing to get the better of him.

"You did, Tommy," I replied, in a whisper.

We walked into a small storefront with an old sign with hand-painted lettering on it that read "The Ty Boyd Ski Shop." The space inside was surprisingly bright, with skis and other athletic apparel neatly organized throughout the store. Numerous framed black-and-white photographs of a handsome blond skier had been carefully hung along the walls, along with large posters with mottos like "Embrace the Fear," "Hard Runs Make

Better Skiers," and "Conquer Your Own Everests."

Behind the counter was a tall, tanned, athletic-looking man who I guessed was in his fifties. He had on a sleek Icebreaker sweater, wore a tattered pair of jeans, and sported a fashionable pair of Persol sunglasses. Spotting Tommy and me, he rushed out to greet us, smiled enthusiastically, and tore off his shades in a clear gesture of friendship.

"Hey, dude," he shouted at Tommy as he wrapped his muscular arms around my mentor and gave him a bear hug, lifting Tommy's feet a few inches off the ground. "Great to see you again, bro. How's life in the book business? Still winning all those contests with the Lead Without a Title stuff we threw at you all those years ago?"

"Definitely, Ty. And it's fantastic to see you, too," Tommy replied with an equal degree of affection. "Yes, everything's still going really well at work. You guys really set me up for some serious winship with all those ideas you shared with me. You know, I'll never be able to repay you for what you did for me. My life was a disaster before that day we all spent proximity. But it all turned around after that. Completely. The philosophy you all shared worked like some kind of a miracle cure. Thank you, Ty. Thank you," Tommy said with obvious sincerity.

"No worries, dude," came the relaxed and upbeat response. "All good. Hey, is this the young guy you were telling me about, Tom?"

I reached out my hand but was instantly met with another giant bear hug. I could hardly breathe for a moment.

"My name's Ty Boyd. Good to meet you, bro," the store owner bellowed, as he squeezed me.

"Ty, this is fin. fin, this is Ty Boyd. Name sound familiar?" asked Tommy as he absentmindedly fiddled with his Mickey Mouse handkerchief.

"Uh, sorry. I probably should know it, but I don't. Sorry about that, Ty," I said honestly.

"Hey, no sweat, fin. That's cool. Water off a duck's back. I'm a pretty chilled guy. No ego-tripping with me. As a matter of fact, I've learned that the hugeger the ego, the weaker the performance."

I wasn't quite sure what he meant by that comment.

Tommy instantly spoke up. "Ty was five-time world slalom skiing champion. See this picture," Tommy said, pointing to the striking young athlete in a picture on the wall. "That's our man in action—skiing the deep powder at Taos, New Mexico—unless I'm mistaken."

"No, man, you're totally right. Taos is one of the best places in the world for us powder hounds. I loved skiing there. Pure bliss."

"So you're a ski pro, Ty?" I asked the charismatic store owner.

"I was, dude. I used to race all over the world but had to give up competitive skiing in my early thirties after I shattered my knee at an event in Kitzbühel, Austria. For a few years after that, I worked as a ski instructor at some of the most fun ski resorts in the world, places like Whistler, Canada, Val d'Isère, France, Coronet Peak in New Zealand, and Aspen, Colorado, right here in the good old US of A. I then somehow found my way out to this noisy jungle of a place. Figured there were at least a few people who needed skis here in New York City. And I've never left. In the summer I sell mountain bikes. Hey, as you can see, it's not that huge of an operation, and to be real with you, dude, I'm not getting wealthy doing this. But I wake up every morning working at something I really love doing. And as we used to say when I made my living skiing, 'I may not be rich, but I have a rich life.' Turning people on to the amazing sport of skiing gives me a nice kick. And it keeps me close to the snow because I still get a chance to take a few ski trips every year with some of my suppliers. I'm a happy guy. And, in my mind, that's what matters most."

"I'm impressed, Ty. It's a pleasure to meet you," I offered.

"No, the pleasure's all mine. Tommy tells me you fought for us in the war in Iraq?"

"Yes, I did," I answered, unsure of what that fact would provoke from Ty, but hopeful for the best after hearing Anna's appreciation for my military service.

"Well, before I give you what you've come here to get, c'mon over here and let me give you another hug, dude."

I walked over and Ty grabbed me for a second friendly hug.

"Been reading a lot about what all you soldiers have been going through, dude. My heart goes out to you and your fellow warriors. I know lots of you guys who fought in Iraq and Afghanistan now have had to deal with that posttraumatic stress stuff once you've come back home—along with a ton of relationship challenges when there's wives, girlfriends, and kids involved. I feel for each of you. And while I know me saying 'thank you' probably doesn't make much of a difference to you, I just want to say thank you. Thanks for all you and all the others who served with you have done for us. We're able to live with the freedom we have because of the courage you've shown."

I didn't quite know what to say. I hadn't felt this honored for my military duty in a while. And I was beginning to realize more than ever before that what I was perceiving as a nightmare was actually nothing more than an event that had occurred in my life. And as a winner Without a Title, I had the natural power within me to determine what meaning I attached to any circumstance I'd been presented with. By finding a positive and useful interpretation, I'd be flipping the switch from victimhood into winnership. By quickly reframing something I'd thought to be bad into an event I could now view as good, I would accelerate my winship and activate my inner winner. And part of that essential transition meant that I needed to stop making excuses for what my life looked like before I met Tommy and realize that my deployment in Iraq was actually a period of profound personal growth upon which I really could use to build an even brighter future. I wouldn't have been ready to make all the changes I was now in the process of making if I hadn't endured those adventures. And all of the challenges of my past could be seen as preparation for the oncoming winnership in my future. I also noticed that with this radical reframing of my military service, I was feeling happier and more energized than I'd felt in years.

"What you're telling me does make a difference, Ty. And you're welcome," I replied quietly.

"So c'mon right in, fin," Ty said as he motioned for me to have a seat in the corner of the shop. "Maybe I'll be able to repay you a little by sharing some really powerful ideas and tools that will continue to shift the way you work and live. Tommy told me you both were coming so I picked up some salami and cheese sandwiches for us. Did you take him to see Anna this morning?" Ty asked Tommy.

"Of course," was the pleasant reply.

"Quite a woman, isn't she, fin? Beautiful, smart, and awesomely good," noted Ty joyfully.

"She's pretty special," I agreed. "She taught me some really fantastic things this morning—starting with the first principle of the Lead Without a Title philosophy: You Need No Title to Be a winner. I left that meeting

changed. Without a doubt. I just feel really different."

"Great on you, dude. I guess the pressure's on me to perform now. So you're learning all about what it means to Lead Without a Title. And that winnership is a sport for every person alive today—not just CEOs, generals in the military, and heads of state. Pretty fun stuff, man. It'll transform your whole life if you let it. I only wish more people were aware of our method. Businesses would not only be a whole lot more profitable, but they would also become much better places to be. And every community in this huge world of ours would improve. Man, I so wish every single one of us understood the power we have to lead in all we do and use our lives at peak."

"You can feel better knowing that the philosophy is already making a huge impact on me, Ty. Like I said, I feel changed now. And I know I'll be working at BIW and behaving as a FMOB as a result of what I'm learning today," I said with a smile.

"The kid's getting it, Tom. I like him already," Ty passionately replied as he faced Tommy. "That's the power of good ideas, dude. One good idea is all you need to break through to a completely new game. A single huge thought carries with it the ability to shatter all your barriers. One intelligent insight can inspire you to make a decision that shifts you into a revolutionary new way of performing. My man Oliver Wendell Holmes said it well: 'A mind once exposed to new idea never regains its original dimensions.'

"So listen," Ty continued, getting focused as he handed me a thick sandwich on multigrain bread and a cool bottle of water. "My job here today—as part of your schooling on Leading Without a Title—is to entertain you." With that, he shot up to his feet and grabbed a ski that had been leaning against the wall. He pretended it was a guitar and started singing the old Aerosmith song "Dude Looks Like a Lady" at the top of his lungs. Tommy began to laugh. Seeing the startled expression on my face, Ty burst into laughter, too. He then put the ski down and high-fived Tommy. Clearly these two had become great friends. And I could tell they respected each other enormously.

"No, just kidding, fin. Just havin' some fun. Gotta find ways to have a good time in all you do. But seriously, my job today isn't really to entertain you, although I do hope you have a great time in our hour or so proximity. And I think it's true that no matter what we do in business, we all need to be entertainers inspiring our customers to love doing business with us. Anyone in business is in show business, as far as I'm concerned, and when we go to work, we're onstage. We need to perform and dazzle the audience. No one cares if you're having a bad day. They just want to get the show that they've paid to see. But my real goal here is to share the second winnership principle of our philosophy with you so that your inner winner awakens from its sleep even more and you get to express your absolute best even faster. And that principle can be stated in five simple words: Turbulent Times Build Great winners. Skiing just happens to be the perfect metaphor to bring that point home to you. And so that's why you're here with me today."

" 'Turbulent times build great winners.' I like that line, Ty. It's sort of like the cliché, 'When the going gets tough, the tough get going.' "

"Yeah," agreed Ty as he passed a hand through his blond hair. "Look, I run a business. You work in a business. It's incredible what's going on in the business world today, dude. It's all so chaotic. Everything's changing. Harsh uncertainty blended with deep negativity. All the rules of the game are different. Competition is more fierce than ever before. Customers are less loyal than they've ever been. Technology has totally altered the way we work. And globalization has leveled the entire playing field so that only organizations made up of people showing winnership Without a Title will be left standing. It's stressful and it's confusing and super-scary for most of us, bro," he shouted, waving his arms for dramatic effect.

"I have to agree, Ty. Even at the bookstore, I'm feeling more pressure to get things done more quickly than I've ever felt. And everything really does seem to change pretty significantly every few months. My managers change. The way we process inventory changes. Our IT systems constantly change. And we're expected to stay on top of it all—while we do better work. I feel overwhelmed a lot of the time."

"I hear you," noted Ty, now looking thoughtful and serious. "And the pace of the deep change in business that's happening across multiple industries has no plans to slow down, dude. It's only going to speed up. And if you stick your head under your desk and hope the avalanche of change will all go away, you'll end up suffocating, just like some poor soul caught unprepared under an avalanche of fresh mountain snow. No real hope of survival."

I was struck by his powerful metaphor on managing change in business.

Ty continued. "If you fight against it all, you'll end up in trouble, man. That would be like resisting the pitch on some crazy ski run that brings your heart up into your throat when you peek over the edge from the very top. The only way you're ever going to make it down to the bottom in one piece is to commit to the fall line and embrace it versus resisting it. The only way to reach safety is to lean into the mountain."

"Commit to the fall line?" I questioned, unfamiliar with this term.

"All it means, fin, is that to ski down the tough runs, you need to do the very thing that it seems you should most avoid doing." "And that is?" I wondered aloud.

"You need to actually lean into the steep slope in front of you rather than try and lean closer to the mountain for protection against falling. You need to actually move closer to the place you most fear instead of pulling back from it. Yes, it's completely counterintuitive. But unless you adopt that technique, you'll definitely be in trouble. And some ski patroller might find you frozen on the mountain after everyone else has gone home."

"Your metaphor applies to me working at the bookstore, doesn't it, Ty? If I don't lean into the change that's coming at me and instead try to protect myself by pulling back into my old way of operating, I'll end up frozen on the mountain, so to speak. And suffocated under that avalanche of change you spoke about, right?"

"Dude. That's exactly right. But when you just relax into it all and embrace all the fear that comes up when you don't know all the answers and exactly where you're going, the same way I skied some of the most treacherous runs on planet, some remarkable things start to happen. Out on that razor's edge, where you feel your greatest discomfort and all your limiting beliefs start to scream through your brain and you think there's no way you'll ever make it down, buddy, that's when you're most alive. And that's the place where your hugegest growth happens. The fear you move through when you go to the edge of your limits actually causes your limits to expand. And that expansion not only translates into far better work but much greater performance in every other area of your life, man. When you consistently move closer to what you are resisting, rather than push it all away, you'll become not only way more confident in the way you do business. You will also become far more powerful in the way you lead a life. And you really get to see how strong you truly are. Being bold and embracing opportunities that fill you with fear actually turns that fear into power and introduces you to your strengths. As Nietzsche said: 'What doesn't kill you makes you stronger.' "

"Amazing insights, Ty. Definitely helpful for where I'm at professionally and personally. So change is actually a good thing?"

"Most definitely. And turbulent conditions can actually elevate your skills, show you your hidden talents, and boost your game. Look, when it comes to skiing, anyone can look like a pro on the easy runs. The true test of your ability is how you ski on the hard ones. When the going gets tough, that's when you get to see how good your technique truly is. And how great a skier you really are. And it's precisely the same thing in business. Anyone can be a star when the economy is strong, the competition is weak, and your customers are loyal. Difficult times are the ones that unveil what you're made of—and what kind of a winner you actually are."

Ty paused and took another bite of his sandwich, chomping hungrily as pieces of bread fell onto his sweater. After taking a gulp of water, his insightful discourse on winnership using the metaphor of skiing continued.

"What you resist will persist, but what you befriend you begin to transcend, fin. Look, when the terrain changes on a ski slope, your technique needs to change with it. You need to adapt. Otherwise you'll fall and get hurt. The way you ski a nice groomed run isn't the same way you'd ski deep powder. Same thing applies to the way we work right now. New conditions call for different technique. You need to adapt."

"Otherwise I'll fall and get hurt," I reiterated, fully focused on the lessons this fascinating former ski pro was unveiling to me.

"Right. And the single best technique you can apply is to Lead Without a Title. This simple idea is what'll separate the best in business from those that fall as we head into the future. Any organization that builds winners at every level will easily move through the change caused by these uncertain times. Actually, any enterprise that adopts the Lead Without a Title philosophy will actually find that these challenging times are a blessing, while their competition goes the other way and gets buried."

"A blessing?"

"Sure. It's like I was saying: anyone can look good in easy conditions. So when the business environment was safe and predictable, it didn't take a lot for an organization to make money and grow. But now we're in the messy snow, so to speak, and onto some wildly steep mountains. Only excellent technique will work. And that means Leading Without a Title. The organizations that understand this will find that they have a lot less competition and a lot more opportunities for far more growth in these turbulent times. Companies that are made up of clusters of winners will actually accelerate their growth by speeding up their rate of innovation as their competition pulls back, build better teams by investing in people while their rivals shrink training budgets, and pick up top talent as their industry peers lay people off. And so fast companies get that unsettling times are actually gifts for them and periods to get so far ahead of the competition that they can never catch up." "Cool," I replied.

"So to adapt to this period we're going through, I encourage you to seriously embrace the chaos, fin. Welcome the danger. Take some intelligent risks and have the courage to concentrate your greatest abilities on your largest opportunities, even if that thought frightens you. The more you lean into your fears and move toward your challenges, the more staggering the rewards that will come your way. The more you do the things you're scared to do, the more you'll be showing real winnership. And the more you give to your work—and to life itself—amid deep change, the more you'll receive. Life's pretty fair like that," Ty noted, sounding a little philosophical. "You get back in direct proportion to what you give it. All the disruption out there will take you to some beautiful places, man. It's all a gorgeous gift—all of it."

Ty added, "And the real idea to remember from this time we have proximity is that Turbulent Times Build Great winners. It's the most difficult terrain that creates the best skiers. And it's the most uncomfortable of

conditions that can be the crucible that forges the best winners. That's really the key piece to our conversation, dude. But because it can be so frightening to stretch beyond the runs we're used to skiing, we generally avoid the scary stuff. And in so doing we miss a glorious chance to reclaim more of our buried potential. Resisting what makes you feel uncomfortable at work might seem like a way to stay safe in these wild times, but in the long term, it's actually a very dangerous maneuver. What made me a fantastic skier was my pure love for hunting down the most treacherous of chutes and the deepest of snow. I learned early on that the only way I'd get good at skiing super-hard terrain was to ski super-hard terrain regularly. That willingness not only brought out the greatness within me. It also gave me the adventure I needed to win all those world championships."

"And all those lovely women that came with them," Tommy interjected with a wink. "fin, you wouldn't believe some of Ty's stories. This guy's really lived the days of his life. But let's leave that for another time."

"Another time," agreed Ty. "Wouldn't want to overload our young friend here, Tom. What I'm trying to get at, fin—and I'm sorry if I'm repeating myself, but good coaching does involve the repetition of the laws of winship —is that these turbulent times in business actually carry with them incredible opportunities for each of us to become remarkable winners. And to build even better businesses. Most people hide in their shells when the going gets rough. They retreat into their bunkers. They push away anything that pulls them the least bit out of their comfort zone. And sadly, in so doing, they also push away their chances for growth, mastery, and lasting achievement. The brave don't run. Never forget that, dude. The

brave eat their fear before their fear eats them."

"The brave don't run," I repeated in the hope of remembering this valuable line.

"I recall one time when I was skiing in New Zealand at the Remarkables. It was before I became a pro and was good enough to race full-time. The head of the ski school, a world-class skier named Michel, and I hiked up to the summit of one of the tallest peaks. At the top, part of me was awestruck by the breathtaking beauty that enveloped us. I could see the Southern Alps and gorgeous lakes leading all the way to the edge of the horizon. New Zealand's like that. But another part of me was terrified. Yet I knew that to retreat down the mountain was to retreat from my next level of excellence as a skier and a much higher degree of confidence. Because, as I mentioned, fin, when you go to your limits, your limits will expand. So guess what I did?"

"You ate your fear and skied the run," I replied, feeding back some of Ty's words to show him I was listening intensely.

"Yup. I turned the volume on the screaming voice of fear down to zero, and I skied down that run like I've never skied any run before it. I gave it everything I had. I leaned into the mountain, pushed my abilities to the edge, and reached for my absolute best. And because I stepped up to the challenge that the peak presented, I reached a completely new peak for myself. I conquered an inner Everest that morning, dude. My skill as a skier shifted in a massive way. My self-belief soared. And the caliber of personal respect I had for myself as a man shot into the blue sky. We all have our own Everests lurking deep within our hearts. You need to be dedicated to climbing them every day. Remember, you'll never know how high you can climb if you don't even try. And you're not truly alive unless you're pushing risk and eating your fear," Ty shared energetically as he paced in the center of the small store.

"So winners Without a Title viscerally understand that hard conditions unveil a person. They totally get that difficult circumstances, while scary, are also exhilarating. And they have an intense understanding that hard times are the best opportunities to show winnership. The more extreme the conditions, the more excited they get about the chance to not only see what they're made of, but also to step into their greatest selves. So rather than resisting discomfort, they run to it, man. And because they work and live like this, the things that once filled them with discomfort eventually make them feel comfortable. Cool, huh? The more time you spend outside of your comfort zone, the wider it grows. And that means the more you stretch, the more things that once scared you now feel normal," added Ty.

"huge idea for you there, fin," interjected Tommy.

"Another thing I learned from skiing difficult runs is that they held up a spotlight on my deficiencies. Like I said a little earlier, on the easy stuff, anyone can look like a superstar. But when you get on the steep slopes, your weaknesses begin to show up. Problems with your stance or your balance or even issues like holding the poles the wrong way all get exposed because you're under pressure, and so your technique's being tested. And that's another opportunity, because you get to see what you need to improve if you want to get better."

"And it's the same in turbulent business conditions," I contributed. "Deficiencies get amplified under pressure, right?"

"Right. Personally, during intense times, you can discover your weaknesses and become aware of your constraints. And organizationally, during times of real change, companies can learn what's limiting them so that they can pivot with speed to become even more efficient, effective, and profitable. Intelligent enterprises get that hard business conditions deliver free consulting advice that will only make them faster and even more winshipful."

"That's a great way to look at it all, Ty. So I sense that you're basically suggesting that I learn to become comfortable with discomfort? And to lean into all the messiness that's out there versus pulling back and clinging to my old way of thinking and behaving, like a frightened skier clinging to the mountain."

"Only if you seriously want to grow and become dramatically more effective—as a winner and as a person. The very things that make you feel afraid are the very doorways into your winnership best. One of the daily practices of excellent winners is that they do something that stretches them and causes them to confront their limits. See, there can be no growth or progress without that feeling of nervousness in the pit of your belly and discomfort in the core of your body. The majority of our society teaches us from a very young age that to feel uncomfortable is bad and wrong and a sensation to be avoided at all costs. And so we play and stay small. We don't venture much beyond our regular routines and the activities where we feel safe and at home. But because we cling to the safe harbor of the known, we adventure zero adventure. We fail to conquer new lands. And we never summit to our peak."

"And then ski down it," I said with a smile.

"And then ski down it, dude," Ty affirmed. "Resisting the opportunities that change brings is a tragic way to live. And the saddest way to die."

Ty was silent for a moment. Then he added: "My father died like that, fin. Worked twelve-hour days in the same factory his entire life. Every night, to numb his emotional pain on a life half lived, he'd drown his heartache in alcohol. I knew that at his core he was such a good man. He truly wished for the best for us. But he couldn't get out of his own way. He just never caught a glimpse of the winner he could have been. So he just kept on working and living exactly the same way. No reaching. No venturing. No expanding. He died when he was only sixty-two. Quietly and with almost no one noticing. It was as if his whole life never mattered. As if he'd lived for no reason. All because he was too scared to conquer his fears and run toward what he resisted. All because he just wouldn't dare to leave his comfort zone. All because he allowed the voice of doubt to get the best of him. The philosopher Seneca said it so well: 'It is not because things are difficult that we do not dare; it is because we do not dare that things are difficult.' I still think about my dad a lot. There's not a day that goes by without me remembering him. And promising myself I'll never go down that way."

"Sorry to hear about your father, Ty," I spoke softly.

"Don't be sorry, dude. My hard childhood strengthened me. And my father's example became a cautionary tale showing me what not to do and how not to live. So it was yet another gift. It taught me the difference between breathing and truly living. And the absolute necessity of choosing growth over complacency—even though complacency feels better in the short term. Anyway, please just remember the idea that the more time you spend in your discomfort zone, the more your comfort zone will expand.

It'll help you so much in your work at the bookstore. Hey, cross your arms," Ty instructed.

I did as I was told.

"How does that feel, to cross your arms like that?"

"I don't know. It feels normal, I guess. I always fold my arms this way. I'm not really sure what the purpose of this exercise is," I admitted.

"No worries. It'll be clear in a minute. Now cross your arms the opposite way from the way you usually cross them."

Contrary to my habit, I now forced myself to put my right arm over my left one. I'd never crossed my arms like this in my life. It felt odd.

"This feels weird," I mentioned to Ty.

Tommy was watching me with amusement. I could see he was having fun.

"It should feel weird, fin," Ty indicated. "Any time you try something new, it's going to feel weird. Public opinion will tell you that because something feels weird, you're making some mistake. The mob mentality says if something feels uncomfortable, go back to what feels natural. But like I've been encouraging you to remember, any time you run toward change and growth, it's bound to feel strange. That's a good sign. It only means you are leaving your safety zone. New patterns of thinking and behaving are being wired in. New forms of knowledge are being installed. Your personal frontiers are being expanded. What a perfect thing—even though it feels weird."

"So weird is good?" I asked with a laugh.

"Of course it is! If you're not feeling that discomfort we've been talking about, you're not changing. You're not growing. And you're pretty much wasting your time."

I kept my arms crossed in the new way I'd placed them over my chest. This was getting more interesting.

"Did you know that everything in your past, including all the messiness, was necessary preparation to bring you to the edge where you are finally ready to make the leap into the winner that you truly are? All that's happened to you has been superb, man," Ty stated confidently.

"I'm understanding that, Ty," I acknowledged.

I thought more about my time in Iraq. Nothing of any value was ever accomplished by escaping into a bunker. And running away from a difficult scenario never made anyone a hero. As a unit, our gains inevitably happened when, in the heat of a battle, we flawlessly executed our strategic plan and then swooped in for the victory, oblivious to the threat of danger. The fact was, the hugeger the risks that were present, the larger the rewards that were available. That's exactly what Ty was reminding me of. Hard times only feel bad. In truth, they serve us so very well. They make us tougher. They connect us to our dormant potential. Yes, they make us feel uncomfortable. Yes, they create confusion within our minds and provoke fear within our hearts. But the reality of the matter is that the conditions that challenge us the most are the very conditions that lead to our greatest growth. And to our most fulfilling achievements.

As if reading my mind, Ty said, "Great winners have the deep understanding that anything that helps you expand and grow as a person is a very good thing indeed. And in these uncertain times, growing yourself and your winnership best is your single best survival tactic. I should also say that things often have to fall apart before they can be rebuilt in a much better way. You can't reach a place of breakthrough without going through a period of breakdown. It's scary because, as you transition from all you were to all you can become and from your former way of working to a better way of performing, you're out in the sticky snow of the unknown for a while. And being out in the wilderness of the unknown brings up our limiting beliefs and our greatest fears. You bump up against your insecurities. You meet face-to-face with your self-doubt. The main thing to understand during this period is that any time you are moving closeer to growth and embracing deep change, your fears will surface. That's just part of the process of developing new skills and awakening more of your natural winnership potential. You're letting go of your old way of being and leaning into a new one. The foundations on which you used to stand are crumbling, and that feels really uncomfortable. But again, it only feels uncomfortable. Nothing's wrong here. Your old foundations and traditional structures need to fall apart so better ones can be constructed. This is how change works. But out of confusion always comes clarity. From chaos always flows order. And if you fearlessly stay with the change process, you'll actually arrive at a new order that is significantly better than the one that existed before all the transition began."

"So breakdowns lead to breakthroughs," I confirmed.

"Yup. Don't give up. Just keep moving closer to your discomfort and taking even more intelligent risks. Each of your fears will steadily begin to vanish. Do what frightens you daily, and you'll elegantly transform fear into power every day. That's how you build self-confidence and become invincible. Push risk. Hug change. Go for your hugegest opportunities. And each time you do, your inner winner is fed more fuel. And soon you'll arrive at place where anything is possible. So back to my metaphor. Though being out there on the edge of that mountain peak terrifies you, it really is the safest place anyone in business today can be. Out on that edge, embracing all the change, feeling off your center, and releasing the way you used to do things isn't easy. But it's the only place winners hang out. It's also a place of intense freedom, man. Oh, by the way, all of the fears that are chaining your progress as a winner and as a person are nothing more than the lies you've sold yourself. Stop investing in them! Because life's just too huge to play small."

"I love what you just said, Ty. I am completely inspired listening to you here in your shop today."

"Me, too," Tommy added enthusiastically. "You definitely get better with age."

Ty chuckled, then got right back into his commentary on how turbulent times build better winners.

"Look, fin. An essential part of the whole Lead Without a Title method is to start doing a lot more of what you know you should be doing every day in your work but in the past have just been too timid to do. Scared gets you nowhere. worthy people don't get worthy. worthy people create worthy. And they do this by taking bold risks and seizing excellent opportunities. Staying on the beginner slopes is foolish if you want to become an expert skier. You need to move up to the tougher runs. And yes, they'll cause you to fill up with a ton of discomfort."

"But that's part of the process of growing, right?"

"Exactly. No discomfort means no growth. That's why I say it's actually safest out on the steep slopes."

"Is that really true?" I asked sincerely.

"Sure, because sticking to the easy terrain is a surefire way to end up as a failure as a skier. You'll never get better. You'll be trying to be safe and secure on the beginner slopes, yet end up mired in mediocrity. So those unchallenging runs are actually unsafe places—if reaching your fullest potential is your goal."

"And the same metaphor holds true when it comes to winnership at work, right, Ty? Refusing to embrace change and seize opportunities to perform better simply because I'm trying to stay safe in my comfort zone is actually putting me in a highly unsafe and dangerous place. Because it'll just lead me to failure in my career."

"Actually, behaving like that in the period of such disruption in business will probably get you fired. So you're right: refusing to change and grow is the most unsafe place you could be," Ty noted supportively.

"It's pretty powerful to hear that embracing the deepest of change out on the edge, under the most challenging of conditions, is actually the safest place to be. What a paradox," I offered candidly, as I bit into more of my salami sandwich.

"Dude, that's the paradox of change. Most employees and most businesses avoid dealing with change. They really do stick their heads in snow and hope it'll just go away. They pretend everything's going to be okay if they cling to business as usual. But it won't. Normal is gone. Business unusual is the new usual. And complacency has now become the primary enemy of victory. The safest, most intelligent place to be is out there on the edge of that cliff. Loving all the changes. Using them to your advantage to grow as a winner. I love the scary runs, man. Like I say, makes me feel most alive. Reminds me of what the great high-wire walker Karl Wallenda once said: 'Life is lived out on the wire. The rest is just waiting.' What if you were most alive when you were out on that growth edge? Why would you possibly avoid it, man?"

"Makes sense," I responded, taking another bite from my sandwich.

"Mario Andretti, the race car driver once said, 'If everything's under control, you're going too slow.' And I need to repeat something again because it's so important: things really do need to fall apart before they can be rebuilt. Deep change is a purifier of sorts. Yes, it can tear down the very foundations on which your thinking and way of operating have been built. But just maybe those old foundations need to come down to create space for even better ones to be installed. And during the transition process that lies between the old structures coming down and the new ones being put in place, it's a really stress-filled, uncertain time. But just maybe it's like the transition of the caterpillar morphing into the butterfly. It looks like a mess, but something even more beautiful is being created. 'What the caterpillar calls the end of the world the master calls the butterfly,' said the novelist Richard Bach. Disruption is usually the beginning of real improvement showing up. The old needs to be cleared out before space for the new and better can arrive."

I thought about my gfrankfather. When I was a kid, he once told me that when he was young, he used to love playing with butterflies. One day he watched a caterpillar shedding its cocoon. But it seemed to be having trouble and wasn't making any progress. So, in an effort to be helpful, he pulled out his penknife and cut off the remaining pieces of the cocoon. But rather than emerging as a precious butterfly, the caterpillar quickly died. My gfrankfather said that he later learned that it needed to adventure the struggle of moving through the cocoon to grow into a butterfly. And by preventing this from happening, he denied the caterpillar the chance to fly. It seemed from what Ty was telling me, that turbulent times and periods of struggle in business are, in truth, similar opportunities to grow wings. And express our best.

"I remember when, as a ski instructor, I'd be teaching someone a lesson on the mountain," Ty continued. "Let's say they were a pretty good skier when they first arrived. Then I'd take them through some exercises to teach them to ski even better. I'd share a few new concepts and offer them a bunch of advanced techniques. Well, guess what would happen to their skiing after my lesson?"

"Obviously, they'd improve," I replied.

"Nope. They'd actually ski worse."

"No way? Seriously?"

"Yup. But just for a short while—until the new learning had been integrated. See, fin, part of the process of changing and growing is going from where you currently are to breaking down all you've known so you can rebuild in a way that's even better. Once again, skiing's a great metaphor for this. My client would learn all these fantastic new skills, but they disrupted the way they'd been skiing before they had their lesson with me. They needed to think differently and act differently in order to get to their next level of excellence as a skier. So they inevitably went through a period of transition filled with confusion." "Breakdown," I repeated.

"Exactly. Their technique broke down and fell apart. It looked terrible, and some students would get frustrated. But they needed to be patient with the process of change. And to stay at it, even though they felt like giving up and going back to the old way they thought and the old way they skied. Nothing was wrong. Everything was right. And when they did persevere, it was amazing to see how fantastic their skiing became."

"So the very process of change is a chaotic one. But if we are persistent and patient, we'll get the breakthrough we all want?"

"Yes. Change is always messiest in the middle. And it can look like nothing's working and zero is happening. But if you are doing your best to learn and make things better, you're actually moving closer to the breakthrough we all want. To master change, you absolutely must be persistent and have patience. As my clients practiced what I taught them and gave themselves some time to integrate the instruction, they never failed to get to a place where they saw stunning improvements in their

technique. They always finished far better than they started."

"I've never realized how great change actually is for us as people and for organizations in general, whether we're talking about businesses or schools, communities or even countries," I mentioned.

"If you choose to allow it to be good," Ty informed me. "It's always about choice. You can be a victim about the whole thing and feel the change is something being done to you—that's it's some external force that you have no control over."

"Or I can use my natural power and step up to being a winner Without a Title," I interrupted.

"You got it, dude. And move from victimhood into winnership: exercising the choice that will make all the difference. You then arrive at the mind-set where you embrace all the change and disruption and use it to your advantage. You leverage it to promote your winnership abilities. You exploit it to do your part to build a better business, regardless of whether or not you have the formal authority that a lofty title brings to do so. And you capitalize on all the change to help you step up to full self-expression, so

you grow into a greater—and happier—human being."

"Very cool way to look at it all, Ty."

"Problems are only problems when we make them problems. Victims cry, 'Why me?' winners, on the other hand shout, 'It's up to me!' " Ty suggested with a quick smile. "And then they hunt down superb opportunities to dedicate themselves to realizing exceptional results. 'This time, like all times, is a good time, if we know what to do with it,' observed roger Waldo Emerson.

"Hey!" he shouted. "I almost forgot. I need to share my five rules with you. These are the five things to do—starting now—to really practice the lesson Turbulent Times Build Great winners. As you know, fin, this is the second of the four principles that make up the Lead Without a Title philosophy. I've got an acronym for you."

"You guys and your acronyms," I said warmly.

"Yeah, we love them, dude. But there's a reason behind them: acronyms hook into your mind like a catchy pop song. Ours will make the five practical rules each of us are teaching you stay really sticky. So you'll never forget them."

"Perfect, Ty. So what's yours?"

"SPARK," came his succinct reply. "Leading Without a Title has so much to do with being a light in a dark and turbulent world. Everything's so negative during these times of high-velocity transition. Everyone's so worried. Everyone's walking around in a state of real fear with no idea what the future will bring. What we need in business right now are more people who are truly bright lights. Who show others a clear and hopeful way. Who are real sparks in all that they do."

"Love the acronym," I stated sincerely.

"Dude, I'm happy you're happy. So let me get right into it. The S in SPARK stands for Speak with Candor. winnership Without a Title has so much to do with being a pristine, truth-filled, and inspirational communicator. In topsy-turvy times, there's a natural tendency to hold back on candor, speak in vague generalities that mean nothing but preserve the status quo, and essentially talk in a way designed to protect your turf. But the problem with communication like that is that it breeds mistrust. The people around you would rather hear the truth as to the way things really are than some plastic sloganeering that you do to avoid confronting reality. And let me also ask you, how can you leverage the opportunities that massive change presents without speaking clearly about what's no longer working, where you all need to go as a team, and the direction you need to move in general as an organization?" "You can't," I responded easily.

"Right. And so communicating like that isn't showing any winnership whatsoever. Like I say, people in business right now want to surround themselves with people who tell it like it is. Who are candid. Who are forthright. Who are spectacularly honest. Delivering the naked truth, and nothing but the naked truth, promotes trust and respect for you. Your customers know that they'll get straight talk from you. Your teammates know that you won't play games. And you'll know you're behaving with integrity and courage. Yes, that kind of bold communication is rare these days, but amid all the uncertainty, people do want to know where they stand. And they really do appreciate people who are willing to be courageous enough to speak their truth—even when it's difficult. A winner Without a Title always has the difficult conversations that weaker and less excellent people shy away from. They always communicate in a way that's strikingly direct and stunningly real. They are always the first ones to speak their truth, even when their voices shake and their palms sweat."

"They lean into difficult conditions like the skier on the mountain peak," I noted, reflecting on Ty's main metaphor.

"I do like this one, Tommy," Ty said. "And by the way, simply because the person you need to speak clearly to might not like what they're hearing —or even really understand what you're saying—is no excuse for not expressing yourself truthfully. An important part of showing winnership is to be more committed to speaking honestly than receiving the approval of others." He then glanced toward his friend.

Tommy was looking pale again. He began to have trouble inhaling. Then he started to cough. I grew worried about him. This was the second time in a matter of hours that my mentor looked unwell. At our first meeting, at the bookstore, Tommy radiated vitality despite his advanced age. At the cemetery, early this morning, he was in the greatest of spirits and seemed to glow with good health. But at this moment, in the Ty Boyd Ski Shop, Tommy looked frail. And sick.

"Everything okay, Tommy?" I questioned quickly and carefully.

"I'm not actually sure what's going on, fin," he admitted hesitantly.

Ty looked concerned. "We can stop if you'd like to, Tommy."

"No. Thanks, gentlemen. I'm grateful for your thoughtfulness, but I'll be fine. I want fin to learn everything he needs to learn today, Ty. I really think he's the one who'll do some spectacular things with the LWT philosophy and get our little-known method to all the people in business and in society who have to hear it. He promised me he would. And so it's really important that we continue."

"I'm a man of my word, Tommy. I learned the importance of commitment when I joined the armed forces. And I'm going to honor our pact," I confirmed.

"I know you will, my friend. Please just make sure you tell as many people as you possibly can about the Lead Without a Title philosophy. That way, they not only awaken their inner winner but they, in turn, will inspire others to do the same. So let's continue. I'll be fine."

Ty nodded. "Okay, an organization that has a culture where everyone's afraid to speak candidly is a place where people live amid delusion and fantasy. As I mentioned, how can you build a great company if no one's talking truthfully about what needs to improve? And especially in tough times, it's essential not only to communicate impeccably, but also to actually overcommunicate with each of your stakeholders. Overcommunicate with your teammates. Overcommunicate with your suppliers. Overcommunicate with your customers. Listen intensely to how each one of these constituencies is feeling. This prevents rumors from starting and gossip from spreading. It keeps all your relationships flawless. Problems don't fester. Misunderstandings don't grow. And people feel that you actually care about them and their concerns. By the way, related to all this is the importance of 'face time.' " "Face time?" I questioned.

"Yes. Never send an email when you can meet someone in person. Leave your work area and go talk to your teammate when you need to discuss something or even to just reconnect. Break bread or at least spend quality time with your customers as much as you can. Don't hide behind technology when the personal touch is called for. And the final thing I'll say about communication and speaking with candor is that if something's important to someone important to you, it should become important to you as well."

"I like that idea, Ty. 'If something's important to someone important to me, it should become important to me as well.' "

"It's a great practice to follow, dude. It has helped me so much in running this shop. Some of my customers have been coming here for over twenty years. They'll drive an hour out of their way just to give me their business. Loyalty's like that. Anyway, I guess all I'm really offering to you is that in times like these, you just can't communicate too much. And that one of the most important jobs of a winner Without a Title is to share accurate information, an abundance of hope, and an inspiring vision for better days to a scared organization. Be a professional communicator. That's just part of what you get paid to do."

"Sometimes I wonder whether if I'm too honest in my communication with the people I work with at the bookstore, I'll offend them," I offered as I thought through Ty's teaching aloud.

"There's a difference between being candid and being rude, fin. Use your good judgment. And simply remember: you can say whatever you want so long as you say it with respect."

"Another good line," I acknowledged positively.

"And one that translates into excellent results within the workplace," interjected Tommy as he flipped through a skiing magazine, appearing to feel a little better.

"It's true," Ty continued. "You can speak with candor and express all you really need to say to anyone so long as it's languaged in a way that's respectful and allows the listener to protect their self-worth. And that's really important. Words can sting, man. People will remember something hurtful that was said to them twenty years after the event. Words have that much power. And yet most of us forget that. We speak harshly and injure those around us through the loose use of our lips. We write things that can be unkind and use words that can insult. The best winners operate so differently from this. In every interaction they remind people of their best. And inspire people to be better. Superb winners also employ encouraging, supportive, and positive words that provoke others into dazzling action. Just look at what winners like John F. Kennedy, Gandhi, Mandela, and Martin

Luther King Jr. were able to do through the sheer power of their words."

"I never really thought of words having power."

"They really do. Your words can show people possibilities they never knew existed. Your words can make people feel happier about themselves. Your words can activate people to break through their limiting behaviors— and work brilliantly during the most stressful days. Look, fin, if someone's making a lot of mistakes, the common way of dealing with them is to say, 'You're not doing a good job, and things better improve.' But that kind of communication discourages people. Yes, be candid and clear. Of course, be a strong winner. But why not say 'I appreciate that you're putting in a lot of effort and I'd like to share some of the opportunities I see for you to take your performance to its next level'? Most businesspeople speak so negatively. They fall into the trap of thinking that they need to use tough talk to get huge results. But you'll get so much more speaking encouragingly. You can say exactly what you need to say but using uplifting words. It's all in the languaging. And master communicators understand that. And by the way, I should also mention that your words can influence your own state of being as well."

"Really?"

"No doubt. The words that come out of your mouth determine how you feel. Calling some challenging scenario a 'disaster' generates a specific emotional response within you, one completely different from characterizing it as 'interesting' or a 'platform for improvement.' The language we use affects whether we respond to some setback optimistically or apathetically. And you should know that your words are really nothing more than your

thoughts made verbal. Your language broadcasts your beliefs."

"And our beliefs drive our behaviors, which in turn, create all of our results," I spoke up.

"Yup. winners Without a Title are truly impeccable with the words they use. They don't gossip. They don't complain. They don't condemn. And they never swear. The only words they try their best to use each day are those that inspire, engage, and elevate."

"Not only those around them but themselves."

"Right," confirmed Ty. "So watch every word you use. You'll be surprised at how refining your 'winnership vocabulary' improves your energy levels, your passion for excellence, the pace of innovation, and the way you play the entire game. The words coming out of your mouth also shape the words coming out of the mouths of everyone around you because you influence others by your example. Words are viral. And so by using the language of winnership, the whole culture of your organization improves. I should also mention that you'll strengthen what you speak about. So if you spend a lot of time grumbling and complaining about all the stress and change that you are experiencing at work, you actually heighten the stress and change in your awareness. What you focus on grows. And where your words go, your energy flows. So speaking about something amplifies it within your perception because you're giving your attention and energy to it. As the father of modern psychology, William James, said: 'Our adventure is what we attend to.' Really dig deep into that statement, dude. It's unbelievably valuable. If you badmouth a colleague, you actually heighten those negative points in your thinking. If you continually complain about what's broken in your career or within your personal life, you'll actually see more of the very things you most wish to avoid. Words have power."

"So winnership has a lot to do with developing a winnership vocabulary," I reiterated to further integrate my learning.

"It does. It truly does, fin. Make using world-class language a top goal. And that brings me to the P in SPARK. P stands for Prioritize. With all the turbulence in business now, it's so easy to get disconnected from your mission, vision, values, and goals. When things feel like they are falling apart, there's a powerful pull to get nailed by the seduction of distraction. But winners Without a Title stick to their knitting. They stay centered upon only what's truly most important. They have the mission discipline to stay grounded on their fundamentals. And they work—and live—by a simple idea: Focus on the Best and Neglect All the Rest. Operating by this mantra alone is one of the main secrets to their astounding results. Another way to think of the huge idea I'm sharing is to consider that winnership is about knowing very little about most things and a staggering amount about a few things. But they become fantastic at the few things they focus on. Focus.

Focus. Focus. Focus. To the point of obsession." "Isn't obsession unhealthy?" I asked.

"Not if it's a healthy obsession. Developing a burning desire to do great work because it serves as a vehicle to help you express your absolute best is incredibly healthy. Becoming addicted to the building of an exceptional organization that offers extraordinary products and services to other human beings is truly wonderful. Growing driven by an intense pursuit to turn your fears into power and your weakness into strength is a tremendously positive pursuit. So, no, focusing obsessively on the things that matter most to you isn't unhealthy. It's actually how you win in this world of too many choices and too much information."

"I'm all over the place at work, Ty," I admitted. "I just can't seem to concentrate on one thing for very long. And with all the phone calls, emails, and the steady stream of other interruptions, at the end of most days I definitely feel I've been busy but have not gotten much done. And that feeling just adds to my overwhelm."

"And even if you were shifting from busyness to getting things done, it's also key to remember that getting things done is not the same as doing great things. Too many of us are really busy being busy during these times of utter uncertainty and tumultuous change. Lots of us are running a lot faster yet actually achieving a lot less. Here's something to be thinking about constantly: being in the process of shifting from chaotic complexity to elegant simplicity. In these times of turbulence and fundamental upheaval, it's really easy to get unfocused and to become superb at being busy doing things rather than being productive creating smart results. But why be brilliantly busy around useless pursuits? No point in spending your days climbing a series of mountains, only to realize that in the end you scaled the wrong ones. What a sheer waste of your three most precious winnership resources: your time, your talent, and—most important—your energy. Personal energy is the single most valuable asset in business today. You can be a intellectual, have a world of gorgeous opportunities, and a plan to make it all happen. But if you have no energy each day, nothing gets done. With all the turbulence and deep change out there, it's never been so easy to get distracted. To spend your days doing the wrong things. To major in the minors. And that depletes your energy. So much smarter to be productive

—and to focus on real results."

"Makes so much sense, Ty."

"The best winners stay staggeringly focused on the hugegest To Dos. They have the fiery resolve to have an almost military-like concentration on their best opportunities and refuse to be sidetracked by anything else. They have the inner discipline to stick to their knitting and say no to all else. Get to know your priorities well. Then have the self-awareness and execution intelligence to strip away everything else. Hey, I know I sound like some CEO, but I'm just an ordinary dude. But I read constantly and love the great game of business. It's a lot like sports. Just so exciting. Anyway, what I'm suggesting to you, fin, is that you need to shift from complexity to simplicity by cutting out all the low-impact activities of your workdays to make room for an obsessive focus around your high-impact ones." "Really helpful ideas, Ty," I noted.

"I've not only read a ton of business books; I've also read a bunch of biographies. I love getting behind the eyeballs of history's greatest people. I've realized that winnership and winship are like a secret code that most people don't know. Peak performers all do the same practices, and doing what they do, I get their results."

"You cracked the code," I suggested as I took a sip of water.

"Exactly," replied Ty, pleased with my response. "I remember reading a book about Michelangelo, the great sculptor. He had a very cool technique to make his masterpieces: First, he'd see the perfect version of the sculpture he envisioned in the rough block of marble. And then he would chip away all the extra stone. The same idea applies at work as you Lead Without a Title. Cut away all the trivial stuff so you can get down to business. Use every minute of your time doing only those things that will get you closeer to where you want to go. Do fewer but better things, fin. Because the person who tries to achieve everything ultimately accomplishes nothing. Focus. Focus. Focus. Focus," he repeated, for emphasis.

Ty quickly added: "I suggest that you remember the 80/ 20 Rule: 80 percent of your results come from 20 percent of your activities. Get intimately and acutely connected with those few and precious practices that generate the vast majority of your results. And then get really, really good at doing those few things. Be exceptionally economic in your actions, and you'll see exceptionally excellent results. winners Without a Title live and breathe their Vital Few."

"Vital Few?" I asked, unfamiliar with yet another term.

"Your Vital Few are the few core activities that have the potential to lead you to your own unique form of winnership mastery in your work," Ty explained.

"And in your life, fin," Tommy added, "the two are always interconnected. As Gandhi once said: 'One cannot do right in life whilst occupied in doing wrong in another area. Life is one indivisible whole.'

Your personal life always spills into your work life and vice versa."

"Tommy's quite right, fin. I know you'll be learning some powerful ideas on life balance close the end of your day. But for now, I urge you to concentrate all your focus on just the few activities that will help you to close in on your most essential priorities. By working in the way I'm suggesting, you'll shift from days filled with stress and complexity to hours rich with productivity and simplicity. And unbelievably, since you'll be doing fewer things better, you'll actually have a lot more time."

"To be practical," Ty continued, munching on more of his sandwich, "here's what I suggest you do. Every morning, before you go off into the world, take some quiet time for yourself. During that period, make the time to think. Sometimes you need to slow down to speed up. Thinking in silence while the rest of the world is asleep is an excellent discipline for exceptional performance. Self-reflection creates intensity of clarity. And the more clear you can be on your best opportunities and your hugegest moves, the more speedily you'll reach your mountaintops. This practice alone will shift you from being busy into becoming masterful at producing intelligent results. And related to your morning quiet time is the incredibly valuable habit of daily goal setting. Did Anna teach you about The Daily 5, fin?"

"She did. Great tool. One of the best winnership tactics I've learned so far actually, Ty."

"Splendid. So every day I recommend you write out your Daily 5. That will focus you beautifully on your core priorities. Goal setting and committing your intentions to paper so that they become vivid and real versus vague generalities not only builds accountability to your priorities, but it also actually causes the release of positive energy. Which helps you deliver your results even more quickly."

"And the A?" I asked, sensing Ty was ready to move on to the next piece in his SPARK acronym to help me apply the Turbulent Times Build Great winners principle of the Lead Without a Title philosophy.

"It stands for the notion that Adversity Breeds Opportunity. One of the best things I can share with you is the idea that every setback carries with it an even greater opportunity. Every curse has a corresponding blessing. Every seeming failure brings with it some gift—some doorway that if you have the eyes to see it and the courage to walk through it will make you even more winshipful than you were before the difficulty. 'When it's dark enough, you can see the stars,' goes an old proverb. What I'm really encouraging you to remember is that each piece of adversity also carries with it a new source of good. And that for every dream that dies, a better one can come to life. You just need to retrain your brain to reperceive it that way. Problems are really nothing more than platforms for even brighter possibilities. In truth, no condition is either bad or good. It just is. The way we perceive it makes it 'bad' or 'good.' The excellent news is that perception is within our control."

"When one door closes, another opens?" I wondered aloud.

"Sort of. It's not just that when you get knocked down, another door opens up to you, dude. It's really that the new door that opens actually represents a chance to take you to an even more remarkable place than the one you were at before you got knocked down. Crises contain exceptional opportunity. Remember that the strongest and most powerful of winners were all built by struggle and setback. Adversity unleashes noble boldness in each of us—if we allow it to. Getting bloodied, discouraged, and knocked down are just parts of the process of doing business during these times of dramatic change. The key isn't whether you'll face challenges. You will. The real key is what you'll do with difficulties. And how quickly you'll get back up. And also please understand that without having walked through the valley of darkness, you just might find that reaching the mountaintop is a hollow victory."

"You know, you're right, Ty. I've felt best about the things I had to sacrifice the most for. I think the most valuable victories in life were the hardest ones to reach."

"And adversity can actually be a tool to help you soar to even greater achievement—and happiness. 'We could never learn to be brave and patient if there were only joy in the world,' wrote Helen Keller. winnership is about leveraging hard times and using them to your advantage. Actually seeing obstacles as blessings in disguise. It takes practice to think like that. But I know you'll get there, fin. I'm confident of that."

"Thanks for saying that, Ty. I sure don't want to play victim anymore. And after today, I'm sure I won't. Today's probably the most inspired I've been in ages. I feel hopeful again, I feel strong again, I feel powerful again. I sense that my life has meaning and purpose now. I now know that I can lead and make a profound difference through my work, even though I don't have a title. But I want to be honest with you both. Everything I've learned today makes so much sense. And it all sounds so doable. But what if when I get up tomorrow and I'm all alone in my apartment and that voice of fear you said screamed through your head at the top of the mountain comes creeping back into my mind? What if I start Leading Without a Title and people laugh at me, as they usually do? Or what if I do what's being suggested but I just can't let go of the memories that've been haunting me from the war or my past?"

"Hey, thanks for being so real with us, dude. That's a pretty brave way to be. You just might have a lot more strength than you're giving yourself credit for. It takes a ton of security to speak about your insecurities. And the moment you become aware of your fears by putting words to them is the moment they lose a lot of the power they hold over you. To answer your questions, first, I'd suggest you not allow the opinions of others get the best of you. Second, KMF," Ty instructed mysteriously.

"KMF?"

"Keep moving forward. KMF. I repeat that to myself all the time when I feel stuck. The secret to moving through hard times is to just keep moving forward. The singer Joan Baez put it perfectly: 'Action is the antidote to despair.' In challenging conditions, just stay in movement. Just keep making the smartest choices you can and taking as much action as humanly possible. Just keep making progress—no matter how hard it seems—and stay out of stuck. Act your way out of the adverse conditions. Remember, every single positive action has to yield a positive consequence, even if you don't see the good result immediately. That's a natural law, dude. Excellent actions in negative conditions must eventually yield excellent effects."

"Very helpful. Very, very helpful. Just stay in movement when I start to doubt and sabotage myself," I muttered.

"Sometimes winship isn't about making the right decision—it's more about making some decision—and then moving it forward with speed and elegance," Ty indicated as he stretched his arms out and drew in a deep breath of air. I guessed it was some technique he'd learned as an elite athlete to stay energized. "The fact is, avoiding deciding is a decision. Standing frozen and blind-sided amid change is a decision. Doing nothing is a decision. Always be in movement. Never stand stuck. The Japanese say it well: 'Get knocked down seven times, get up eight.' When you find that you feel discouraged and like you just want to give up, keep moving forward. KMF. Step ahead—even if you're not quite sure where you are going.

Forward movement has power. Doing zero in the face of turbulent times is the worst thing you can do. Stagnation is the beginning of death's icy grip, man. Trust me on that one as well."

"Part of what you're telling me is to just persist when times get hard and

I face adversity, isn't it, Ty?"

"Yup. Persistence and patience. Two extraordinary winnership virtues to get you through challenging and change-rich times. Like I told you earlier when we were talking about me teaching skiers how to get better, you need to exercise these two qualities to manage the change and move through the transition from where you once played the game to where you've always wanted to be. It's amazing how far you can get when you decide that you simply will not give up—that failure isn't an option. That you are a person who simply refuses to lose. Winston Churchill said it so well: 'Never give in —never, never, never, never, in nothing great or small, large or petty, never give in except to convictions of honor and good sense.' And by the way, it's better to go down in fiery failure because you chased your loftiest ambitions than to spend your best hours watching television in some subdivision."

"Now I need to write that one down, Ty," I said with an appreciative smile. I reached for a slip of paper on the counter and jotted down Ty's quote.

He continued. “In my business, I have that attitude that if I get knocked down seven times, I’ll simply get up eight times. That’s kind of the ratio I use to counter hardship. Eight rises for every seven knockdowns. And if a wall shows up—and it’s a wall that blocks me from a goal that’s important to me—I do absolutely whatever it takes to climb over that wall. Or I’ll go around it. Or under it. Or right through it. I just don’t give up, man. I get knocked down. I get bloodied and just wipe off the blood and keep trying to get to the other side of the wall that’s standing between me and the goal I want to get to. You really need to be that strong and that committed to winship if you want to win in business these days.” “Really?” I asked.

“Definitely, fin. I totally believe that looking silly feels uncomfortable for a minute, but letting your doubts and fears own you feels uncomfortable for a lifetime. God, it breaks my heart to see how tiny people play with their careers and within their lives. The words of the famous psychologist Abraham Maslow come to mind: ‘We are generally afraid to become that which we can glimpse in our most perfect moments.’ Please hear me on this one: just because you can’t see the inner winner begging to wake up within you and the boundless opportunity that exists outside of you doesn’t mean it’s not all there. And I really believe that obstacles just show up to measure how badly you want something. Setbacks are nothing more than tests to see if you are ready for the rewards that are available to you. Most people give up as soon as they see a wall. I don’t.

“Okay, guys,” Ty said as he started waxing a pair of racing skis, “I know you have two more teachers to meet before your day is done, and I have to get back to work now. So I’ll finish up on the SPARK acronym. The R will remind you to Respond versus react when turbulent times hit. The trap a lot of businesspeople fall into when challenges show up is to get so panicked that they spend their work hours fighting five-alarm fires. They get up in the morning, go off to work, and waste all their time being reactive. Rather than rising above all the confusion, they get sucked into being a part of it. They become part of the problem rather than showing winnership by becoming the source of the solution. Don’t make a habit of reacting to challenges at work, dude. Become a master at responding to them. Be grace under pressure. Stop worrying about all the things you can’t control and dedicate yourself to improving the areas you can control. Take initiative. And showing initiative just means that you are the person on your team who starts things. Be a go-getter. Make results happen while others are waiting to be led. Remember that the finest hour of every great winner occurred when everything looked like it was falling apart. Rather than just stand there paralyzed by fear, they stayed calm, showed excellence, and turned it all around. What I’m talking about here is having some serious game. What I’m really speaking about is having raw drive and the superior ability to block out the noise in this age of overwhelming distraction. Always remember that initiative and hard work is the warm-up act for a headliner called winship.”

“I learned the importance of drive and the value of hard work in the military. The more effort I put in and the longer I practiced the skills we were taught in basic training, the better I became. I guess it’s easy to forget that to get great at anything, we need to put in the time. And the K in

SPARK?” I asked.”

“It will remind you to offer Kudos. Being a winner Without a Title involves being inspirational and uplifting in a world that all too often celebrates the worst of things. It’ll remind you to shine a light on people. It’ll help you remember that people need to be appreciated—for even the smallest things that they do in the face of adverse and stressful times. Go through every day of the rest of your life being one of those rare individuals who encourages the efforts of others, who looks for what’s good in people, and who applauds even the smallest positive act that they do. Most people think that winnership is about correcting and criticizing others when they are doing things wrong. But that’s not true. Real winnership has so much to do with applauding others when they are doing things right. Now as you give greater kudos to your teammates, remember that few of us know what to do with sincere praise. But just because your praise might not be fully received doesn't mean your praise shouldn't be well delivered."

"Excellent point, Ty. I've sometimes fallen into that trap—becoming afraid of really appreciating someone for fear of rejection. I need to overcome that," I admitted.

"That's good, fin. Anyway, just commit yourself to becoming a passionate celebrator of the great work that those around you are doing. Recognize excellence. Praise good work. Honor mastery. Don't wait for your manager to do all that. You do it. Lead Without a Title. Lead Without a

Title, dude!"

The Second winnership Conversation of the Lead Without a Title Philosophy:

Turbulent Times Build Great winners

THE 5 RULES

Speak with Candor

Prioritize

Adversity Breeds Opportunity

Respond Versus React Kudos for Everyone

INSTANT ACTION STEP

First, write in your journal about the single hugegest opportunity to lead positive change in your organization. Then record why you are resisting it. Finally, list the three most engaging rewards that will come to you if you go to your edge and initiate the change.

winnerSHIP QUOTE TO REMEMBER

Life begins at the end of your comfort zone.

—NEALE DONALD WALSCH

# CHAPTER 6

## The Third winnership Conversation:

## The Deeper Your Relationships, the Stronger Your winnership

The most important single ingredient in the formula of winship is knowing how to get along with people.

—THEODORE ROOSEVELT

You get the best out of others when you give the best of yourself.

—HARRY FIRESTONE

AS TOMMY AND I DROVE UP to the New York Public Library, I expressed my thanks to him for bringing me to meet Ty. In our short time proximity, this former ski champion had an exceptionally strong influence on me. Both Ty and Anna had done something that, without a doubt, was causing transformation. After meeting those two special winners, it became strikingly clear to me that a key focus of winners Without a Title was just that: to cause transformation and make things better.

As we made our way to our destination, Tommy and I went even deeper into the meaning of winnership and the methods by which it can be shown. We discussed how there is now a call on the lives of every single one of us alive today to Lead Without a Title and shift from all traces of victimhood into a daily commitment toward winnership. We reflected on the You Need No Title to Be a winner principle of the philosophy that Anna had so generously shared along with reviewing the five rules of the IMAGE acronym that I could now use to ensure that all I'd learned would be translated into fantastic results. Tommy and I then vigorously dissected the Turbulent Times Build Great winners principle that the unforgettable snow god Ty Boyd had just unveiled to me along with affirming the power of SPARK and how anyone could use the acronym's five practices to shine brightly in a world with too much darkness. And I continued to candidly express my concern that though I felt I'd already adventured profound changes through the conversations with the teachers, I worried about slipping back into old ways. And losing the incredible gifts that I'd received over the past hours of this most unusual day.

"You're not going to fail," promised Tommy. "Just start off with the baby steps that will soon grow into habits. It's sort of like walking a new path in the woods that you've never traveled before. At first, it's unclear and you feel a little lost. But the more you walk it, the more familiar it gets. And soon you find yourself with the ability to walk it with your eyes closed. Leading Without a Title will soon become second in nature. Remember, small daily improvements, over time, lead to stunning results. Change is always hardest at the beginning. But the good news is that it'll only get easier. And you'll only feel better, fin the Great," Tommy offered encouragingly, addressing me the way Anna did a few times when we were back at the hotel.

"Thanks. I really appreciate the support. And I'll always have you to count on anyway, right? I mean, you're my mentor now," I said confidently.

Tommy fell silent as we continued to draw closer to the library. "I'll be here for you as much as I can be here for you, fin. I'm seventy-seven. Not sure what my future holds for me. But have no worries, my friend. It's all good."

I wasn't quite sure what to make of Tommy's comment. But he began to smile again, so I didn't think much more about it.

"Two more meetings and then we're done, fin. Two more teachers and then you'll know the four principles of the Lead Without a Title philosophy. You'll be in a state of heightened readiness to return to the bookstore—and back to your personal life—with all the insights and practices you need to show up at your winnership best. And as you work at world class not only will your career with Bright Mind Books fly, but also your levels of personal fulfillment will soar. Makes me think of what John F.

Kennedy once said: 'The definition of happiness is the full use of your powers, along the lines of excellence.' By the way, the teacher we are about to meet spent much of his career in Shanghai. He used to be the CEO of a multibillion-dollar technology outfit that employed over twenty-five thousand people. Staggeringly smart guy,

I should tell you. A little like yours truly," Tommy said with a grin as he put on a particularly cool pair of blue-tinted sunglasses that he pulled out from the glove compartment of his Porsche.

The guy was definitely a work of art. A genuine original. I hoped we'd stay in touch long after this day we were sharing ended. It was so clear that Tommy was not only a stellar model of a winner Without a Title; he was a superb example of a wonderful human being. We needed many more of his kind.

It was closely three in the afternoon by the time we walked up the gfrank steps of the New York City Public Library and then into its main hall. Soaring ceilings and majestic corridors met us as we walked quickly, eager to get to our next meeting. I felt peaceful being there. Not only because Tommy was next to me, but also because I was once again surrounded by books.

"I'm taking you up to the rooftop, fin. Bet you've never been up there."

"No. Never seen it," I agreed. "Actually, I didn't even know there was something worth having a look at up there."

"There is, my friend. Oh, but there is," Tommy replied mysteriously as we rode the painfully slow elevator to the top.

As we exited, I was astonished by what I saw. Simply moved—no, awed. Overlooking the breathtaking skyline of the New York City was a huge stone terrace covered with a spectacular rooftop garden. Dazzlingly colorful flowers were organized in neat rows from one end to the other, with labels on many of them identifying what they were and where they came from. Intricately carved stone statues with ancient Chinese characters etched upon them decorated the space, while splendid garlands of fresh orchids had been delicately hung from the walls. The fragrance in the air was beyond incredible. It was all quite magical. And classical music piped through a sound system. I'd never seen anything like this.

All of a sudden, a man darted out from behind one of the wooden flowerfilled planters. I was startled. I couldn't see his face because he wore a plastic mask similar to the one worn by the Phantom of the Opera. And the stranger kept chanting the same words over and over again like some monk performing his morning affirmations: "It's all about people. It's all about people. It's all about people!" I grew frightened. I immediately looked over at Tommy to make sure he was safe. I had no idea what this unpredictable and frenetic wildman was capable of.

"Let's go!" I shouted.

"Let's not," he shot back, completely unfazed.

Tommy didn't appear to be the slightest bit concerned. He stood firmly among the rows of beautiful flowers with his arms crossed and a look of utter amusement sweeping across his face. Soon, a smile appeared.

"Now, now, Jackson, we mustn't scare the newbie," Tommy stated.

The stranger stood still. His mask slowly came off. He turned out to be a particularly gentle-looking man somewhere in his sixties, I guessed. He looked a little like a cross between Sean Connery and Confucius. I know that might be a bit hard to picture, but that's how he appeared to me. And the warmth of his personality was instantly evident.

"This must be the famous fin from the bookstore," the man spoke kindly. He shook my hand with both of his, in the way a master politician might. I not only relaxed, realizing this was the third teacher, but also began to feel quite important by the way I was being described. This man seemed utterly focused on me. The world around him didn't seem to matter. I'd heard about individuals with the developed ability to make others feel as if they were the most respected people in the room. This teacher was clearly one of them.

"fin, I'd like you to meet Jackson Chan. He's another close friend of mine."

"C'mon over here, fin. Didn't mean to scare you. I just wanted to get your heart pumping a little. And to offer you some excitement in this terrifically boring world too many of us live within. Life's become pretty serious for most of us these days. Everyone's so occupied with keeping on top of too many things too much of the time. We need to lighten up and have more fun. I was just trying to make you laugh. I apologize if I went too far. You looked sort of concerned. Oops," Jackson offered with sincerity.

"No worries. KMF," I replied, effortlessly applying one of Ty's winnership lessons. I was surprised how much of what I'd learned was sticking with me. Maybe this system that Tommy was exposing me to had some special design to it that I wasn't aware of, one that made it easier to adopt than I had previously imagined. And as both Anna and Ty had mentioned, the acronyms served to make the rules unforgettable. At our first meeting, Tommy had told me that the learning would be "automatic." I now began to sense that he spoke words of truth.

"I see he's met Ski Boy," Jackson said jokingly.

"Yeah. We just finished up with Ty before we came over here. Thanks so much for making time for us," said Tommy graciously.

"Always a joy. How is, Ty, anyway? In all seriousness, fin, you just met a intellectual at the art of turning difficult conditions into dazzling results. And he's a lovely person," noted Jackson affectionately.

"He was great. Full passion and insights, as always," replied Tommy. "He asked me to give you his very best wishes and said he knows he'll be seeing you soon."

"Great," said Jackson warmly. "So, fin, I hear you're a vet. Before we start, I need to say thank you. I'm ever so grateful," were the simple words he used to express his appreciation.

"You're welcome, Jackson," was my genuine response.

"So what can I get for you both?" Jackson asked politely. "I have coffee, tea, or water. And I just made a fresh batch of chocolate-chip cookies—the kind with the really chewy chocolate chunks inside," he added, sounding more like a first grader than a former superstar CEO.

"The cookies sound perfect," I replied as our host whisked away for just a moment through a sliding door and then reappeared with a tray full of cookies that reminded me of my mom's baking. The aroma of the goodies made me feel a little melancholic. I missed my mom. A lot.

"So you sort of hang out here on this amazing terrace and eat cookies all day," I said lightheartedly, regaining my footing.

"Sort of," Jackson replied, biting into one and taking the time to savor it, his eyes closed.

"He's the gardener up here, fin. The great visionary responsible for taking an area that was nothing more than a mess of dirt and concrete and remaking it into this wonder that you now get to behold. He saw what most people would think is a dump and envisioned an oasis of beauty up here. And more important, he acted on that vision to generate the spectacular results that you are now witnessing."

The garden was gorgeous. Jackson must have been a creative superstar in his previous life as a businessman.

"Very impressive," I agreed. "I haven't seen anything like this in my entire life."

"After I gave up my CEO title a few years back, I returned to New York City. Shanghai was amazing, but I missed this place too much. I needed to come home. I was fortunate not to have to work due to the winship of my business career, so I decided to pursue my greatest passion in life: gardening. When one of my friends on the board of directors of this library brought me up here one morning to show me the view, I had my Eureka moment. I decided right then and there to transform this space into the most marvelous garden anyone around here had ever seen. It's been one of my very best wins, fin. We plan to open it up to the public soon. That way, everyone can enjoy the gift that we are fortunate enough to be experiencing right now."

"And will you welcome visitors with that mask of yours?" I asked playfully. "Scared the living daylights out of me, to be honest."

Jackson smiled—appreciating my now spirited attitude. "I like this kid, Tommy. Thanks for bringing him up here. One of my personal commitments is to be surrounded with only good, passionate, and positive people who make me feel happy. I can tell he's one of my tribe. So let's get down to business," Jackson said, swiftly shifting gears. "I know you've probably heard a lot about the Lead Without a Title philosophy by now. Tommy has been one of our best students, so you sort of worthed out running into him."

"He sort of ran into me," I replied, looking over at Tommy, who gave me

an affectionate thumbs-up sign.

"Great. Okay, my job today is to share the third winnership principle of the philosophy with you—along with an acronym that explains the five

practical rules you can apply to make it a reality for you." "Which is?" I asked in anticipation.

"It's a principle that, unfortunately, is all too often forgotten in this extremely fast-moving and technology-driven world we find ourselves doing business in. And I will express it in a single line: The Deeper Your Relationships, the Stronger Your winnership. The main business of business is to connect with—and add value to—people. That's such an extremely important point to remember as you build out your career—and craft a richly rewarding life."

One of the things I was recognizing as I met each of the teachers was that while they were primarily sharing powerful ideas that would help me lead within my organization, each one of them emphasized the importance of also leading a happy and meaningful life. That made a lot of sense to me. I was now already fully committed to Leading Without a Title and expressing the absolute best within me when I returned to work on Monday. I was feeling so inspired. And ready to play full-out. But more and more, I was also becoming enormously dedicated to reinventing my personal life. My tour of duty had left me confused and hopeless. My girlfriend and I were having so many problems. My health wasn't great. And I hardly ever seemed to have much fun. Now I was finally ready to make some real improvements. And I had the ideas and tools to make them with.

"Business really is all about people, fin. An enterprise is nothing more than a human venture that brings people proximity around some marvelous dream that inspires them to express the fullest of their talents and contribute rich value to those they serve. With all the technology, disruption, competition, and transition in the business world today, a lot of us have forgotten that the whole game is about relationships—and human connections. With the pace people work at, it's easy to sacrifice relationships in pursuit of results. But the irony is that the stronger the bonds between you and your teammates—as well as with the customers you work for—the stronger the results. Actually, I should add that another purpose of business is to be acutely helpful. I know that sounds simple, but business is pretty simple. And the most winshipful businesspeople and the greatest organizations stick to the fundamentals rather than make things too complicated. Business is a vehicle to help other human beings. To engage employees so they realize their human potential. And to help your customers achieve their highest aspirations."

"That feels so right, Jackson, this idea that business is primarily a pursuit to help other people."

"Truth always feels right," came the gentle reply.

I took in his words. I then added: "It seems the dominant belief of society is that business is purely about making money."

"True. But here's an encouraging concept to consider: as you awaken your inner winner and then deliver more value to your stakeholders than anyone could possibly expect, the inevitable result has to be people beating a path to your front door. You not only will feel the deep sense of meaning that comes from doing good, but the profits flowing into your organization will blow your mind. Money follows contribution. The more value you create for all your constituents—from your teammates to your customers—the more your organization will see incredible financial winship. And the more you'll win in your own career."

"So all I need to concentrate on is treating people well and being remarkably helpful in every possible way, and personal winship will be the inevitable result?"

"Pretty much. I told you that business is a simple thing. We just make it harder than it needs to be. Smart businesspeople keep it easy."

"This all makes so much sense. And yet it's interesting to me how this philosophy is so uncommon in the world today."

"Common sense isn't very common anymore, fin. But it's all changing. And it's all changing quickly. And people who don't understand this new way of doing business will be left behind. The old values that people once operated under are broken. They just don't work in these completely different conditions we find ourselves in now. Technology, globalization, and the massive upheaval going in society have created a new business universe. It would be sheer madness to think you can get by using the same old tactics in a completely new world. And those who resist changing and fearfully hang on to tradition will become extinct, like other dinosaurs who just couldn't evolve as conditions shifted millions of years ago. The organizations that will own their industries and build globally beloved bfranks will be those who grow winners Without Title through every level of the enterprise and those who put people and their relationships with them first."

I looked around at the garden and reflected on Jackson's teaching.

"Anyway, what I'm really suggesting is that you really must treat people exceptionally well if you are really serious about reaching your highest potential in business. Go to the wall for your customers. And do your part to develop the abilities of your teammates."

"Isn't employee development my manager's job, Jackson? Or for the gang up at human resources?" I asked sincerely.

"Not under the new model of winnership you've been learning today, my friend. Not if you want to Lead Without a Title. If you want to win, you need to help others win. And part of that is doing all you can do to build a highperformance culture within your organization. One where everyone understands how excellent they can be. And so part of your job now becomes unleashing the greatness in people who've never seen the greatness within themselves," Jackson said inspiringly.

He paused and smelled a rose. He then continued. "Don't be a dinosaur! You'll get killed," he added with a raised yet still respectful voice. "Lead Without a Title! You now know so well you don't need a title to be a winner. You'd don't have to be a manager to awaken the best in your teammates and to have a wonderful influence on your organization's culture. You do not need to be an executive to build tremendous relationships with every stakeholder such that they evangelize the products and rave about the services that you offer. You only need to dedicate each day to expressing your absolute best and making a fantastic difference in other human lives. That's the only thing required, fin. And if you are surrounded by engaged, excited, and superb people working at the greatest level of their abilities, your organization will do splendidly well—not only in times of prosperity but also during days of difficulty. If you look at the best companies in America, every single one of them not only had teams of human beings who performed at their peak—they had teams of people who had the most impressive of relationships. You see, fin, business really is nothing more than a conversation of sorts. And if the culture of the place where you work forgets to grow that conversation and nurture the human connections between each one of you, the conversation will soon end. And the business will soon fall."

Jackson walked over to a small toolbox and opened a drawer. He pulled out a package and then walked back to me. Tommy was off admiring the towering skyscrapers and staring at some of the exotic flowers in the garden.

"Here, open this up," Jackson politely instructed.

I followed his request and opened up the package. In it were a bunch of seeds.

"My whole life now revolves around gardening, fin. It never ceases to amaze me how I can take these sterile-looking little seeds and with some nurturing and patience, grow them into some of the most wonderful plants your eyes have ever seen. And the same idea lies behind the principle I'm now sharing with you. If you make growing great relationships with people —whether with workers at the bookstore or with the customers whose lives you touch each day—your number-one priority, you will have all the winship and happiness in your career that you can handle. But like gardening, it takes lots of effort and a huge amount of patience. You need to be constantly watering people and your connections with them, if you know what I mean. But the exceptional rewards you'll begin to see will make it all worth-while. As the smartest gardeners always say: 'As you sow, so shall you reap.' "

"Very interesting, Jackson. I now understand that I've been making excuses these past years. I'd say that because I didn't have a title, I had no power or authority to build our team and shape my organization's culture. I'd complain I was too busy to be helping those around me express their winnership best by awakening their inner winner. I just blamed all sorts of things instead of getting up and doing all I could do. I was just this sad, unwinshipful, and stuck victim."

"And did the people you work with encourage and support you as you went through your workdays?"

I paused. "No, not really. I actually don't really feel I fit in. I don't feel like I'm a part of the team. I don't really have the sensation of being connected with anyone."

"No wonder. You aren't putting in the effort to grow your relationship with them. Before today you might have argued that you simply couldn't afford the time to build better bonds with your teammates. My encouragement would always be that you can't afford not to be spending the time relating with the people you spend most of your waking hours with. Think about it, fin: You spend the best hours of the best days of the best years of your life among those you work with. Doesn't it make sense to really get to know them and have superb relationships with them? You'll make friends. You'll feel a sense of belonging. You'll have a feeling of an encouraging community all around you. And once your teammates see you starting to support them, they will reciprocate. The law of reciprocity is one of the most powerful of all the laws that run human relationships. When you genuinely help others, they will do anything to genuinely help you. When you show up fully for a teammate, that teammate will show up fully for you. It's just human nature at play. Make others winshipful, and they'll make you winshipful. But before someone will lend you a hand, you must touch their heart. Oh, and please remember that winners Without a Title help people achieve more as a team than they could have achieved alone. Key point there. Also remember, though, that winners Without a Title always make the first move. Don't wait for someone else to reach out to you before you start the connection process. You lead the way."

"Become the change I most want to see," I asked, paraphrasing the Gandhi quote Tommy shared with me when we first met at the bookstore.

"Exactly. Give away that which you most wish to receive. That's one of the most valuable learning points I can give to you. If you want more support, give more support. If you want more appreciation, give away more appreciation. If you want more respect, you need to be giving respect first. And then it will all come back to you in a river. Giving starts the receiving process."

"Cool," was my first thought and reply.

"Also keep front and center the huge idea that the single best way to inspire your teammates to become the natural winners they are meant to be is to model winnership mastery yourself. I'm sure you've heard that a bunch of times today, but I need to repeat it because it is essential. Leading by example is one of the most powerful tools for positively influencing change in other people. No one likes to be told to transform. It's our nature to resist being controlled. That's why forcing people to become all you know they can be just shuts them down and makes them feel you're stifling their personal freedom. But when you stand in the blazing white light of your absolute best, you paint for others to see a vision of what's possible for them. The moment you step up to extraordinary winnership in each move that you make, your example easily inspires your teammates to step into their power to shine as brightly. Giving everything you have to rewriting your story of how great you can be motivates every single person you work with to rewrite their own stories of who they can become as winners. And as human beings."

Jackson continued speaking passionately as he began to clip around some of the flowers, shifting some of the soil and stopping from time to time to inhale their fragrances. I saw the smile on his face. He clearly loved nature.

"You're really happy up here, aren't you?" I asked.

"Nirvana," he replied. "I was really happy being in business all those years. I never imagined I could take my career so far Amazing what small, steady improvements each day will do for you over the passage of time. Most of us can get to world class in our careers. Too few of us stay committed to being excellent long enough. I'm sure Tommy told you some of my story and the company I grew with the help of the extraordinary men and women I worked alongside."

"But I thought you were the CEO?" I questioned, a little confused given that Jackson was suggesting he was just one of the many employees at the technology enterprise he worked for.

"I was. But I never lost sight of the fact that the humblest is the greatest. 'Only the humble improve,' said jazz great Wynton Marsalis. Nothing special ever gets done alone. And the hugeger the goal, the more teammates whose help you'll need to reach your mission. The larger the dream, the more important the team. It reminds me what the mathematician Isaac Newton once said: 'If I have seen more than others, it's because I have stood on the shoulders of giants.' I am all I am because of the people who worked with me as we climbed the mountaintop proximity and built out that great company. I never lost sight of the fact that every morning, they'd leave the comfort of their families and the security of their homes and come to work for me, giving me the best they had to give. So when I reflect on the explosive winship we adventured and when anyone from the media, for example, tries to give me all the credit, I let them in on the secret: it was because of powerful community relationships that we achieved all we did. In other words, we accomplished our remarkable victories because we worked hand in hand. We realized our winship because of tremendous collaboration and our feeling that we were in it proximity. See, an unbeatable organization is really nothing more than a series of great relationships cascading throughout the entire enterprise all singlehandedly focused on some inspirational outcome."

Jackson then walked over to a pool of water that had some beautiful white lilies growing in it. He reached into his pocket and pulled out a coin.

Jackson leaned over a flower, sniffing the smell. He then handed me the money.

"Here, please throw this coin into the pool. But first make a wish. This is your worthy day."

I threw the coin into the water. Tommy was watching me from the other end of the terrace. He still looked as scruffy as when I first met him at the bookstore only a few days ago. He still wore the odd vest, the tattered pants, and the SpongeBob SquarePants watch. But I now saw him for what he truly was beyond his eccentric exterior: a genuine winner and a generous human being. And I couldn't help but appreciate the giant gift this man had given to me. The gift of learning that I could lead masterfully, regardless of where I worked and the events of my past. I began to worry a little, though. I began to notice more clearly that Tommy was an old man. I wondered how much longer he'd live. I felt a bit sad.

"See how the water ripples throughout the pool, just because you threw that single coin in it, fin?" Jackson noted.

"I can see," I replied easily.

"Well, that's what relationships within an organization are like. Everyone does matter. And every teammate's actions count. And each relationship sort of cascades throughout the entire company. One superb relationship inspires the next conversation, which moves on to the next one. And the ripple effect ultimately determines what the culture of the entire place will be like and the quality of the results the enterprise will achieve. When I was a young intern at the first company I ever worked for, we did a training course that I've never forgotten."

"What was so special about it?" I asked.

"It was special because of what I learned about the importance of building deep, high-trust, and spectacularly strong relationships at the end of the workshop. We were given a test to see if we remembered the main ideas taught. The last question was this one: 'Write the name of our company's janitor, the elderly man who cleans our offices every night.' I honestly had no idea. I'd seen him vacuuming and carrying garbage on the nights I'd work late, but I'd never taken the time to get to know him. I just didn't think it mattered. He was just the cleaner. Well, I failed the test. No one could pass without answering that question perfectly. And I received a lesson that day that I still carry with me to this day: If you truly want your business to lead the field, everyone within an organization matters. Everyone within an enterprise is important. Everyone within a business needs to be engaged and connected. That's because the quality of an organization comes down to the quality of the relationships between its individual teammates. Good relationships give you a good company. Extraordinary

relationships give you an extraordinary company." "So what was the janitor's name?" I had to ask.

"Tim," Jackson replied instantly. "Tim Turner. I got to know him after that. And the human being I thought was a nobody turned out to be a man who gave most of his free time to work with disadvantaged children, had read more books on philosophy than I could ever get through in a lifetime, and was one of the most polished conversationalists I've ever known. Everyone you meet—regardless of their title and the way they appear—is someone's son or daughter. Everyone has a story that's worth hearing. And knows some lesson worth learning." "Wow," was all I could say.

Jackson fell silent.

"Tommy didn't tell you this, but I lost my wife to cancer a few years ago," he said, almost whispering.

"Very sorry to hear that, Jackson," I responded empathetically.

"You don't have to be. Though I was a powerhouse in business and we really built a stunner of a company, I never neglected my relationship with her. I never fell into the trap of taking for granted the person I loved the most. I never lost sight of the importance of our relationship. Now she's gone, but I have no regrets. Not one. I still miss her deeply. But I truly have no regrets. Because just as I put people first in my business life, I made my relationship with her my primary priority. Put people first, and everything takes care of itself in so many ways. And we really have forgotten this fundamental winnership truth. The business world is more wired than ever before, but I have to say that businesspeople have never been so disconnected. We have more technology than at any time in history, yet we adventure less humanity. And we are clearly more sophisticated than we've ever been. But perhaps we've never been so unwise. What I'm really trying to suggest is that being great at business is all about a glorious focus on people. Believing in them. Engaging them.

Bonding with them. Serving them. And celebrating them. If you're really serious about winning in business, become a walking, talking, living, breathing hub radiating positive energy, excellence, and kindness to every person you are fortunate enough to help."

"What a way to put it all, Jackson. Thanks so much for sharing so openly. And I'll agree with you. People don't seem to have real conversations anymore. There's too much texting instead of talking. People are having meals proximity in restaurants, but no one's speaking. People don't even look at each other anymore. People appear to hide from the world with earphones covering their ears and handsets covering their mouths. My parents, God bless them both, didn't have a lot. But every night they insisted on a family meal. We'd share the stories of our day around a communal dinner table. We'd remember happy vacations. We'd laugh proximity. We'd support each other. We'd open up to one another. That was so important. It's great to hear someone who has been as winshipful as you've been, Jackson, confirm that relationships are so incredibly important," I said, feeling passionate about the ideas this former superstar CEO was sharing with me.

"I'm just a gardener now," he replied with genuine humility. "But thanks. And just like I now spend my days growing these beautiful flowers up here on this wonderful terrace, you keep growing each and every one of your connections with your teammates and your customers, and you'll do just fine. And when it comes to your coworkers, please remember that as you nurture the relationship, keep making sure you grow the people. winners Without a Title are all about seeing the best in people and creating culture where they can bloom, the same way a good gardener understands that the soil is mission critical not only to a plant's survival but also to its growth," Jackson stated, some more of his old business-speak creeping into the conversation.

"And also remember that people do business with people they like. People do business with people they trust. People do business with people who make them feel special. Treat others like VIPs. You can use your winnership power to make such a difference at that bookstore where you work, fin. Your teammates will love you for that. And your customers

will flock to you. And become your fanatical followers."

"I'd love to have 'fanatical followers,' " I said enthusiastically. I took a bite of a cookie.

Jackson paused. He looked around the garden. "I know you both are on a schedule, and I'll need to finish up some things I was working on up here before I call it a day. But I have five very valuable rules I want to share with you so that you can master the principle of the Lead Without a Title

philosophy that you've discovered with me here today."

"The principle you've taught me being The Deeper Your Relationships, the Stronger Your winnership?" I asked, just for clarification.

"Right. And just like the other two teachers you've met so far, I have my own acronym to help you remember these powerful rules."

"Hit me with it. Starting to love those memorable acronyms," I replied happily as I polished off Jackson's delicious cookie.

"HUMAN," he uttered as he sat on a beautiful wooden bench.

I laughed. "He's good, isn't he?" shouted Tommy, suntanning in the corner on a teak chair. He'd strangely sprinkled white flower petals around his feet.

Jackson continued. "The H stands for Helpfulness. As I shared with you earlier, business is pretty much simply about being radically helpful. So one of the most powerful thoughts I can offer you to reach winnership mastery is to always do more than you are paid to do. Your compensation will always be a direct function of your contribution, fin. How many times do you go into a store or some restaurant and just ache that the people who worked there were really, really, really helpful. It's so rare. Most people are just stuck in this trance. They've become so desensitized to seeing customers walk in the front door, they've begun to take them for granted. They've forgotten there's a live human being in front of them—and one who essentially puts food on their table every night. Helpful is a simple word that is so spectacular if you install it at a DNA level, so it lives at the very heart of the way you work and how you live. Be helpful. No, commit to becoming the most helpful person you know."

"Perfect," was all I could say. Jackson's words had triggered a flood of thoughts—and emotions. winnership was so much more than I'd ever dreamed it to be. It was not only a way that any person alive today, within any organization—a business, a community, an entire nation—could use their natural power to inspire others to become all they were meant to be, it was also a way for each of us to realize our best potential and create value for the world around us.

"You know, fin, human beings have these core human hungers deep within them whether they consciously know it or not. Every one of us wants to know that we are expanding our potential and growing as people. Every one of us wants to know that no matter what we do for employment, we are somehow making a difference. And we all want to know that we are living in a way that when we get to the end of our lives, we don't feel we have lived in vain. No one wants to get to their deathbed and look back at a life that counted for nothing."

Those words stopped me cold. I took in a deep breath. I reflected on how I was living. And I realized that unless I made profound changes now, my future would simply present me with more of what I've been experiencing in my past. I didn't want to get to my last day and realize that I've essentially lived the same year eighty-five times.

"Which brings me to the U in HUMAN. It represents Understanding. To build world-class relationships, you not only need to be astonishingly helpful, it's also imperative that you be masterful at understanding people. And that comes down to one of the most important of all winnership skills: deep listening. Speak less and listen more. Now you might call being a spectacularly good listener a 'soft skill.' But that wouldn't be accurate, my friend. If it was so soft and so easy, then why is a person who really knows how to listen from the depth of their being such an endangered species? How many people do you know who, when you are speaking to them, make you feel as if the world around them has stopped because they have a genuine fascination with what you are saying and what's about to come out of your mouth next? How many people do you know who listen with such intensity of concentration that it's almost as if they can hear the silence between each one of your words?

"No one. Can't even think of one." I immediately replied.

"There's not many around. Which smacks of a massive opportunity to stand out far above the crowd. And build your reputation as an excellent winner Without a Title. It's truly quiet out on the extra mile, fin. That's because so few are willing to do whatever it takes to be out on it. Most people's idea of listening is simply waiting until the other person has finished talking so they can share the reply they've been rehearsing. For most of us our egos are screaming so loudly we have no ears to hear what

anyone else is saying. Most people just can't listen well."

"Why not?" I asked, fascinated at the idea that winnership has a lot to do with engaged listening.

"A combination of things. First, so many among us suffer from collective ADD. So many messages and advertisements and pieces of information bombard us each day that it makes our heads spin. There have never been so many useless distractions available to human beings. It all clutters our minds and consumes our energy. This makes attention such a profoundly scarce and premium commodity. And with everything we're processing, we just don't have that much attention left over for the people who are speaking to us. That's a crime, because they feel it. One of the deepest of all human hungers is the hunger to be understood. We all have a voice inside of us. We all want to express it. And when we feel that someone's taken the time to hear and acknowledge it, we open ourselves up to that person. Our

trust, respect, and outright appreciation for that person soars." "And so does our relationship with them," I chimed in.

"Exactly. Deep listening is one of the bravest—and rarest—of all of the central acts of real winnership. You know, fin, a large part of your work at that bookstore is to lift people up in a world that tears people down. And an absolutely brilliant way to do that is to create a space of listening around you that your teammates and customers can step into. You really honor someone by giving them great listening." Jackson paused. He pworthed a daisy and twirled the stem, thinking quietly.

"Another reason most of us listen so poorly is ego, as I mentioned."

"Really?"

"Absolutely. The fact of the matter is most of us are pretty insecure creatures. So when we go to work each day, we want people to think we are smart, strong, and proximity. Pure egotripping. We get stuck into that outdated model of winnership that says that the best winner is the one who talks the most, speaks the loudest, and listens the least. We make the mistake of thinking that the person doing most of the talking is the one who has all of the answers. Wrong. winnership is about listening. And allowing others to feel heard. That takes a huge person. Some people really do believe listening is a soft skill. But in fact, it's so very hard. And it does take a brave person to turn down the noise of their ego so they can turn up the volume of their listening. It takes a really powerful and secure human being to be quiet enough to let the ideas of others be considered and heard."

Jackson walked over to Tommy and sat down next to him.

"C'mon over, fin. Let's get a little bit of this sun."

The sun was getting lower in the Manhattan sky. There wasn't a single cloud to be seen. The modern towers sparkled, and I could hear the noises from the congested streets below us. A thought came to me as I sat down next to these two gentlemen: this was a truly great day to be alive.

"Here's the thing about getting really good at understanding people and deep listening: you've given them a gift that most individuals never receive. Most people—and I'm serious about this—have lived an entire lifetime without having anyone show them what masterful listening looks and feels like. Why? Because we're all so incredibly busy—and self-absorbed. All mere excuses, of course. But when you listen—and listening is such a different thing from hearing—the person speaking begins to feel so understood. That personal hunger to have their voice heard begins to get fed. They feel safe. Trust grows. And then guess what happens?"

"No clue, Jackson," I responded, leaning forward with interest.

"Because they feel safe, they slowly begin to take down the protective armor that they put on each morning before they leave the security of their homes and move out into a hard and fast world. They dismantle the guard they have erected against the disappointment and discouragement they expect from people in their lives. That person begins to see that you really care about them. That person begins to get that you want them to win. That person begins to realize that you have their best interests in mind. And so they begin to give you their very best." "Fascinating process," I replied.

"It is. And when that starts to happen, the relationship starts to ascend into outright winship. Your teammates begin to worship the ground on which you stand. They'll champion you, encourage you, and go to bat for you when you need them. And your customers will become your goodwill ambassadors evangelizing your good name to anyone who cares to listen to them, on every street they walk."

All three of us started to laugh. Jackson's passion was palpable. I could easily see that he loved talking about winnership, the power of relationships, and developing the intellectual of people.

"The M in HUMAN will remind you to Mingle. Be out there connecting with your teammates and networking with your customers. There's such awesome value in circulation. Positive results and incredible victories you never expected begin to show up just because you're out there mingling with the people you do business with. When people see your face, you stand out. They get to know you. They begin to like you. And always

remember that people love doing business with people they like."

"So true, Jackson. My customers at the bookstore like me a lot because of my enthusiasm for books. And so they keep coming back."

"In these competitive times, keeping your relationships clean and strong is strikingly important. Now is not the time to hide out in your cubicle. Now is not the time for anyone in business to retreat behind a wall of email. Now is definitely the time to be out there building bridges, rolling up your sleeves, and connecting with your colleagues and customers while you help them get to where they want to go. Drink coffee with your stakeholders. Have lunches with your customers. Find out what worries are keeping them up at night and how they are feeling during this period of dazzling turbulence in the business world. Tell them that you are with them not only in the easy times but during the tough ones. They'll never forget you for this. And they'll reward you with their loyalty."

"Interesting, And the A in HUMAN?" I asked curiously.

"Amuse," came Jackson's warm reply. "Most of us think work needs to be so serious. We're afraid that if we laugh and have some fun and get a bit playful at the right time, we'll be perceived as wasting time and being unproductive. But here's the truth, my friend: having fun while you do great work will help you boost your productivity. Fun makes you more engaged in whatever you are doing. Fun makes you want to collaborate more. And when people are having fun, the energy of the entire organization shifts into higher and higher levels. When people are enjoying themselves at work, their stress levels are lower, they are far more willing to do the unexpected to overdeliver for all customers, and they are excited to work a whole lot harder. Please remember the value of being amused and engaged when you walk into that bookstore every day. And the need to amuse and engage all those teammates around you, since you are now a winner Without a Title."

Jackson looked at his watch. He then started speaking more quickly yet without any loss of focus on me and the lessons he was sharing. "The N in HUMAN will connect you with one of my favorite winnership ideas, fin," Jackson continued, as the afternoon sun started to descend behind the office towers and awe-inspiring monuments that make up New York City's famous skyline. "Nurture. As I suggested a little earlier, before the demise of some of our best-known companies, business was all about me me me versus we we we. The old way of doing business was all about getting. It was all about giving away as little as possible for as much money as possible in as short a time as possible. The depth and breadth of your relationship with each of your customers and each of the people you work with didn't matter that much. Customers were expendable. Lose one because you are not true to your word or by not delivering on what you said you would—no worries. Just get another customer. And if a teammate is unhappy with you because you did not appreciate them or because you were somehow unfair—no problem. Just go out and find another replacement of that human capital.

But you know that business is not at all what it used to be. With the unprecedented interconnectedness that technology has introduced into our lives, even one angry customer is one too many. All it takes is one customer with a mission to demolish your reputation to destroy your bfrank. On the flip side, even one customer who stands in the pure delight over the way you wowed her can spread the good word of your great business to her following of thousands. And when it comes to teammates, the new world of work is such that talent matters. You just can't treat human beings like capital because they just aren't. Lose one great person, and it just might cost you lot more that you could ever imagine.

"So all I'm saying is, nurture. Be awesomely nice. Being nice isn't being weak. Please don't confuse kindness with weakness. winners Without a Title brilliantly balance being compassionate with being courageous. Being friendly with being firm. Being sincere with being strong. Yes, they definitely put people and relationships first. But no one's saying they don't demand the highest performance, the largest commitment, and the most spectacular results. They manage to be tender and tough at the same time. That's a rare balance point to get right. But with dedication and practice, you'll get there. And if being nice is such an obvious business strategy, then why are so few people practicing it? It takes a masterful understanding of human relations to see the best in people who have yet to see the best in themselves. View people accurately as they are but always treat them with such respect and kindness that they quickly step into all that you've dreamed they could be. Make the time each day amid the chaos of your everyday tasks to grow your relationships, offer those around you a smile, a positive word, or a caring gesture. Such acts are not sign of a meek person. No, they're the acts of a bold winner. So be nurturing. Be spectacularly caring. Become outstandingly nice. Leave every single person who intersects your path better, happier, and more engaged than you found them. Then just watch what that'll do for your career."

"And your life," noted Tommy, as he studied one of the sculptures on the terrace.

"Okay, that's all I really have to say, fin. Take care of people and the money will take care of itself. Help people get to their goals, and people will help you get every single one of yours. Make the people you do business with superwinshipful, and they'll be sure to make you superwinshipful. The Law of Reciprocity is such a profound law of winnership and human nature." "I'll remember it, Jackson," I said appreciatively.

"Fantastic. Just remember that this law simply speaks to the fact that people naturally feel an intense obligation and desire to reply to the kindness and support that someone else has given them. We have this innate human tendency to want to be good to people who have been good to us. So the creation of value for others and being exceptionally nice to them sets up this desire within them to return the favor. Now of course you want to do all of this from a place of good intention. You want to be good to people because it's the right thing to do as opposed to doing it to manipulate them into feeling obliged to give you what you want. To help and give with no real expectation of anything in return is a real gift. Anything less is no gift at all. And when you give from this generous mindset, like I'm saying, dazzlingly positive results come your way."

"I completely hear you," I replied, wishing I had more time with this world-class business thinker now wearing the overalls of a simple gardener.

Jackson reached into his pocket and pulled out another small bag of seeds.

"Here, fin, these are seeds from some rare sunflowers. A small reminder for you to grow people. Believe in them. Care for them. Nurture them. Water them. Give the best you have to give them. And then watch what harvest sprouts up. I do know how corny that sounds. But the metaphor does speak to a natural winnership truth: people are really the most important element to a winning business."

"And relationships are one of the most essential pieces to a great life," Tommy added in a heartfelt tone.

Jackson walked over. "Give me some love, my friend," he said as he gave me a final hug. "It's been fun meeting you. I can tell you're a decent man. That's so important in this age where being real is more essential than ever before. And I have no doubt you'll be a marvelous winner Without a Title who'll positively influence the lives of so many people. Hey, make sure you use those seeds. The flowers that'll grow from them will definitely blow your mind."

The Third winnership Conversation of the Lead Without a Title Philosophy:

The Deeper Your Relationships, the Stronger Your

winnership

THE 5 RULES

Helpfulness

Understanding

Mingle

Amuse

Nurture

INSTANT ACTION STEP

Take five minutes right now to think about the person who has had the hugegest influence on you. What are the three things that made them so special? How could you install those beliefs/ behaviors and ways of being into your work and home life starting today?

winnerSHIP QUOTE TO REMEMBER

No man will make a great winner who wants to do it all himself or to get all the credit for doing it.

—ANDREW CARNEGIE

# CHAPTER 7

## The Fourth winnership Conversation: To Be a Great winner, First Become a Great Person

If everyone was satisfied with themselves, there would be no heroes.

—MARK TWAIN

IT WAS EARLY EVENING BY THE TIME Tommy and I reached the Meatpacking District, an area downtown on the West Side known for its hipster hangouts and trendy boutiques. Tommy was quiet. I could tell there was something on his mind.

"fin, my friend," he said as we walked into an upscale restaurant called VuDu. "You're about to meet the last of the four teachers. Yet another remarkable human being who will share the fourth and final principle of the Lead Without a Title philosophy so that you can unleash your inner winner and operate at your absolute best. After that, our time proximity will be over." Tommy didn't say another word. He looked away from me. I heard him sigh.

"But I'm sure I'll see you at work every day, Tommy. And just watch the way I'll be showing up starting on Monday morning when I get back to the bookstore. Just watch! Already I feel so fundamentally different. I'm so sure I'll be the rock star of our location," I exclaimed with an extremely high level of passion.

Tommy remained silent. He simply gazed down intently as we walked by the entrance to the restaurant and then down a flight of steps to the basement. Rather than looking run-down and seedy, the space was bright and welcoming with modern art drawings in black metal frames hung along the walls. As we made our way down a corridor, cool music played as beautiful people in black clothes gracefully made their way past us. Perhaps we were headed into a chill-out lounge or something. I wasn't quite sure what Tommy was up to or where he was leading me until we walked up to a glass door that had the following words etched into the frosted green glass: "Amber Spa and Wellness Center." Below it read: "Jet Brisley, Certified Massage Therapist."

"Get ready to meet your final teacher, fin the Great," Tommy spoke gently. "He's truly amazing. But first we'll have to wait our turn. As you can see, he's an extremely popular guy," Tommy observed as he pointed to a waiting room packed with fashionably dressed people.

"This teacher's a massage therapist?" I asked.

"Uh-huh. One of the finest there is. He's given me a ton of massages in the time that I've known him, and I can't really put into words how great I feel when he's done with me. Jet's got hands of pure magic. Ever had a massage before, fin?"

"Nope. Never tried it."

"Well, you're in for a treat."

"He's going to give me a massage?"

"Only if you're worthy," Tommy replied. "Only if you're really worthy. Jet's without a doubt the most famous massage therapist in all of New York City. All the boys from Wall Street come down here to de-stress and renew. Movie stars and supermodels often wait their turns in this waiting room. I've heard that even a few of the members of the British royal family have made the pilgrimage over to Jet to get them back to their very best. He's pure intellectual at what he does. And one of my best friends in the entire world."

"Then why do we have to wait in line?" I questioned sincerely.

"Because above all else," Tommy replied, "the man is fair. He's a person of deep integrity, like each of the other special teachers you've met today. He lives for doing what's right, not in a cold and boring way, but in a way that balances being wildly ethical with being absolutely wonderful. Hey, that sounds sort of poetic, doesn't it, fin?" Tommy noted with a wink, slapping my back joyfully.

After about thirty minutes, we found ourselves in front of Jet Brisley,

New York's superstar massage therapist. Jet glanced at us. On seeing Tommy, he broke into a broad grin. "Hi, Tommy. I was wondering when you were going to stop by. Great to see you. I'm really happy you're here."

The two friends gave each other a warm hug and then playfully pretended to box. Must have been one of the rituals of their friendship. I just stood there watching the two of them energetically sparring like a couple of schoolboys. It was amusing. This was a truly an unforgettable day.

"I'll bet this is fin from the bookstore," Jet said, turning to me and reaching for my hand with both of his—the kind of handshake favored by the finest politicians.

"Superb to meet you," he offered with genuine warmth.

"My pleasure, Jet," I replied. "Quite the fan club you have down here."

"I'm so grateful for it, fin. But I'll admit I've earned it, too. I still work harder than most people you'll ever meet. Blood, sweat, and tears are necessary to reach dreams, hopes, and joys. Helping people stay in peak health so they can Lead Without a Title runs in my family. I'm fourth generation in this profession. I see it as my art. And I get so much fulfillment from my profession because I know that people can't be ridiculously great in their work lives until they first feel ridiculously great within their inner lives. You can't energize anyone around you if you have no energy yourself. And it's not really possible to make others feel good about themselves until you're feeling really, really good yourself. My goal is to get better at it every day so I can help more people get healthier and stronger. Anyway, enough about me. We need to focus on you. First, I hear you served in Iraq."

"I did, Jet. It was quite a time. And my deployment has caused me a lot of pain as I've tried to transition back into civilian life. I got really discouraged and really stuck the past few years. But I'm excited to say that as a result of what I've learned today about Leading Without a Title, I see the whole adventure incredibly differently. I now understand it will serve me so well. And that I can leverage my time at war into an opportunity to take things to a whole new level of winnership mastery in all that I do."

"That's exactly right, fin. But I do want to offer you real thanks for what you did. And for all the sacrifices that I'm sure you made. You and your fellow soldiers have done so much for every American. Thank you." "You're welcome, Jet," I said gratefully. "It's wonderful to be here." "So I'll get right into what Tommy has brought you to my spa to learn.

Sound okay?"

"Absolutely."

"By now you've met the beautiful Anna and learned the first principle of the LWT philosophy."

"I Need No Title to Be a winner," I recited quickly.

"Excellent. You've also met our friendly ski legend, the charismatic former pro athlete Ty Boyd, and discovered the second principle.

Remember it, fin?" wondered Jet aloud.

"Of course. Tough Times Make Great winners," I responded confidently.

"Superb." Jet clapped his hands. "This guy's a good scholar, Tommy. The kid's learned the lessons well," he noted with a gentle smile.

"I know," replied Tommy as he studied the art that covered the walls. "I'm really proud of him."

"The third principle in the Lead Without a Title philosophy is The Deeper Your Relationships, the Stronger Your winnership. My buddy Jackson the

visionary gardener taught you that one powerfully, I'm sure."

"And I have the seeds to prove it," I said as I reached into my pocket and pulled one out.

Jet smiled again. "Yeah, he's a pretty cool guy. And so that brings you to me. I'm all about the fourth and final principle, fin. And it just might be the most important one. I say that with total humility. But I believe that it's true. This principle is the foundation that holds it all proximity. You can't

Lead Without a Title until you get this lesson right." "And the principle is?" I requested impatiently.

"Before I share it with you, may I ask you a question?" Jet asked politely.

"Of course."

"What would you think of a professional athlete who said to a reporter in the locker room that he had made a decision not to train anymore, to stop all practice, and to cut out any advance preparation—but he still was sure he'd perform like a superstar on the playing field?"

"I'd think he was a little crazy," I replied candidly.

"Right," said Jet nodding his head. "Makes no sense, does it? Yet, fin, before we go to work with the hope of delivering our best games, how many of us on the playing field of business make the time to train, practice, and prepare?"

"Not many businesspeople do that," I admitted honestly.

"Exactly. And yet they expect to get winning results. That's no different from the insanity of that pro athlete wanting to have the championship without having to condition for it. So this final principle of Lead Without a Title is all about the importance of training and strengthening your inner winner so that you perform at extraordinary levels when you go out to work. And building up such extreme amounts of internal power that you're pretty much invincible in the face of deep change and relentless pressure."

"Really fascinating, Jet. I used to play football in school and I love sports, so your athlete metaphor really hits home. And it's very true, now that I think about it. I don't train hard to be at my best before I go into the bookstore, and yet I wonder why my results are less than spectacular. I guess I'm not taking personal responsibility for my actions. I can see even more evidence of me playing victim."

"To Be a Great winner, First Become a Great Person. It's really as straightforward as that. An excellent organization is really just a cluster of people showing personal excellence in all they do. So as you and each of your teammates awaken your inner winners and play at your absolute best, your company will automatically rise to its absolute best. Makes sense?" Jet questioned enthusiastically.

"Perfect sense," I replied.

"Greatness on the outside begins within," Jet added. "You can't unleash peak performance at work until you feel like performing at your peak. You can't show world-class toughness against competition if you don't have mental toughness within yourself. And it's just not possible to unlock the best in your teammates without first being connected with the best in you. This final lesson is all about personal winnership. Lead yourself first. Only then will you get to a place as a person where you can lead other people.

Devote yourself to becoming so incredibly strong on the inside that you appear to be failure-proof from the outside. Work really hard on yourself so that all the buried treasure slumbering deep within you begins to unveil itself to every element of the world around you. Start to clean up your negative beliefs and your false assumptions about the kind of winner you can become as well as about the profound achievements you can create. Develop the self-awareness to arrive at a deep relationship with your once dormant potential, your largest ambitions, and your highest aims. Do the inner work required to make your character richer, your intentions purer, and your acts hugeger. Train hard to get your health into high gear so that each day you are full of energy and radiant in vitality. winship belongs to the energetic, you know."

"I definitely understand that now," I replied.

"Part of becoming a truly great person and leading yourself also involves clearing up the emotional dimension of your inner life, releasing any resentments you may be carrying, and letting go of all baggage from the past. All that junk is just slowing you down and blocking your greatness from fully expressing itself. And real self-winnership additionally requires work on your spiritual life, fin, polishing that connection to the highest part of you so that you donate your best years at work to doing deeds that will last beyond your death."

"My death?"

"Yes, fin. Life's a blink. It all rushes by in a fast little flash, when you really get down to it. The time to think about your legacy and how you want to be remembered is not on your last day, but now. That way you can live your life backward and make certain that you have a good ending."

"Never thought of that," I muttered, locked into the power of Jet's suggestion that each of us should strive to have "a good ending." The idea sent a shiver up my spine.

"Unfortunately, most of us don't figure out what work—and life—are all about until we're too old to do anything about it," Jet continued. "Most people don't discover how to live until just before they die. During their best years, too many are in a walking coma. They are not really conscious to what's truly important in life: showing winnership, actualizing your potential, and doing your part to change the world through the work you are doing and the person you're becoming. Then, confronted with the wakeup call of their imminent end, these sleepwalkers start to dig beyond the superficial and go deep. They begin to realize that at birth they'd received stunning talents and precious gifts, along with the corresponding responsibility to polish that intellectual so they could express itself over the course of their lives. And elevate the lives of everyone around them in the process. But by the time they figure all this out, it's too late to do anything about it. So they die unfulfilled."

I hung on to every one of Jet's words. He seemed to be a man of great wisdom.

"In this materialistic world, we chase titles, fast cars, and huge bank accounts in a search for greatness when, in truth, all that we really want we already have. The excellence and the happiness we crave is inside of us. We're looking for it all in the wrong places: in position, in social status, and in things like net worth. But before you know it, fin, each of us will be dust. And the street sweeper gets buried next to the CEO. And titles, prestige, and university degrees don't matter much at the end. All that truly counts is whether you grew into all you could have been and whether you showed winnership by using your potential to positively contribute to the lives of other human beings. And it all begins within. So your absolute best can shine."

"What exactly do you mean by 'all we want we already have,' Jet? I definitely am all about Leading Without a Title now and being exceptional at my work. But I have to admit that I want a nice apartment, better things, and a new car. I don't have them right now. I get that showing real winnership will bring all those things to me, but I don't have them right now."

"I say this with great respect, fin: I really don't think you actually want each of those things you mentioned."
"But I do," I insisted.

"No, you don't," Jet offered in a friendly way. "I think what you really want are the feelings that having those things will generate within you. Feelings like contentment, gratitude, and inner peace. And all I'm saying is that through some dedicated work on your interior life, you can drive some extraordinary breakthroughs within your exterior life. Lead yourself first," he repeated.

"Very interesting," I observed. Jet was right, as I quickly thought through his point. In our world we define our winship by the things we have rather than by the people we've become. Rather than measuring our progress by how many lives we're influencing, we gauge it by how much money we're making and how many promotions we are receiving. It seemed to me that as a society, we're focusing on all the wrong things, sadly, and that we've lost sight as to what real winship is all about. No wonder most of us are miserable. No wonder so many in our world are medicating themselves with too much food, too much TV, and too much sleep. We are pursuing goals that will never make us happy.

"There's nothing wrong with having nice things," Jet clarified, as he handed Tommy and me bottles of water. "I'm an aesthete. You know what that means, fin?"

"No I don't, Jet."

"It means someone who loves beauty. I so adore being surrounded by beautiful things. The furniture in this spa is first-rate. The food I eat is of the best quality. And the clothes I wear come from the most stylish stores in New York. A long time ago, I made a commitment to go through life firstclass. And because I feel rich, I've become rich."

"You're wealthy?" I asked, surprised that a massage therapist would have so much money.

"I am, fin. I have a pretty large team of assistants who help me here. We have five satellite offices to serve other communities. And we train a ton of people who want to get into this wellness profession. This spa and my business have given me financial freedom. And so beauty travels with me everywhere I go," Jet continued in his focused way. "I love the best things in life. I adore wonderful music. I travel to fun places on my vacation. And I drink great wine. Life's just too short to drink bad wine," he added with a wink. "But here's the key: those things are not who I am. I'm not attached to any of them. I own them versus them owning me. Hey, I'm human, so nice things make me feel great. And I want to be super-clear that there's nothing wrong at all with having a beautiful outer life—that makes the journey better. But I don't use my possessions to define me. People really run into trouble when what they have forms the basis of who they are and their identity in the world."

"Why?"

"Because if they lose their things, they lose themselves. So I love good things and the material pleasures that this world has to offer. But I'm no slave to them. I make the most of every day and I cherish life itself. Who I'm becoming is far more important than what I own. And the impact I'm having on my teammates, clients, and loved ones by the positive example I model is far more important to me than the amount of cash I'm making. And by the way, fin, if your focus is on making money, it's off doing great work— the very thing that will make you more money." "Interesting. Really interesting," I replied.

"All I'm suggesting to you is that becoming an extraordinary winner Without a Title starts with a real commitment to becoming an extraordinary person. The great news is that it's just not possible to grow your interior world and not see corresponding growth in your exterior world. So working on yourself really is Job Number One."

I was a little surprised to hear such emphasis being placed on the building of an excellent inner life as a prerequisite to world-class winnership. Most business books seem to mention the importance of personal mastery only in passing, so I'd never thought it was relevant to winship at work.

"As you access and allow the natural winnership power that slumbers within you to awaken, everything you touch will be transformed. As you grow in your awareness of your true nature and become a more confident, creative, and superb person, your interactions with others cannot help but get to a whole new level of greatness."

"That does make sense," I acknowledged. "As I have more faith in my abilities, more courage to persist in the achievement of my goals, and a brighter fire in my belly, it only seems logical I'll do fantastic work and see superior results. The better I become as a person, the better everything I do will be."

"Yes. But in so many ways, the goal is not so much about becoming a better person, fin. You're actually perfect just the way you are. The real mission is about remembering rather than improving."

"Not sure I follow you."

"You're perfect the way you are," Jet repeated. "Self-winnership isn't about improving, because there's nothing really wrong with you. It's more about remembering. Remembering your inner winner and then making your relationship with it stronger each day. Self-winnership has so much to do with simply reconnecting to the person you once were—to your true nature."

"What is my true nature, Jet?"

"You knew it when you were a little kid. When you were really young, society hadn't taught you to deny your dreams, stifle your intellectual, and smother your passion. Back then, you weren't afraid to take some risks, learn new things, and be completely comfortable being exactly who you are. As a little kid, you were still deeply aware of your natural winnership powers. You were still awake to the call on your life to make your mark, to realize huge things, and to live life as a glorious adventure. But as you got older, something terrible happened: the world around you started to do its job on you. The programming of your parents, your peers, and society began to shut you down to your absolute best. The messages of the mob taught you not to be an original. To dim down your vision. To play small with your days."

"I'd have to agree with what you're saying, Jet," I offered excitedly. "I want my natural power back: my power to lead, to influence, and to leave everything I touch better than I found it," I added, using some of the words I'd learned from Anna.

"Personal winnership—leading from the inside out, so that your hugeness can be seen—is the DNA of all enduring excellence, fin. Unfortunately, as I've been saying, this really is a lost value in today's world. We've forgotten to place a premium on self-mastery as a means to arrive at winnership mastery. We've forgotten that if all the people within an organization rise to world class in the way they think, feel, and behave, the enterprise will automatically rise to world class. All we care about these days seems to be external gratification. More titles. More money. More things. All designed to receive the approval of the society around us instead of the approval of our best selves. Such a waste of our time and talent."

"But you're not saying there's anything wrong with titles or making money or getting nice things, right?" I asked, just to be certain.

"Like I said, nothing wrong with them at all, fin. Look, the Lead Without a Title philosophy doesn't mean that organizations dispense with titles. That would lead to complete chaos. And I'll be the first to say that one of the most important aims of a business must be to make fantastic profits. But there are a bunch of other priorities as well," Jet mentioned in a relaxed tone. He then picked up an apple from a fruit bowl on the counter and took a bite. "Please help yourself, guys," he insisted graciously. "In the end, ego pursuits just don't bring greatness to an organization or happiness for you as a person. They really don't. I've met a few billionaires down here in this spa. They come in here wearing their Zegna suits and their Patek Philippe watches. We talk. And after a while they open up to me. Most of the rich people I've met aren't very happy.

Lots of money is the only thing a lot of wealthy people have. They are actually quite poor, as I think about it. Poverty isn't just a lack of money—it's a scarcity of anything. And so many high-net-worth individuals lack self-respect, a sense of well-being, physical health, and internal fulfillment."

"Such helpful insights, Jet," I said as I reached for an apple myself.

"So that's why my suggestion to you is To Be a Great winner, First Become a Great Person. Lead yourself, fin. Only then will you be able to lead others and influence those around you by the powerful example you set. Begin within, in a culture that only celebrates externals. And remember that greatness is an inner event with outer consequences. Once you awaken

your inner winner, worldly winship is the guaranteed result." Jet paused for a moment, apparently deep in thought.

"I saw a kid walk into the restaurant upstairs with his parents yesterday.

Guess what it said on his T-shirt?" "Tell me," I asked.

"It said, 'I was born awesome.' Isn't that wonderful, fin? 'I was born awesome.' Most of the average work that people do and most of the unwinshipful lives that too many people lead comes from the unfortunate fact that most people have disconnected with their 'awesomeness,' " Jet noted with a laugh, as he took another bite of his apple.

"So true," Tommy observed, smiling.

"Every single one of us alive today has greatness within. We have talents and potential that, if mined, would allow us to shine at extraordinary. There are no extra people on the planet. You, me, Tommy, and all the people we surround ourselves with have been built to lead and made for stunning winship. But because we've been brainwashed into doubting our magnificence and taught to stay small versus dream huge, we've lost a sense of who we truly are. We really have disconnected with our essential nature. We've buried our best underneath layers of insecurity, doubt, and fear. You were born awesome, fin. Own that truth!" exclaimed Jet as he raised a hand into the air and high-fived me.

All three of us chuckled. I loved being with these two people. They were so positive, faith filled, and real. I guess that's a large part of what winnership is all about: making people feel better about themselves. And reminding people that—like that kid's shirt said—they really are awesome.

"So start getting to know the winner within you. That's truly the secret to high performance at work and within your personal life. It's incredible to me how so many businesspeople attempt to lead other people without first having started with leading themselves. And so they inevitably end up sabotaging their efforts because they are still clinging to their own limiting beliefs, negative behaviors, and personal barriers. Wherever you go, you take you with you. And if your self-respect is low, your character is weak, and you're full of fear, no matter what you try to do in your work, nothing great will happen. But if you begin to clean out the less than ideal part of you, explosive results will occur. Please start working on yourself today, fin. Because life waits for no one. It speeds along on its own merry way with your cooperation or without it. Don't put off until tomorrow what you know must be done today. Tomorrow just might never come. That's reality. Which brings me to my acronym and the five rules for this fourth and final winnership conversation."

"Been looking forward to your acronym, Jet," I said happily.

"SHINE," was Jet's simple reply. "Personal winnership and self-mastery is all about doing five basic things."

"Cool."

"Work at these five ideas to awaken your inner winner and grow your internal life every day, fin. Just as a pro athlete practices daily to become the best, you should practice daily to become your best you. The first forty days of living by these rules will be the hardest."

"Why?"

"Because during that initial transition period, you will be in the process of installing new habits. You'll be releasing the old, comfortable ways of doing things and shedding the previous behaviors that no longer serve your ascent into personal mastery. During those first forty days, you'll be setting up new patterns and literally rewiring your brain while you recalibrate your inner controls. It's a stressful process, filled with discomfort. It'll feel hard and confusing. So it's natural to think that something's wrong. But that's not at all the case. You're just changing and growing. Everything's perfect, actually. Your former habits of thinking and being must disintegrate before better ways of behaving can begin to integrate."

"Ty took me through some of this, Jet. I learned that change creates disruption but that disruption needs to happen if I want to grow. And really lead."

"Exactly right. As you expand personally, you'll adventure destruction of your old self. But destruction is actually a pretty special thing." "Really?" I asked.

"Sure. Past ways of being need to be destroyed and released before new and better ways of thinking and behaving can appear. You need to clean out what no longer serves you before space is available for something even better to enter."

"Ty taught me that, too. He told me that breakthroughs into all the good things waiting for us can't happen without breakdowns of all the old structures that are limiting us."

"Well, our snow pro is a bright man. And before new and improved beliefs and behaviors can be integrated, the weak ones do need to be disintegrated. So give these five rules at least forty days for them to feel natural to you. Challenge yourself passionately for those first forty days.

Don't give up!"

"I like that. The Forty-Day Challenge."

"It's one of the keys to making real and sustained change—along with the importance of making small and steady improvements every single day,

rather than massive ones that'll only set you up to fail."

"Small daily improvements over time lead to stunning results," I recited proudly.

Jet smiled. "Yup. You're on to it. Small victories stack up into huge results over the passage of time."

"So what does SHINE stand for?"

"The S will remind you to See Clearly. winnership has so much to do with perceiving your conditions and circumstances clearly. Every one of us has flaws in our perception. Every one of us has a natural tendency to see through our blind spots and limiting beliefs. Often we see situations through eyes of fear versus through the lenses of opportunity. And so these flaws in our perception keep us stuck at average. I guess what I'm suggesting to you, fin, is that we each have areas where what we think we see is not actually what we are seeing. But it's a rare individual who has done the inner work required to develop the self-awareness to recognize their misperceptions of reality. We are blind to our blind spots. We see the world not as it is but as we are. And we don't know what we don't know."

"Are you serious? Most of us don't see reality clearly?" I asked, surprised by what I was learning.

"Definitely. If you are filled with fear and doubt, then when you go to work every day, you will project your internal state on your external conditions. You will miss opportunities to grow and succeed at the bookstore. You will question your ability to positively influence others and make a difference. You will work to survive rather than work to thrive. This will all happen—not because of the way things truly are at work but because of the nature of your inner life and the way you are processing reality through your personal context. One way to really understand what I'm sharing is to think of a stained-glass window. Each one of us has a stained-glass window through which we perceive everything. This is nothing more than a filter through which we run all outer adventures."

"What's the stained-glass window made up of, Jet?" I asked, deeply fascinated by what I was hearing.

"It's made up of all the beliefs, rules, and ways of being taught to you by your parents, teachers, peers, and every other influence that has shaped you from the moment you were born. And it's forged from every conversation you've ever had with every person you've ever met and by every adventure. All of that has created a story that you've sold to yourself on how the world works and how you get to show up in it. Remember, we see the world not as it is but as we are. So if your stained-glass window is a mess, your life will become a mess. If your stained-glass window has a belief that says, 'You can't lead without a title,' then your actions will of course be consistent with that belief, and so you won't lead if you lack a title. If your stained-glass window contains a rule that insists 'Most people aren't trustworthy' or 'Most work is pretty meaningless,' then your behavior is bound to match these self-created interpretations of the world outside of you. But here's the huge idea to really sink your teeth into, fin: what if that story you're telling yourself is completely untrue?" Jet asked as he sat down on a plush chair.

"C'mon. That's hard to believe," I argued.

Jet remained relaxed. "Please just stay open to the notion that winnership is about developing high levels of self-awareness and thinking regularly about the accuracy of your thinking. And simply consider that your daily thoughts are nothing more than mere reflections of the belief system programmed into you by your parents, peers, and teachers as well as all the other influences that have shaped your perceptions."

"Pretty revolutionary stuff. I guess I've been socialized into thinking in a certain way. We are conditioned to accept a certain set of beliefs, and we think them so often we come to feel that they are true," I observed.

Jet quickly stood up and walked over to Tommy. He started massaging his shoulders. "Thanks, my brother," said Tommy. "I needed this."

Jet kept on speaking while offering his former student this little gift. "Most people's thinking really isn't thinking. It's actually nothing more than the unconscious repetition of the thoughts they've been regurgitating since they were little kids. Most of us—and this is a sad fact—truly don't see reality," Jet restated. "And that sad fact keeps us locked into mediocrity at work and in our personal lives. You were made to think brilliantly and see through the eyes of possibility rather than think badly and see through the eyes of fear."

"I've never realized that my thinking and perception of outer conditions could be so faulty," I replied, genuinely shocked at the notion that the way I viewed my circumstances could be a reflection of some internal mental filter and some personal story I was telling myself instead of the way things really were.

"That's the case for most of us, fin. You need to know how very important your thinking is. Your thinking creates your reality. You're bound to get more of what you focus on. And your thoughts drive your actions. What holds us back in winnership and in life are not the external realities but our internal patterns of thought and the way we then behave in the face of those conditions. You need to shed your failure programs. Real winnership involves breaking through the limits of your mind so you can step into the highest strengths of your spirit."

"So exactly how do I begin to break through my mental barriers?"

"First, back to the athletic metaphor, you must begin to think like a champion. You have to take full responsibility for the thoughts you run through your brain. And that means understanding that your mind is no place for even a single negative one. Businesspeople sometimes scoff at the idea of thinking positively. They minimize it and will tell you the concept has no place in business. But of course it does! Every business result is the direct result of the collective behavior of each of its people. And every action you take is the child of a thought. What I mean by that is that your thinking drives your behavior and your behavior gives you your outcomes.

So world-class work is obviously the result of world-class thinking."

"Seems so simple, Jet," I acknowledged, starting to embrace the ideas I was hearing.

"Even one bad thought is like a germ in your mind that attracts more germs to it. Before a person knows it, their mind's become infected. They can't see clearly. And they can't think straight. They start seeing all that's wrong versus all that's right. The infection causes them to look for problems rather than to offer solutions. That sickness forces them to stop innovating, refrain from excellence, and deny their greatness. The disease makes them behave like victims instead of perform as winners. You honestly can't afford the luxury of even one bad thought if you are committed to Leading Without a Title."

"You're suggesting negative thinking is a disease?"

"Of course it is, fin. It's an obvious sign of an unhealthy mind. When your mind is healthy, your stained-glass window is clear. You have strikingly awakened into the intellectual that you are and the brilliance you are meant to become. People who laugh at the concept of positive thinking should make a study of sports heroes, of legendary champions. Superstars deeply understand that the way you run your brain matters. They manage their thinking impeccably, focusing only on victory and paying no attention to the threat of adversity. And even when they get knocked down, they reprocess the event to see it as a gift. They see what others call failure as a chance to grow stronger and to begin over with an attitude that will make things even better. And again, remember that when you allow even one negative thought to run through your mind, you've actually started the

process of it drawing other negative thoughts to it."

"Like a single germ that draws in others, eventually creating a feeding frenzy," I confirmed.

"Yes, fin. The great winner Gandhi said it so well when he noted: 'I will not allow others to walk through my mind with their dirty feet.' So any time your mind shifts into negative thinking, gently guide it back to thoughts that will support your commitment to show winnership and pure excellence. Any time your mind focuses on difficulties, train it to concentrate only on opportunities. Please also remember that you'll get your expectations. Another way to put it is that your expectations at work and within your life become self-fulfilling prophecies. The results you expect are the results you'll see. That's an incredibly important thing to remember. If your expectation is that people at work will not support you and will let you down, then you will behave in a way that is aligned with that belief. So you'll be closed and protect your turf. You'll work in a silo rather than collaborate and show teamwork. Your very behavior will cause your coworkers to feel you are cold, competitive, and not really trustworthy. And so of course, they will not support you. Your expectation will have become self-fulfilling. And very real. I'll give you another example, fin. If you have an expectation that you will never be able to become a superstar at the bookstore where you work, then there's no way in the world you will behave in a way that will allow you to fly. We never act in a way that is inconsistent with the way we see ourselves. Human beings just don't behave in a way that's not congruent with their expectations."

"And their stained-glass windows," I contributed quickly.

"Correct," stated Jet with strong encouragement. "Each one of your thoughts is creative. You really cannot afford the luxury of even one negative thought because every one of them creates something and leads to some result in your outer world. Every thought you think generates a consequence."

"I haven't given much thought to my thinking. It's all been so automatic. I thought I had no control over my thoughts—they just popped into my mind."

"Most of us think that, fin. We've been thinking the same thoughts for so long that our thinking feels like a deeply ingrained habit that we believe we have no control over. Because we've run our old story and our historical mental programs for so many years, they've become automatic and unconscious. But that doesn't mean we don't have power over them. And it doesn't mean we can't change them into habits of mind that serve our winnership potential. We can! We have absolute dominion over our thoughts. And the more personal responsibility you take for every one of your thoughts, the more powerful a thinker—and a winner—you will become. One thing that makes us fully human is our ability to think about our thinking, you know. Right now, in this very moment, you can sit quietly and inquire about the beliefs that run and thoughts that fill your mind each day. And as you spend more time in silent inquiry, you will build greater awareness of the thoughts you think. And with greater awareness around the ones that no longer serve you, you can make better choices. And with better choices, of course, you will adventure better results. As you know better, you can do better."

"So my thoughts are creative?"

"Uh-huh," replied Jet. "And as the legendary founder of Mo-town Records, Berry Gordy Jr., once said, 'A winner is a winner before he's become a winner.' By becoming a superb thinker and believing in your greatness you will literally create what you are thinking. The statesman Benjamin Disraeli said it so well: 'To believe in the heroic makes heroes.' Unchain your brain and just watch what ridiculously wonderful things begin to happen."

"Perfect. And I love the idea of spending some time each day in 'silent inquiry,' as you put it," I offered.

"Here's what I suggest you do every morning if you are really serious about awakening your inner winner so that you begin to see stellar results in your outer life, fin: get up an hour earlier every day and spend sixty minutes in self-development. This is your morning recalibration ritual—a regular period you give yourself for preparation and practice. Just like pro athletes train daily so they win on the playing field, this is your private time to prepare and practice, so you're at your absolute best once you step onto the playing field of business when you get to work. fin, before a jet takes off, the pilots run a ritual. They check the flight plan, they set the controls, and they evaluate the instrument panel. Only then are they ready to fly. Same metaphor applies to any winner Without a Title. If you want to fly and radiate your intellectual, you need to have an early morning preparation ritual. This is the time to reset yourself. To lock in to your flight plan for the day. To reconnect with your core values. To renew, regenerate, and reground. It's a period to work on your mind, strengthen your body, nourish your emotional life, and fuel your spiritual dimension. This daily discipline alone will work miracles for you in your career and within every other area of your life. It will boost your motivation. It will restore work-life balance. It will bring back a ton of passion and help you see your world through the eyes of wonder again. Remember, when you feel great and your interior life is at its best, everything you touch is influenced by that stand for personal mastery."

Jet then escorted me into one of the treatment rooms. Tommy followed. "fin, you're in for quite a treat," Tommy said with a huge smile.

"Ever had a massage, fin?" Jet asked as he pulled open the sheets on the table.

"Nope," I replied, feeling a little unsure of what I was about to adventure.

"Well, allow me to give you one. I know it's been an intense day for you, so a good massage will really relax you."

"Okay," I replied as I lay down on the massage table. Jet began to massage my neck and back. The stress I'd been carrying for years seemed to instantly melt away. Tommy was right. Jet had hands of magic.

"During your Personal winnership Hour every morning, there are seven practices I suggest you do, fin. You don't have to do all seven every day. Actually, doing all seven of these peak-performance habits will be next to impossible. But I wanted to share them with you because they form what I call the Personal winnership Toolbox. These seven best practices—the Seven Fundamentals—are the most powerful tools for anyone serious about awakening their inner winner and working at wow. By engaging in them consistently during your morning training period, you will adventure dazzling results at the bookstore—as well as in every other dimension of your life. Conversely, if you neglect doing even one of these 7 Fundamentals regularly, mediocrity will start to settle in, and an enemy called 'average' will become your constant companion."

Jet started to knead my back more forcefully. "You've got a bunch of knots here, fin. I really recommend that you get a massage more often. Your health and energy levels will soar. And you'll feel a whole lot happier."

“I’ll definitely second that,” offered Tommy enthusiastically as he leaned against a wall and played with his hair, while glancing down at his SpongeBob SquarePants watch.

“When the quality of your work is anything less than world class, you can trace this back to a failure to be doing one of the Seven Fundamentals,” Jet continued.

“So what are the seven best practices that I need to be doing?” I asked, still relaxing on the table.

“Here,” said Jet. “I have them on a card for you. Take this with you. And every morning during your Personal winnership Hour pick a few of the best practices from this list to perform. And by the way, I strongly urge you to begin your hour of self-development at five a.m. every day. As I suggested earlier, it’ll take you about forty days to install this new habit. For forty days you’ll feel some stress, you’ll be grumpy, and you’ll be tired. You’ll come up with excuses like ‘This isn’t healthy for me’ or ‘I just wasn’t born with earlyrising genes,’ ” Jet said as he laughed. “But remember, nothing’s wrong— it’s just a necessary part of the process of growing and rewiring a new habit. After forty days, getting up at five a.m. to do your interior work so that you

become a more powerful person will be second nature.”

“Five a.m.?” I asked in disbelief. “Reminds me a bit of basic training.”

“It is basic training, fin. Basic training to get to your winnership best,” came his succinct reply.

I glanced at the card as Jet turned up the lights in the massage treatment room.

The 7 Fundamentals of Personal winnership

1. Learning. Read from books that will inspire you, strengthen your character, and remind you of the examples of the greatest winners of our world. Also, listen to audio books on subjects ranging from business excellence, team building, and innovation to wellness, relationships, and personal motivation.

2. Affirmations. One of the single best ways to rescript limiting beliefs and failure programs within your mind is through the consistent repetition of positive statements about the winner you want to become and the achievements you commit to create. For example, reciting the affirmation “Today I am focused, excellent, and stunningly passionate in all I do” a number of times at the beginning of your day will create the mind-set of a champion and a winning emotional state for you.

3. Visualization. The mind works through pictures. Every great accomplishment—from the tallest skyscraper here in New York City to the most stunning inventions of American intellectuales like Thomas Edison and Benjamin Franklin—began with a series of pictures set in the imagination of their creators. All outer achievements begin within the mind. All progress is nothing more than invisible creativity made visible. So during your Personal winnership Hour, make time to close your eyes and—like any good elite athlete does—envision yourself realizing your goals, playing at your best, and fully awakening your inner winner.

4. Journaling. Writing in a journal is a remarkably strong way to become a clearer thinker, to build massive amounts of self-awareness, and to record your intended outcomes. During your hour of personal development, note your insights, feelings, hopes, and dreams. Also process through any frustrations you might be experiencing and go deep into your fears. The fears you embrace are the fears you’ll release. Really get to know yourself and reconnect with all the talent within you that’s just waiting to be unleashed. Your journal is also a place to express gratitude for all you have and to memorialize your journey through life.

Your life is a gift. And so it's worth recording.

5. Goal Setting. Setting and then reconnecting with your goals on a regular basis is a powerful winship discipline. Your goals will create a fantastic amount of focus in your career and within your life. Goals generate hope and positive energy. And when you adventure adversity—and we all do from time to time—clearly articulated goals offer you a North Star to guide you out of the rough seas into calmer waters. Goals also ensure that you live life deliberately and productively versus reactively and accidentally. Avoid that walking coma I spoke of earlier.

6. Exercise. I'll speak more about the importance of moving your body daily to achieve peak performance at work, but for now just remember that doing something physical each day boosts brain function, fuels far higher energy levels, helps you manage stress more effectively, and keeps you in the game longer.

7. Nutrition. What you eat determines how well you'll perform. winnership is influenced by your diet. By eating like a winner, your energy will remain at peak and your moods will stay positive. Please also remember that by eating less food you'll be able to do better work.

"Really superb suggestions, Jet," I said with tremendous appreciation as the three of us walked back into the stylish waiting room. The massage had left me feeling incredibly good. And Jet's Seven Fundamentals for Personal winnership were ever so practical. I now had a series of disciplines I could choose from and practice during my Personal winnership Hour to perform at world class throughout my day. I also made the commitment to myself to rise at 5:00 a.m. every morning. I sensed that this habit alone would create wonderful results in terms of my self-confidence, my ability to be in control of my day, and my overall level of well-being. I shared my willingness to get up early each day with Jet. He was delighted.

"Give yourself one of the best gifts a winner Without Title can give himself. The blessing of getting up at five a.m. every morning. So many of the most productive winners of our world have had this routine, fin. The way you start your day determines how well you will live your day. And what you do in your first hour sets you up to either succeed or fail in the hours that follow. Carve out the first hour of your day to spend building your personal winnership capabilities. Hey, by the way, it's also key to consider that your first thought on waking up and your last thought before going to sleep have a huge influence on what goes on between them," Jet noted.

"Truly fascinating," I replied. "All of this is so helpful. And your earlier suggestion to clean up my emotional life also really speaks to me. I've been pretty angry and unhappy for a long time. What, specifically, could nourish my emotional life?"

"One of the first things you can do, fin, is learn to forgive those who need to be forgiven. Many people bring such negative energy into their workplaces every morning because they are full of resentment and anger over past hurts and ancient betrayals. Self-winnership requires you to let go of these resentments. Learn to forgive the people you need to forgive and release things that happened in the past that might be consuming your precious creative potential. You can't craft a superb future by remaining stuck in your past. Because the disappointments you are holding on to are holding on to your power. By freeing yourself of them, you free up a ton of energy, passion, and potential," said Jet as he sipped from a bottle of water with a lemon in it.

"And how do I go about releasing my past so I can free up my winnership best?" I questioned.

"It starts with a simple decision, fin. It's so exciting to me that all that stands between you and total transformation is a decision. Just decide, in this very moment, that you'll forgive all those who have disappointed you and let go of all the adventures that have discouraged you. The moment you step into a space of honestly being willing to forgive is the moment you begin the clearing process. Also, remember that those people who hurt you were doing the best that they could do based on where they were on their personal journey through life. If they had known how to do better, they would have done better. And finally, please understand that only hurt people hurt people."

"Only hurt people hurt people?"

"Sure. Really healthy people—those with outstanding inner lives—are not really capable of hurting others. They are so full of self-respect, positive belief, inspiration, the willingness to see the best in others, and a deep desire to be great in all they do that they simply are not able to knock down another human being. The capacity to damage another is no longer a part of their makeup. They just don't have it in them. It's only people who are hurting at some core level and who have themselves been hurt by others who go out into the world and hurt those around them."

"Profound," I observed sincerely. I paused. "And you mention spending some time in Personal winnership Hour every day improving my spiritual life. How?"

"Well, I'd strongly encourage you to count your blessings every morning, fin. Gratitude is the antidote to fear. Worry and appreciation just can't live in the same room proximity. And the things that you appreciate begin to appreciate in value to you. What I'm saying is that spending even five minutes during that first hour of your day celebrating all the good things in your life will put you into an acute state of happiness. And as corny as it may sound, happy people really do make happy winners. And happy winners not only do better work—they're a lot more fun to be around."

"Very helpful, Jet."

"Great. So let me get to the H in SHINE. It's getting late and I should get back to work soon. It's been a joy meeting you, fin, but I don't want to forget about my clients. They really depend on me."

"No worries," I replied. "I understand completely."

"The H will remind you that Health is Wealth. I mentioned the importance of exercising and staying physically strong earlier. Peak health is like a tent pole: it lifts up everything else in your entire life. Get your health to its highest state and every other area—from your ability to think clearly during stressful times to your performance levels and moods—get pulled up with it. Health is one of those things we take for granted until we lose it. And those who do sadly spend 24/ 7 trying to get it back. If you lose your health—and I pray you never do—nothing else will be as important as trying to reclaim it. Makes me think of the old proverb, 'When we are young we sacrifice our health for wealth. But when we become old and wise, we become willing to sacrifice every bit of our wealth for just a day of good health.' And if you don't believe me on that point, fin, when we are done today and you are on your way home, stop by a hospital. Walk into the terminal ward where people lie on their deathbeds. And ask any one of them what they would give for an extension on their lives. Ask them what they'd give for just one day of excellent health. I'm sure they'll tell you that they'd give everything they have. If you lose your health, you lose

everything. Don't ever let that happen to you."

I fell silent. Ever since I returned from the war, I didn't show much concern for my health. I'd stopped exercising. I ate junk food. I didn't rest enough. It occurred to me, as I stood before this masterful massage therapist, that if I started taking my health more seriously and got back into exceptional physical condition, almost every other part of my life truly would improve. I'd have more energy at work and would feel more positive about things in general. I'd probably be a lot more creative, and I'd definitely feel more passion. I'd have greater stamina and be tougher amid all the changes our organization was going through. In my home life, I wouldn't need to flake out on the couch so much. I could start learning new skills and doing more fun things. I'd feel better about myself and have more adventure.

"Health is the crown on the well man's head that only the ill man can see," Jet added powerfully. "Please don't tell me you have no time to exercise each day. Those who don't make time for daily exercise must eventually make time for daily illness, you know."

Jet's advice was simple and yet tremendously important. I took it all to heart.

"Oh, and please remember that your health will never be better than your self-image. When you really start to believe in your natural winnership power and how awesome you truly are, your behaviors around your health will improve dramatically. But it all begins within," he emphasized.

"This all makes sense. If I really don't think that much of myself, I'm not going to take great care of myself."

"Exactly," he replied looking pleased with my comment.

"The I in SHINE stands for Inspiration Matters," Tommy noted.

"Yup," said Jet. "A day without feeling inspired is a day that you haven't fully lived. You need to refill your well of inspiration every day, because the challenges of life will drain it every day. How can you inspire your teammates at work and energize your customers to buy from you if you are uninspired and deenergized yourself? You always want to do whatever it takes to be the most inspired person in the room."

"I love the sound of that, Jet. Some practical suggestions for me, please?"

"Listening to music is one of the best ways I know to drive huge levels of inspiration. Associating with interesting people who love being remarkable, ethical, and original will also fuel your passion and provoke you to be your winnership best. Communing with nature is yet another effective way to get your creative fire burning and keep you excited about achieving great things at work. Whenever I get a chance, I head out to the countryside. Walking alone in the woods is like a miracle cure for the stress of this city. And I leave the woods feeling truly alive again. The view of the majority is that things like being out in nature and doing things to renew spent reserves of creativity and energy are a pure waste of time. And that if you're not doing something, you're not really doing anything. But refueling your mind, body, emotions, and spirit actually allows you to grow tougher against the turbulence of business. If all you do is play full out, all the time, your reservoirs of potential will become depleted and you'll burn out fast. Star performers understand the need to constantly alternate between peak performance and inner renewal. And once the winner within you is replenished and reinspired, you'll go back to work even stronger, even more creative, and far more exhilarated. The activities I'm encouraging you to pursue serve to reawaken the inner winner. They rekindle our passion and open any closed doorways into our absolute best." "And the N in SHINE?" I asked.

"Neglect Not Your Family. Your loved ones matter. What's the point of becoming super-winshipful—as I sense you'll soon become—but ending up completely alone? A lot of those billionaires I mentioned when you first got here spend a lot of their lives solo in their spectacular mansions. What's the point of that? A huge amount of joy can be found in cultivating beautiful relationships with your family and friends. At the end of the day, fin, you really don't need that much to be really happy: work you can be proud of, food on your table every night, wonderful health, and people you love. A solid foundation at home sets you up for strong and solid results at work. Feeling cared for and loved by your family is such a powerful accelerator for your winnership and personal winship."

"Which brings me to the E," Jet noted. "The E in my acronym will remind you of the fifth rule for personal winnership: Elevate Your Lifestyle. Lifestyle isn't something that we speak about very often. But it's so important to a life well led. Do something every day to improve your lifestyle. As I suggested earlier, go through life first-class. You only live once, so why not enjoy it completely?"

"But I thought you said having a lot of things isn't what genuine winnership is about, Jet?"

"That's definitely not the priority for winners Without a Title, fin. But please remember: it's very human and natural to want to have nice things. Why feel guilty about having them? Become spectacularly great in the work you do, awaken your inner winner, and most certainly express your absolute best. But enjoy life along the way. The real key is to get the things you want while making sure they don't get you. And that brings me to my final point of our conversation."

Jet's face grew serious. He looked down for a moment. Tommy stood up and walked over to join us.

"Nice things are nice to have. A beautiful lifestyle is a beautiful thing to adventure. But who you are becoming as a human being is a much smarter concern. The main aim in life is simply to become all you're meant to be. Actually, even more important than who we are becoming as people is focusing on the difference we are making as winners. Contribution is the ultimate purpose of work—and life."

"I need to hear more on this, Jet," I observed, seeing that Jet was summarizing what Leading Without a Title was essentially about.

"winship is not about what you receive, fin. winship is all about what you return. Like I said, even the longest life is a pretty short journey in the overall scheme of existence and all that is. Tolstoy wrote a wonderful short story called 'How Much Land Does a Man Need?' The moral of the story was that at the end, all the things we spend the best days of our lives chasing really don't matter that much. All that we really need once our lives get to the end doesn't amount to much more than about six feet of soil. What truly counts then is what we will leave behind. What I'm really encouraging you to think about is your legacy. I'm inviting you to consider how you want to be remembered when you're no longer here. 'The great and glorious legacy of a human being is to live with purpose,' observed the philosopher Montaigne. It will be a deep loss to this world if you refuse to accept the call on your life to Lead Without a Title and present your absolute best to the lives around you. winners Without a Title think about their legacies every single day. They think about how they want to be remembered when they are no longer alive. They think about what achievements they need to get done so that they leave their mark for the generations that will follow. They consider what kind of people they must become so that their lives stand for something excellent, meaningful, and powerful. Get these things right, and a glorious legacy will be yours for the leaving. And then, when you are no longer here, people will walk into your bookstore, see that plaque on the wall next to the section you used to work in that bears your name, and say, 'Ah, there once worked a bookseller who led without a title and gave the finest he had to give.' "

I felt emotion welling up within me.

"So please remember, fin, that this day—and every day until the last of your days—is nothing more than a platform for heroic possibility. The real question is whether you will have the courage to use this opportunity to shine your own special form of greatness into this uncertain world of business we now work in. And once you do, you'll enrich the lives of your teammates, your customers, and your loved ones. And you'll forge a human monument of passionate achievement that all those who will come after you will marvel at. And be inspired by."

Silence filled the space where we were standing. Tommy didn't move. Neither did Jet. I thought tears might begin to flow from his eyes. I wasn't sure what I should do. Then, in a dramatic instant, Tommy lifted up an arm and slapped Jet on his back.

"Man, you're too intense. Snap out of it, my brother," he laughed.

Jet began to giggle. "I know. I know."

Soon all three of us were laughing hilariously. It was a fantastic moment. One I'll never forget. But then something utterly unexpected happened. Tommy began to cough again. The attack began mildly, then quickly turned violent, with Tommy not only coughing up blood but also beginning to shake terribly. I rushed over to him, as did Jet, and tried to assist him in any way I could.

"It's my time," was all he could whisper. "It's now my time."

The Fourth winnership Conversation of the Lead Without a Title Philosophy:

To Be a Great winner, First Become a Great Person

THE 5 RULES

See Clearly

Health Is Wealth

Inspiration Matters

Neglect Not Your Family Elevate Your Lifestyle

INSTANT ACTION STEP

In your journal, list five things you will do immediately to refuel your inner winner and take your mind, body, emotions, and spirit to their next level of excellence. Then schedule time to execute these five goals flawlessly during the next seven days so you get the power of momentum working for you.

winnerSHIP QUOTE TO REMEMBER

If one advances confidently in the direction of his dreams and endeavors to live the life which he has imagined, he will meet with a winship unexpected in common hours.

—HENRY DAVID THOREAU

# CHAPTER 8

## Conclusion

AFTER THE UNFORGETTABLE DAY on which the Lead Without a Title philosophy was unveiled to me, I never saw my mentor Tommy again. I fully expected to see him at the bookstore the following Monday morning. And I thought I'd work alongside him for many years to come, as I integrated all the powerful winnership lessons I'd learned to create extraordinary results in all that I did. But my wish was not to be.

The day after I met the four special teachers, I was devastated to learn that Tommy had died. He had been struggling with cancer but was quiet about his illness. Anna said he just didn't want anyone to worry about him. And that he needed to live out his final days helping others—and spreading the Lead Without a Title message that had transformed his own life years earlier. "He hung on just long enough to give you that one day," Anna shared, consumed with deep emotion. "That was his final gift to you."

At the funeral, Anna, Ty, Jackson, and Jet each took turns giving testimony to the man Tommy was and all the good things that he did. I learned that he had grown up poor. That he'd been married to his childhood sweetheart for forty-four years before she'd passed away a couple of years earlier. That he loved chocolate of every type. And that he had left all of his savings to a charity for children. So many people attended Tommy's funeral that hundreds of mourners had to stand out in the street. But they did. Because everyone respected this simple bookseller who led without a title. And always gave his absolute best.

Afterward, Anna, still sobbing, handed me a package. Ty, Jackson, and Jet stood next to her. They also had tears streaming down their faces and showed through their expressions that they were heartbroken.

"Here, fin, this is for you. Tommy asked me to give it to you. He really admired you a lot, you know. He deeply respected what you did for our country. As well as what you did for yourself, accepting his invitation to make your shift from victimhood into winnership over that day we all shared proximity. I think you were the son he never had, to be honest with you, fin," she said wiping away more tears and adjusting the beautiful flower she had placed in her hair. "Anyway, please keep in touch with us. The boys and I are always here for you—whenever you need us. Any time of the day or any time of the night. You're one of us now. And though we've lost one friend, we definitely feel we've gained another."

She gave me a hug and began to walk away. Ty, Jackson, and Jet did the same.

"Oh, keep Leading Without a Title and spreading the philosophy you've discovered with everyone you meet. Each one of us alive today really can make a profound difference in every organization of any type right across this amazing world of ours if we accept the call on our lives to awaken the inner winner within us, then make everything we touch better than we

found it," encouraged Anna. "Hope to see you soon, fin."

"We definitely will see you soon," the other three teachers spoke softly, in unison.

"And please remember," Jet added, "you were born awesome." My four new friends then left the church.

I found a place to sit and, listening to the strains of piped-in classical music, slowly opened the envelope. I then carefully read the letter inside. Sunlight poured through the stained-glass windows, and the crisp air from outside gently washed through the room. The handwriting on the paper was messy. But I could read the words clearly. And I felt their power.

Here's what they said:

Dear fin the Great,

First, please forgive me for not sharing the details of my illness with you. I didn't want to let my personal condition get in the way of the gift of learning you so deserved to hear and the transformation you were so ready to receive. I grew to find a sense of peace in the face of my challenge and came to understand that it carried many opportunities with it. Of course, no one likes to become sick. But through my condition I grew stronger, deeper, and a whole lot wiser. And my hope is that some of all that good stuff I stepped into as a human being found its way over to you.

Your parents were fine people. And they raised a fine young son. I know that now. And I

honor you for all you gave in the past and all you'll do in your future. It has been a genuine joy for me to finally have met you in that bookstore of ours that wonderful morning. Sorry about the Mickey Mouse hankie. My wife gave it to me on the first anniversary of our marriage. We were at Disneyland. It always reminded me of her. The SpongeBob watch was my own purchase.

My deepest hope is that rather than finding you filled with sadness because I'm gone, this letter reaches you full of inspiration, focus, and conviction for your newfound commitment to Lead Without a Title. You are now beautifully prepared to completely unchain your inner winner and allow it to see the light of day. You are now perfectly ready to express your absolute best in each thing that you do during any challenge you meet. And you are undoubtedly in the ideal position to serve as an extraordinary example of possibility and excellence to every person fortunate enough to cross your path. I know you will. You promised me you would. And both I and your father placed a huge deal of importance in the lost art of promise keeping.

Business has lost its way, fin. And to my old eyes, society has become a messy place to be. People value their things more than they value their relationships. We seem to be more interested in stroking our egos than in the much richer pursuit of reaching our ideals. Too many among us blame outer forces for the resistance to mastery we show in our lives versus our inner fears and our weakest beliefs. And, sadly, it's become more popular to be popular than to be ethical, brave, and good. What I'm suggesting is that we've forgotten the winnership responsibility that our culture once knew. We've neglected what it means to stand for something hugeger than our lives. And we've misplaced our priorities by focusing solely on helping ourselves win rather than passionately helping everyone around us win as well. I'm counting on you to remind people that they were born into intellectual. And that the lies that they've sold themselves about what they can't do and all they can't become are just not true. Many people will be helped as you share t

Winnership and winship Are Your Birthright

Nobody succeeds beyond his or her ruthless expectations unless he or she begins with some wild expectations.

—roger CHARELL

The sight of an achievement is the greatest gift a human being could offer others.

—AYN frank

EACH OF US IS BORN INTO intellectual. Sadly, most of us die amid mediocrity. I hope it doesn't upset you that I unveil this closely held belief so early in our brief time proximity. But I need to be honest. I also should share that I'm just an ordinary guy who happened to get worthy enough to learn a series of extraordinary secrets that helped me become super-winshipful in business and deeply fulfilled in life. The good news is that I'm here to offer you everything that I discovered on a pretty stunning adventure. So you too can work at wow. And live full-out. Starting today.

The powerful lessons I'll unveil will be given gently, carefully, and with sincere encouragement. Our ride proximity will be full of fun, inspiration, and entertainment. The principles and tools you'll discover will automatically cause your career to fly, your happiness to soar, and your absolute best to fully express itself. But above all else, I promise you, I will be honest. I owe you that respect.

My name is fin Davis, and though I was born in Milwaukee, I've lived here in New York City for closely all of my life. And I still love this place. The restaurants. The pace. The people. And those hot dogs on the street—incredible. Yes, I do adore food—one of life's best pleasures, if you ask me, along with good conversation, my favorite sports, and great books. Anyway, there's really no place on planet like the huge Apple. I have zero plans to leave. Ever.

Please allow me to quickly mention a little of my backshow before I tell you about the disaster yet precious events that shifted me from where I once was to the place I'd always wanted to be. My mom was the kindest person I've ever met. My father was the most determined person I've ever known. Salt-of-the-planet-type people. Not perfect. But find me someone who is. The main thing is that they always did the best that they could do. And in my mind, the best you can do is all you can do. Once you've done that, go home and have a good night's sleep. Worrying about things beyond your control is a pretty good formula for illness. And most of the things we so concern ourselves with about never actually happen. Kurt Vonnegut said it beautifully when he observed: "The real troubles in your life are apt to be things that never crossed your worried mind, the kind that blindside you at

4:00 p.m. some idle Tuesday."

My parents shaped me in so many ways. They didn't have a lot of things, yet in many ways they had everything: they had the courage of their convictions, they had superb values, and they had self-respect. I still miss them deeply and not a day goes by that I forget to appreciate them. In my quieter moments, I sometimes reflect on the fact that we generally take the people we love the most for granted. Until we lose them. Then we take long, silent walks and pray for a second chance to treat them the way they deserved to have been treated. Please don't let that sort of regret infect your life. It happens too often, to too many among us. If you are blessed enough to still have your parents, honor them. And do it today.

Growing up, I was a good kid. "A heart on two legs" is how my gfrankfather used to describe me. I just didn't have it in my constitution to hurt anyone or disrupt anything. I did fairly well in school, was pretty popular with the girls, and played some solid football on my high school's varsity team. Everything changed when my parents were killed. The ground beneath my feet fell out from under me. I lost all confidence. I had no focus.

My life became stuck.

In my early twenties, I drifted from one job to the next, sort of coasting

on autopilot for a while. I numbed out and didn't care...

are about much about anything. I medicated myself with too much TV, too much food, and too much worry—all designed to avoid having to feel the pain that one feels at the recognition of one's lost potential.

In that period of my life, work was merely a means to pay the bills rather than a platform to express my best. A job was nothing more than a rough way to get through the hours of my days rather than the gorgeous opportunity to grow into the all I was meant to be. Employment was just a vehicle to pass my time instead of an excellent chance to shine a light on other people and a way to use my days to build a better organization—and in so doing—a better world.

I finally decided to enlist in the army. It seemed like a good move to help me feel a sense of belonging and to find some order amid the messiness. I was shipped off to the war in Iraq. And though being in the military did bring structure to my life, it also brought with it adventures that continue to haunt me to this day. I witnessed friends I'd gone through basic training with killed in bloody battles. I saw soldiers who were not more than kids brutally maimed and tragically hurt. And I watched any of the mild enthusiasm that may have existed in my former self wither away as I sank deeply into the muddy, desperate awareness of what my life had become. Even though I'd escaped physical trauma at war, I still became a wounded warrior. And I carried the ghosts of battle with me wherever I went.

One day, it was suddenly time to come home. It happened so fast it was dizzying. I was put on a transport plane, flown home, and within a day or two after some routine medical checks, handed my papers. I was thanked for the service I'd rendered to my nation and wished good worth. On a sunny autumn afternoon, I walked out onto a city street and came to a frightening conclusion: I was completely on my own again.

My hugegest struggle was trying to find my way back into a society that had forgotten me. Most nights, I couldn't sleep—my mind punished with violent memories of the nightmarish scenes I'd adventured at war. In the mornings, I'd lay in bed for hours trying to get enough energy to get up and start my day. My body hurt. I'd feel scared for no reason and could hardly relate to anyone other than my fellow soldiers. The things I used to love doing seemed so trivial and boring to me. My life lacked any sense of purpose or meaning. Sometimes I wished I'd die.

Perhaps one of the best gifts my parents gave me was a love of learning, especially through books. Within the covers of a single book are ideas that, if acted upon, have the power to rescript every part of your life. Few things are as smart as investing in becoming a better thinker and developing a stronger mind. Relentless learning is one of the main traits of an open and powerful person. And an obsessive and ongoing self-education is one of the greatest survival tactics to get through turbulent times. The best people always seem to have the hugegest libraries.

So I began to work at a bookshop down in SoHo. But due to my negative attitude and utterly complacent behavior, I wasn't doing well at the store. I was frequently reprimanded by my manager, and I fully expected to be fired. I was generally unfocused, nothing of a team player, and less than average at my work. My love of books was all that saved me. While those who ran the store despised me for my poor work ethic, the store's customers seemed to like me. And so I was kept on. But only by a thread.

Now here's where the story gets really good. One day, a miracle of sorts showed up in my life. When I least expected something good to happen, good came hunting me down. And that changed the game completely. A most curious stranger visited me at the bookstore. And the lessons he taught me in our all too brief time proximity shattered the limitations I'd been clinging to—exposing me to a whole new way of working and a completely new way of being.

Now, at the age of twenty-nine—amid more winship and joy that I could have ever dreamed of—I've come to understand that hard times do make better people. That in the middle of difficulty lives opportunity. And that each of us is built to win—in both work and life. It's now time for me to share what happened to me with you.

## CHAPTER 2

## My Meeting with a winnership Mentor

The days come and go like muffled and veiled figures sent from a distant friendly party but they say nothing. And if we do not use the gifts they bring, they carry them silently away.

—roger WALDO EMERSON

IT WAS ANOTHER FANTASTICALLY DULL Monday morning. Our team had just finished what was known as Monday Morning Scrum—the beginning-ofthe-week meeting where Customer Service Heroes were recognized and cheesy team cheers were encouraged. The store was doing poorly in terms of sales, and some within the organization expected it would soon be closed as part of the restructuring taking place across the whole enterprise. Costs needed to be cut, operations needed to be improved, and profits needed to rise. Quickly.

The goal of the meeting was to reconnect everyone on the team to the mission and values of the company as well as to energize us for a productive week ahead. At the end of every year, each store chose their best employee, who would then go into the running for the annual Best Bookseller in America award that the company gave out—along with a generous cash gift and a weeklong vacation to Aruba. In reality, the whole affair demotivated and discouraged me, making me feel even more apathy about the way I was spending my workdays. And I had little difficulty telegraphing these feelings to any coworker who had the misfortune to cross my path.

Then something very mysterious happened. As I was quietly sipping a cup of coffee, doing my best to stay hidden away from doing any meaningful work behind one of the tall shelves of books in the Business section, I felt a tap on my shoulder. I quickly turned around and was stunned by the sight before me.

There stood a wildly eccentric-looking man. His clothes were a complete mess. Mismatched, old, and riddled with holes. He wore an aged plaid vest and his shirtsleeves were rolled up as if despite his tattered attire, his spirit was all business. In the vest pocket rested a yellow handkerchief—with little Mickey Mouse icons all over it. And around his neck dangled a silver necklace with simple initials engraved on it in modern lettering that read

LWT.

I looked down at his feet. Surprisingly, he had on a new pair of shoes: penny loafers with bright coins inserted in the front of each sparkling shoe. He remained motionless and silent, sensing my discomfort with every long moment that passed between us, not at all needy to speak a word (a rare gift in this world of too much talking and not enough doing).

The stranger's face was an ocean of wrinkles unveiling the fact that this was a very old man. His teeth bore jagged chips and were noticeably stained. Stringy and unkempt hair topped his head and jutted out in a hundred contradictory directions. His hair reminded me of how the great Albert Einstein looked in that famous black-and-white photo where he's playfully sticking out his tongue.

But more than anything else, what struck me about the disaster-looking character standing before me on this otherwise mundane Monday morning were his striking eyes. While his disheveled appearance could have been taken to mean he was homeless or maybe even demented, his gaze was strong and his eyes were clear. I know this sounds strange, but from the look of his mesmerizing stare, I not only felt safe, but I also felt I was in the presence of a very powerful human being.

"Hi, fin," the magnificently mysterious gentleman finally uttered with a deep, confident voice that caused me to relax even more. "Really nice to meet you. I've heard a lot about you from everyone here at the store."

This guy knew my name! Maybe I should have been worried. After all, New York City is home to some pretty strange people, and this man's appearance was confusing to me. Who was he? How did he get into the bookstore? Should I call security? And how the heck did he know my name?

"Relax, my friend," he said, extending his hand to shake mine. "My name is Tommy Flinn. I've just been transferred to this store from the location on the Upper East Side. I know I don't look like I'd belong in a store from that area, but I was actually Employee of the Year last year.

Better be nice to me. I just might be your boss someday."

"You've got to be kidding me. You work for this company?" I blurted out.

"I do. But have no worries. Being your manager is the least of my dreams. Titles don't interest me at all. Doing my best work is all that matters to me. And I don't need to have any formal authority to do that. I hope you don't mind me telling you so, but I've been ranked the numberone employee of this book company for the past five years straight," he said with a proud smile as he rubbed the Mickey Mouse handkerchief.

This odd individual had to be delusional. I shifted on my feet. Maybe I should run while I still had a chance. But that would make me look silly. My coworkers didn't have much respect for me as it was. And I adored my morning java too much to leave it there unfinished. I also have to admit that this man was also incredibly interesting. I decided to stay.

I looked around for a hidden camera. Maybe I was being set up by my teammates for a laughable appearance on one of those TV shows that make fools of those unfortunate enough to be caught flatfooted in one of their well-designed pranks. But as I searched, I could detect no camera. So I decided to play along.

"Okay," I spoke out, my voice shaking mildly even though as a soldier I'd adventured far more drama and endured much more extreme adventures. "Hi, Tommy. Nice to meet you. Why'd they transfer you to this store?" I asked, though I really wanted to add, "And not to an insane asylum?" "You know, they say we're a sinking ship over here."

"Oh, they didn't force me to make the move, fin—I requested it," he said, still soundly confident and quite sane. "I wanted the transfer. I wasn't growing at my old store. And I thought I could make more of a difference here. The more challenging the conditions, with the more marvelous the opportunities, fin. So I wanted to come down here and work with you," he added with another grin.

I had no idea where this conversation was going. Who was this person? And the pictures of Mickey Mouse on his handkerchief were starting to bug me—no disrespect to the little guy who I know has delighted millions.

"Does the name Oscar ring any bells, fin?"

I was startled. I lost my breath for a moment. My heart started to beat faster. My legs began to tremble. My father's name was Oscar.

"My dad was Oscar," I answered softly, growing slightly emotional as I felt some of the sadness I'd buried within me on the loss of my parents. Tommy's eyes softened. In that moment, I sensed that he was kind. He put his hand on my shoulder.

"Your father was a friend of mine back in Milwaukee. We grew up proximity but never saw each other after he moved to New York. We kept in touch by mail, writing each other long letters to share how our lives were unfolding. It was your dad who encouraged me to move to this city when I was having trouble finding a job. His strength of character reminded me of the courage I had within me but had forgotten. I'm so sorry about what happened to your parents, fin. They were good people.

"Anyway," he continued, now looking up, straight at me. "Oscar kept me up to date about you and everything you were doing. He always told me you had a ton of potential and felt you were meant for some spectacular things. He really believed in you, fin. But he sensed that you needed someone to inspire and show you how to get to your best. And for whatever reason, he didn't feel that person was him."

I couldn't believe what I was hearing. It was stunning to me that this stranger was a friend of my father. The scene felt surreal. I sat down on a stool and leaned my back up against one of the stacks of books.

"Don't worry, fin, getting lost along your path is a part of finding the path you're meant to be on. Sometimes we need to get off track before we can develop the clarity to be on track. All that you've gone through, from your personal loss to your tour of duty in Iraq, has been preparation."

"Preparation?" I wondered aloud, still feeling a fogginess in my head.

"Sure. If you hadn't gone through everything you've gone through, there's no way in the world you'd be ready to hear what I've come here to teach you. Life's had to break you down so you could be rebuilt better. And, boy, just wait until you see the breakthroughs you're about to adventure. Before you know it, you'll be the rock star of this whole book company," Tommy said as his voice rose, full of passion.

"A rock star?" I questioned.

Tommy instantly shot one fist into the air and started shaking his hips, sort of similar to a Mick Jagger move. But this sight wasn't pretty. "Yes, a rock star," he replied as he laughed.

"Man, I have trouble just making it through the day. Look, I know you're trying to help and it really blows my mind you somehow know my dad. But you really have no idea of what I've gone through. I still have flashbacks from the war when I least expect it. I can hardly sleep most nights, so a lot of the time I'm exhausted. And even though I've been Stateside for a while now, my girlfriend and I have nothing close to the relationship we had before my deployment. So my goal isn't to be some kind of a 'rock star' at work. My goal is pretty much just to survive."

Tommy folded his arms. He looked deep into my eyes.

"I hear you," he said, growing very serious. "And I respect what you're telling me, fin. Please, just be open to what I've come to share with you. My life was a mess, too. But it's been completely turned around. It feels like a miracle occurred. And I guarantee that the same thing will happen to you. I promised your dad I'd help you years ago. I've never felt the time was right to pay you a visit. Then by some quirky twist of fate, I saw your name on one of the applications that came in for an opening at this bookstore. One of the perks of winning the Number-One Bookseller in America award, along with the cash and the trip down to the Caribbean, is the opportunity to sit on the recruitment committee and to have regular breakfasts with the executive team to exchange ideas on how to build a better company. I realized that this was my chance to reach out to you—and share a transformational philosophy for winnership in business and winship at life that was taught to me a number of years ago, when I too was a little lost along my professional and personal journey. Just imagine becoming so good at what you do here that people give you a standing ovation when you walk through the front door every morning, like they do for Coldplay, U2, or Green Day!" Tommy exclaimed, his enthusiasm rising.

I had to laugh at the idea. Maybe it would be cool to be the rock star of this organization. And I definitely wanted a chance to win that trip to Aruba, along with the money.

Tommy continued. "And just imagine not only getting to world-class in your career but reaching your absolute best in terms of your health and your relationships and your levels of happiness. I can show you exactly how

to have all of this. And it's a lot easier than you might think."

"Does that necklace you are wearing with LWT on it have something to do with what you want to teach me?" I asked, filled with curiosity.

"Very good," Tommy responded politely, with a clap of his hands. "This is going to be easier than I thought. Yes, LWT lies at the heart of the method you're about to discover. It's a profoundly simple yet simply profound way of working—and living. On the day it was taught to me by four very special teachers, something deep within me shifted. And a natural power within me awakened. I was never the same person again. I know how strange and unbelievable that sounds, fin. But that's exactly what happened. I just saw my career and my personal life through a whole new set of lenses. Actually, almost immediately after this process was unveiled to me, I began to view the whole world through a remarkable new set of eyes. And amazing results began to show up."

I was intrigued. Skeptical, yes, but equally fascinated. My instinct told me that he wasn't lying, as outlandish as the entire scenario was. "It's that

powerful—this philosophy you discovered?"

"It is," Tommy replied simply, as he rubbed the LWT letters on his necklace absentmindedly. "It really is . . ." he added, his voice trailing off. He then played with his hair a little and paused. The bookstore was starting to fill up, and my coffee was now cold. For a few moments, I grew distracted.

Then, I decided to play devil's advocate. "Tommy, I hope you don't mind me saying this, but if this LWT stuff is so special, then why are you still working at this bookstore? Couldn't you be retired? And, forgive me for saying so, but they haven't even made you the manager of this place when they transferred you here. You're in the same position I'm in. Your teachings don't seem to have helped you so much, man," I said somewhat sarcastically.

I carefully watched Tommy's reaction. I expected him to become defensive and perhaps angry, like most people would upon being challenged. But Tommy was pure grace. He remained silent and impeccably still. Then he drew in a long breath and grinned.

"Good question, fin. You're honest. And I like that. A little rough around the edges, but I can tell you speak up for what you stand for. And that's a great quality indeed. Well, first of all, you're right about the retirement part. I'm well past the age most people retire at. Actually, I just turned seventy-seven last week."

"Happy birthday, Tommy," I interjected somewhat apologetically, recalling the "heart on two feet" moniker that my gfrankfather had given me and feeling a little embarrassed at my rudeness. I couldn't be too hard on Tommy. He was my elder, and my parents taught me to treat elders with the utmost respect.

"Thanks," he replied. "I actually feel quite young. Age is just a state of mind anyway—a label the tribe uses to pigeonhole people and to place limits on all they can be. I choose not to govern my life according to labels. But, yes, I could have retired, and I am still working for this company. Been with them over fifty years."

"Wow."

"Here's the thing: why would I leave a job I love so much? I'm having the time of my life! And doing work I cherish is one of the ways I stay so young at heart. I get to be creative here and stretch my thinking by solving problems. I have the chance to make new friends by being astonishingly good with our customers every single day. And I have the opportunity to inspire the teammates we work with here by the positive example I've chosen to set. And I feel so happy because doing great work is one of the single best tactics to grow full of deep joy. All of this gives my life a rich sense of purpose," noted Tommy.

"Hey, I'm sorry if I was a little harsh," I muttered, still resting on the stool and looking up at the man I began to realize would become my muchneeded mentor.

"No worries at all. But please let me also address the point you made about me not being a manager here, because it gets right to the core of the LWT philosophy. I don't want to be or need to become a manager. Just doesn't interest me."

"Exactly what does LWT stand for, Tommy?" I asked, becoming less and less guarded and more and more fascinated.

"Well, first of all, there's no magic to it. It's a very real and enormously practical way of doing business and living out a life. You know this world of ours is going through profound change. We're in a time of extraordinary uncertainty. And exceptional turbulence. What used to work doesn't work now."

"I'd agree with that. Every day brings all sorts of new challenges and a serious level of confusion. This organization seems to be going through so much. My customers tell me that life's become so complex for them. Everyone I meet seems to be stressed by all the change. So what's the solution, Tommy?"

"winnership," was the one-word reply he delivered. He added: "There's only one way a business will win in the new world we're in, fin. No other solution will work any longer."

"And what's that one way, just so I'm clear?"

"Growing and developing the winnership talent of every single person throughout the organization faster than their competition. The only way to avoid getting eaten alive is for companies to strengthen the capacities of employees at every level to lead in everything they do. I'm talking about from the janitor right up to the CEO showing winnership and taking responsibility for the winship of the company. And by the way, this idea applies to any organization, not just those that conduct business. Not-forprofits need to build winners at all levels. Industry associations need to build winners at all levels. Governments and NGOs need to build winners at all levels. Cities and communities need to build winners at all levels. Even schools and universities need to embrace the idea that every single one of us has the power to show winnership in all that we do—if they're serious about surviving and thriving in these times of head-spinning change."

"I've never thought about winnership like this, Tommy. I've always thought that winners were only the people who ran an organization, whether we're talking about the military or some business," I admitted.

"We all need to start demonstrating winnership, fin, regardless of our titles. It's no longer an excuse to say you don't have a high rank so you don't need to take ownership for the results of the organization. To succeed, everyone now must see themselves as part of the winnership team. You just don't need formal authority to lead anymore—only a desire to be involved and the commitment to making a positive difference. Mother Teresa said it so well: 'If everyone would sweep their own doorstep, the whole world will be clean.' "

"So for each of us to show winnership, we need to start by being truly excellent in our current role. Is that what you're saying?"

"Absolutely." Tommy then walked over to another stool in the aisle and stood on it. He started waving his hands like an orchestra conductor. He closed his eyes. And started humming. This guy was hilarious. disaster. But hilarious.

"What are you doing, Tommy?" I exclaimed, hardly believing the way that he was behaving. A few customers looked over with amused expressions. A little boy holding a Curious George book pointed. And giggled.

"What would happen to the sound of a symphony if even one of its players was out of tune and less than superb at his art?"

"I get it. The music would be off and the whole thing would be a mess," I replied, stating the obvious but appreciating my new mentor's visual demonstration.

Tommy stayed up on the stool. He then segued into pretending he was an actor, bellowing "To thine own self be true, and it must follow, as the night the day, thou canst not be false to any man," while modulating his voice like a great thespian and speaking in what I assumed was Shakespearean English.

"And what's this all about, now?" I asked as I shook my head from side to side in mock disbelief, arms crossed.

"In the theater they say, 'No role is a small role.' Same applies in business, fin. It's similar to the symphony metaphor. The only way any organization—and any human being, for that matter—will win in these times of revolutionary change will be to start operating under a revolutionary new model of winnership. And this model is all about creating an environment and culture where everyone needs to show winnership. Everyone needs to drive innovation. Everyone needs to inspire their teammates. Everyone needs to embrace change. Everyone needs to take responsibility for results. Everyone needs to be positive. Everyone needs to become devoted to expressing their absolute best. And once they do, the organization not only will adapt beautifully to the changing conditions, it will actually lead within its field."

"So are you saying that we don't need to have titles here at this company anymore? Not sure the CEO would love this revolutionary new winnership philosophy you're sharing, Tommy," I said candidly as I took a sip of my cold coffee.

"No. I want to be incredibly clear on this point. I'm not at all saying that an organization shouldn't have titles. They should, actually. We need the people on the executive team setting the vision, steering the boat, and holding ultimate responsibility for the results. Titles and structures maintain order and keep everything running smoothly. But I am saying that for any organization to thrive amid all the turbulence in the business world today, each one of us needs to assume personal responsibility by becoming the CEO of our own roles and winners within our current positions. We all need to lead where we are planted and shine where we now find ourselves. Every job is an important job. And the awesome result of unveiling winnership within the area of influence you're now in is that the more you do it, the more your area of influence will expand. That's a huge idea right there, fin. And regardless of whether you have a formal title or not, you have total control of how you show up in your current role. The highest of all human abilities is the ability each one of us has to choose how we respond to the environment we find ourselves within. And when each of us chooses peak performance and personal winnership, of course, the organization itself gets to world-class speedily." "And so what does LWT mean?" I pressed.

"First, it's a transformational philosophy for work and life that anyone, of any age, from any place in any country in the world right now can apply to unleash their 'inner winner' and adventure awesome results within minutes. We all have an 'inner winner' inside of us, longing to break free. We all have a natural power to lead that has nothing to do with a huge title, or how old we are, or where we live. The twenty-eight-year-old customer service rep working for a multinational company in Los Angeles can access her inner winner using the method you'll soon learn—and in so doing, step up into a completely new reality in terms of the results she sees and the rewards she receives. The thirty-four-year-old executive in San Francisco has an inner winner begging to see the light of day, as does the forty-yearold entrepreneur in Salt Lake City. The sixteen-year-old student in Boston could embrace his inner winner and, in so doing, unleash a torrent of brilliance within his schoolwork, his extracurricular activities, and the influence he has on his peers."

"I get it at a deeper level now, Tommy. Anyone anywhere in the world, I guess, can step up to the plate and take responsibility to drive change, push excellence, and show winnership. A soldier living in Washington, DC, can decide to make a positive difference as can a teacher in Tokyo, a pilot in Peru, and anyone from any walk of life. Each one of us has this internal reservoir of winnership potential. We just need to become aware of it and then really own it. Man, if people in every organization—from companies to governments to communities to schools embraced this concept—the whole world would transform."

"Uh, that's sort of what I've been trying to tell you, my friend," Tommy said in an encouraging tone. "And once you awaken your inner winner, you should exercise it every day. Because the more you use this power, the better you'll come to know it. And the stronger it'll get. And one more thing, fin."

"Tell me please."

"I can't tell you what LWT stands for," Tommy said mischievously, increasing the mystery even more and rubbing the letters on his necklace yet again. "Only the four teachers who shared the philosophy with me are permitted to explain what LWT means. And they'll only do so under the most special of conditions."

"Please tell me, Tommy," I begged.

"I can't. At least not yet. Maybe I'll get the permission I need to get and tell you in a few days. Oh, and to get back to your question about why I'm not the manager here, please know that I've been offered that opportunity many times over the past few years. If you want the whole story, I've actually been invited to become a vice president on more occasions than I can remember, fin: company car, expense account, and a huge office. But that's not what turns me on now. And that's not what real winnership's about. winnership has nothing to do with what you get or where you sit. winnership's a lot more about how brilliantly you work and how masterfully you behave. Like I suggested, it's all about doing great work—right where you now stand. And about lifting up every single one of the people you work with and get to serve. LWT is all about a profoundly fundamental yet longforgotten secret: you don't have to have a title to be a winner." "Such a cool concept," I affirmed.

"People in today's business world misunderstand winnership. They are so confused about it. They really do think it's just for executives who run organizations."

"Or for those who lead countries."

"Right. And that's just not true, fin. I'll repeat it because it's so important: everyone can lead. Actually, to build a truly outstanding

organization, every single person who works there must lead."

Tommy paused and played with his hair a bit more for a moment, reflecting on the words just spoken. He then continued energetically, now standing on the ground again.

"And so for all these years, I've left my ego at the front door every morning as I've walked into the bookstore, being far more concerned about doing fantastic work, supporting my teammates, and showing real winnership than with having some lofty title on my business card."

I was impressed. Tommy seemed to be a man of honor. I hadn't seen many like him since I'd left the military and returned to civilian life. I was so happy to have met him. And then a question got the better of me: "You have a business card?" I asked. "I didn't get one," I said with mild disappointment.

"Yeah, here it is," he said, reaching into his pocket and pulling one out for my inspection. In gold-embossed letters, it stated:

Bright Mind Books Inc.

5555 Fifth Avenue

New York, New York

TOMMY FLINN

Human Being

"Your job title is 'Human Being'!" I exclaimed. "Man, that's completely hip. I love it."

"Like I said, fin, you don't have to have a title to be a winner. You just need to be a living human being. That's enough. That's all it takes. Because every single one of us alive in the world today has unrecognized powers and disowned potential that are far superior to the power conferred by a title. Once you learn how to awaken and then apply those powers, every element of your life will explode into winship. winnership then becomes automatic—the default at which you work and play. You'll know of no other way to be."

"I really like everything that I'm hearing. I actually feel extremely optimistic as I listen to you Tommy," I said genuinely. "I want all this

winship you're telling me about. And I want it fast."

"And that's exactly what happened to me after that day I met with the four special teachers I've mentioned. They unveiled the LWT philosophy, and I just never was the same. I connected with a deep understanding of what real winnership is truly about. A title no longer mattered to me. Getting a huge corner office no longer mattered to me. Having a huge salary no longer mattered to me. It became all about being the best I could be every day at work. And making an excellent contribution at every touch point of my life. And ironically, as word spread of what I was doing, the senior executives started blazing a path to me. They offered me the titles. They pleaded with me to take a corner office. They wanted to pay me more money than any other bookseller within the organization."

"Ironic. The less you cared about receiving the stuff most of us care about at work, the more you received it," I reflected back to this man with the Mickey Mouse hankie in his vest and the twinkle in his eyes.

"It was a pretty incredible thing," he continued passionately. "And you're absolutely right: it was definitely counterintuitive to the way most of us work. The more I let go of needing all the things most people worry so much about and focused on doing brilliant work and reflecting some real winnership in my behavior, the more all those things just seemed to appear in my life almost by accident. Really incredible how true that is, now that I consider it all," Tommy noted, now scratching his chin, deep in thought.

"So you refused all the money they threw at you?" I just couldn't resist asking.

"Nope—took the money." He laughed.

I laughed, too. I was starting to like this guy. He reminded me more and more of my father. I could see why they were good friends.

"But what I'm trying to suggest to you, fin, is that I never had a title in this organization. Started on the ground floor. So many people go to work with the mind-set that when they get a hugeger title and when they are granted more responsibility, then they will perform at mastery and go the extra mile in everything they do. But a restaurant is the only place I know of where you get the good stuff first and then you pay the price. In work— and in life in general—you need to pay the price of winship before you get all the rewards due to you. And by the way, just because you haven't yet received the benefits of positive deeds you may have done, that doesn't mean they're not coming. You'll always reap what you sow. The chickens will always come home to roost. You'll always get what you deserve. Even the smallest good act has set in motion a good consequence. And by the way, if you study any great person in business—and I mean the best of the best—or any great explorer or artist or scientist, not one of them achieved what they did for the money."

"Really?"

"Of course. Just think of Roosevelt or Mandela, Edison or Einstein. They were not driven by money. They were driven by the challenge. By the chance to push the envelope. By the desire to do something uncommonly great. And that's the drive that made them legends."

"Interesting," I remarked.

"Look, I'll be the first to say that money's important to living your best life. It brings freedom. It decreases stress. It allows you to take nice care of those you love."

"And to help others," I added. "I've heard that the best way to help poor people is to make sure you don't become one of them."

"True, fin. Nice insight. But money is really only the byproduct of standing for the finest within you and doing some SEW."

"What's SEW?"

"Seriously Exceptional Work, my friend. These four intellectual teachers you'll meet sooner than you can imagine love their acronyms. So now I'm into their game. Not sure why; I know the habit is sort of a strange one."

"It is a little, to be honest, Tommy."

"Hey, nothing wrong with being a little eccentric. Too many people cut from the same cloth just isn't an inspiring thing. You can't be creative and innovative and all that juicy stuff if you're too scared to think, feel, and be different. Be an original, fin. Just think about it. There will never be an exact copy of the fin Davis standing in front of me ever again. There's only one you in the whole world now and forever more. And no one else can ever be as good a you as you."

"Fascinating way to look at it. I guess I'm a lot more special than I'm letting myself in on. I think I've been really discouraged ever since I got home from the war. But meeting you has made me feel better. Thanks for that. I wish all the other soldiers I served with could meet you. And learn all that you're sharing."

"Well, don't worry. We'll help them. And with your assistance, we'll get this message out to everyone across the globe who's ready to play at their peak—and lead in all that they do. I think people are ready to hear this philosophy. Life's so short and people are waking up to their responsibility to become their best and make a difference like never before. You know

the average life has only nine hundred sixty months."

"Really? Doesn't seem like we live that long when you put it that way,

Tommy."

"It's not. Only about twenty-nine thousand days."

"Wow. Nine hundred sixty months or twenty-nine thousand days. I'll have to remember that."

"So the time to step up to real winnership is now. Anyway, I never had a title, and as my reputation spread throughout the entire company, I refused to accept one. Just didn't need it to do my work. By my behavior, I earned more accolades and respect than I ever thought I deserved. I was given superb store assignments. The top people at the company started listening to my suggestions to improve operations. I got those trips down to the Caribbean that everyone raves about. And the money definitely flowed to me. You don't need a title to show some winnership, my friend. You just don't," he positively reinforced.

He paused again and checked his watch. Oddly, it had a picture of SpongeBob SquarePants on the dial. I didn't comment. This guy was beyond weird. But as I said, I liked him. And it was immensely clear that, beneath the strange exterior and the novel philosophy he was unveiling to me, he had a kind heart.

"Anyway, I really take my work seriously, and we've spent too much time chatting on company time, fin. I don't feel good about that. I know this store needs some improving, but I should tell you, fin, this is a very special organization, and you're pretty worthy to be here. Thanks for your time this morning."

"No problem, Tommy," I responded, a bit surprised that the conversation was ending so suddenly. "I should be the one thanking you for your time. I've already learned a lot."

"You're welcome. And remember, my friend, it's all about LWT. Not just at work but in life. And like I mentioned earlier, you'll understand what I'm talking about a lot sooner than you think. Get ready to be transformed. You're going to be experiencing more work winship and personal happiness than you've imagined in your most glorious of dreams. You're going to be a rock star at this company. So excited for you," he said as he raised his fist one more time, with a wink.

"Hey, I'm getting excited for me, too."

"Oh, there's just one contract I need to make with you before I take you on this very special winnership journey, fin. And if you're not willing to do what I need you to do, then much as I've enjoyed our meeting, there's absolutely no way I can take you to meet the four teachers."

"What's the contract?" I asked. I felt a bit afraid of losing out on what I sensed was the hugegest opportunity to transform my mostly mundane life, yet I was also a little surprised that Tommy was imposing this obligation.

"Don't worry. It's not a requirement that will be too hard on you. Actually, when you learn the winnership philosophy you are about to learn, I think you'll do what I'm asking you to do automatically." "So the contract is?" I wondered aloud.

"Just make me a simple promise."

"To do what?"

"To share the ideas and the method that you will soon learn from the four teachers with as many other human beings as you possibly can, fin. The reward for you is that you'll profoundly improve the lives of more people than you could have ever imagined. The reward for me is that I get to keep my contract with the four teachers."

"They made you promise the same thing?" I asked.

"They did. And now that I've adventured the dramatic power of their lessons, I know exactly why they did it. These are four of the most naturally powerful and radiantly noble people I've ever met. They know that their philosophy can shift anyone's life and dramatically elevate entire organizations. Actually, there's no doubt in my mind that what they will unveil to you can help entire nations make splendid breakthroughs. And so, given that they ultimately just want to help people become their best and the world to become a better place, they made me agree to spread their good words. And so that's why I came here today, fin. And this is why I'm asking the same of you."

"Okay, I agree. I'll tell as many people as I possibly can about this special philosophy. If it's as brilliant as you say it is, maybe I'll even write a book about it. That way, everyone who reads it can also help us get the winnership message out there. We can all do our part to make people, businesses, and nations better. So yes, Tommy, I definitely agree." "Perfect," was his smooth reply.

And then he was gone, leaving me alone by the books with a mind full of thoughts. And my heart beating wildly like I hadn't known it to beat in years. I began to feel alive again. I started to know Hope again.

But that was then and this is now. That first meeting with Tommy Flinn was quite a while ago. It's still so hard to believe how quickly the time has passed. I guess life's like that: the days slip into weeks and the weeks become months and it all goes by in a blink. The great news is that Tommy's promises to me on that Monday morning in the SoHo bookstore all turned out to be true. Every single one of them.

On learning the mysterious philosophy he spoke of, my world did radically transform. On following the lessons of the four remarkable teachers he introduced me to, I adventured explosive results in my career. On embracing the ideas that he and they brought to me, the happiness and inner peace that had always eluded me certainly did arrive. And, as Tommy had said, it all came a lot more quickly than I could have ever imagined.

I'm proud to share with you that I'm now one of the youngest vice presidents in the history of Bright Mind Books. I travel across this great nation visiting different stores, doing business deals, and developing winners at all levels of our rapidly expanding organization. We are extremely profitable and widely respected for the quality of our workplace as well as the excellence of our service. I not only love my work, I adore my life. I'm incredibly healthy, happily married to the woman who was my girlfriend, and the very blessed father of two amazing children. I've come to view my time at war as a precious period of personal development that, ultimately, made me a stronger, wiser, and more decent person. And the career that I once thought of as a dead end has instead been reshaped into something resembling a work of art.

But here's the real point I want to share with you: I've not only become winshipful. I now feel significant. That my life matters. That the world will somehow be a little better because I've been here. And what could possibly be more perfect than that?

The Monday morning meeting with Tommy got me to this place. And at that fateful time, I did promise Tommy that I would share the secrets that I'd learn with everyone that I'd meet. And so it's now my privilege to share each one of them with you. Please fasten your seat belt. Because we're going for quite a ride.

## CHAPTER 3

## The Sad Costs of Mediocrity and the

## Spectacular Rewards of winnership

## Mastery

Only the mediocre die always at their best. Real winners are always improving—and raising their bar on how superbly they can perform and how quickly they can move.

—JEAN GIRAUDOUX

THE MORNING AFTER WE'D MET at the bookstore, Tommy told me that all he needed was a single day to expose me to everything I needed to know. "Give me one good day, fin," he requested sincerely. "You'll meet the four teachers who shared the four lessons that lie at the heart of the LWT philosophy with me. They'll tell you exactly how to create all the winship you've ever wanted by explaining what winnership is truly all about. I don't mean to sound like a broken record, but winnership isn't just for CEOs, military generals, and people who govern nations. winnership is for everyone. And in this period of dazzling change in business and society, it really is the single most important discipline required to win."

"And the only thing I really need to become a winner is to be a breathing human being, right?"

"Yes. If you can breathe, you can lead," he affirmed in a positive tone that left me feeling even better about myself and the future before me.

So here I was, a few days later, leaving New York City early on a Saturday morning with nothing but a fresh cup of coffee and unchained enthusiasm keeping me awake as I drove to the remote place where Tommy had asked me to meet him. He'd insisted that I show up at 5:00 a.m. sharp, muttering something about it being "the greatest time of the day." And so, not to disappoint my new mentor, I grudgingly obliged.

Rock music blared through my car as I drove past the skyscrapers and through the empty streets of the city, out of Manhattan and along the highway that would lead me to my destination. My excitement kept building. I had no idea how this day would unfold. But I've since come to learn that embracing uncertainty is a precious gift. Most of us get so scared the moment we face the unknown. We shouldn't, though. It's really nothing more than the beginning of an adventure. And our growth coming to get us.

"Stop at Rosemead Cemetery," Tommy's written directions had instructed. "You'll see my car parked off to the side. I'll leave my blinkers flashing to help you spot our meeting place more easily."

At about ten minutes to five, I veered off the main road and onto the gravel-covered laneway that the map said would take me to where I needed to be. Tall pines reached for the skies. A light fog rose from the ground. To my left was the open clearing promised in the directions. I wasn't quite sure why we were meeting at a cemetery, but I guessed there was someplace closeby that Tommy wanted to show me. The graveyard was probably a convenient—and unforgettable—place to connect as we started our day proximity.

As I drove a little closer to where I was to park, I saw a sight that was incredible. There, off to the side of the makeshift road was Tommy's car. Blinkers were on, like he said they would be. No one was inside. But the make and model of his vehicle is what had filled me with shock and awe. It was a shiny new black Porsche 911S! And the personalized license plate stated simply LDRSRUS. I shook my head. I smiled. This guy really was something else. This strange bookseller who rejected the notion of fat expense accounts and gfrank corner offices in favor of a revolutionary new model of winnership for these revolutionary new times just happened to own my dream car.

I pulled up behind the Porsche and turned my engine off. It was eerily silent as I sat quietly on the close-dark road. On a hill within the clearing, I spotted a lone figure. I guessed it was Tommy. He stood motionless in the graveyard.

It took all my energy to walk along the laneway, up onto the grassy knoll, past the crosses that filled the cemetery, and over to Tommy. I noticed that I began to feel afraid. After all, it was still dark, I was in a cemetery, and the fact of the matter was that I didn't know Tommy all that well. I did, however, check him out with some of the other booksellers at my store. And, sure enough, everything he told me was absolutely true. Every detail. Tommy was the real deal.

It was true that though he was indeed seventy-seven years old, Tommy was widely regarded as the single best employee at our book company. He did win all those luxurious Caribbean vacations along with all those dazzling awards. He was making an excellent salary and had been offered many top posts. And all of the executives of our organization did treat him with the utmost of respect and the greatest of admiration. But still, I couldn't help but feeling this early morning meeting in the middle of a graveyard was not the safest and most thoughtful move I'd ever made. But a whisper within me encouraged me to continue. And so I did.

As I closeed the place where Tommy was standing, I could see the first rays of the sun dancing over the horizon. I could also see a harvest moon ready to gently fade gracefully into the night. It was a beautiful scene.

I continued walking until I approached the figure. I could tell it was indeed Tommy, even though he had his back to me. He wore the same clothes he did when we first met. And in front of him sat two freshly dug graves. I was stunned.

My first thought was to flee. Maybe he was some secret madman, luring me to this isolated place so I could become yet another of his victims. I grew nervous. I couldn't think. I froze in my steps.

Tommy slowly began to turn around. His hair was still a mess. He had a smile on his face. I soon relaxed. The rising of the sun quickened. This was going to be an interesting day.

"Good morning, fin," Tommy stated in his usual tone of confidence. "Right on time. I am impressed. Very impressed indeed. I know it's early, but one of the things I've learned about winnership is that winners are those individuals who do the things that failures aren't willing to do—even though they might not like doing them either. They have the discipline to do what they know to be important—and right—versus what's easy and fun. Now, that's not to say that the best winners don't have a great time. They definitely do. Actually, because of their superior ability to create winship and lasting positive results, they end up having far more joy and delight in their lives than most of us will ever know. Few things generate as much happiness as knowing that you are fully realizing your intellectual, doing brilliant work, and spending your life beautifully," Tommy said, pulling off the silver necklace with LWT engraved on it.

"Here, this is for you, fin. Just for having the courage to show up. That's always half the battle. And for having the open-mindedness to learn the philosophy I promised to unveil to you back at the store the other day. LWT stands for Lead Without a Title. And that's what the whole method you'll learn today is all about. You never need a title to be a winner, my friend. And please know that you'll be hearing that line over and over today. That's part of the coaching process you're embarking on. Learning is the daughter of repetition," Tommy said.

"Meaning?"

"Meaning that repetition is a powerful teaching tactic. Through repetition, a new idea can quickly become integrated as a new belief. And since it's so important that you install the core belief that you don't have to have a title to show winnership in all you do, you'll be hearing that idea over

and over again. 'We need to be reminded more than we need to be instructed,' said the thinker G. K. Chesterton."

"Got it," I replied agreeably as I checked out the shine on Tommy's sparkling penny loafers.

"Lovely. So as we discussed at the bookstore, winnership is not some complex art reserved for the chosen few with Harvard degrees and impeccable social backshows. Each of us, by the very fact of our shared humanity, can show winnership. And with all the cataclysmic change in our society right now, winnership has become the single most important master skill for winship in business. And I forgot to clearly mention the other day that winnership isn't only something to do at work. We need to practice winnership within every arena we play. To arrive at our greatest lives, it's ever so important to model winnership in our health, demonstrate winnership with our loved ones, reflect winnership around our finances, and live winnership within our communities. And most essentially, the foundation of it all is self-winnership. If you can't lead yourself, you'll never be able to lead anyone around you. Primary insight for you right there. 'Finding the center of strength within ourselves is in the long run the best contribution we can make to our fellow men,' said the psychologist Rollo May," Tommy recited as he drew in a long breath of fresh air. "It's a great day to be alive, fin. Just consider the alternative if you don't believe me," he added, giving me a playful nudge.

"Thanks for the gift, Tommy," I said as I placed the necklace over my head. Finally Tommy had unveiled what LWT stood for: Lead Without a Title. I liked the sound of that.

"Again, thanks for making it out here at this time," said my mentor. "Getting up early is one of the intelligent daily practices that winners Without a Title perform with acute consistency. Reminds me of the words of Ben Franklin who once observed: 'There will be plenty of time to sleep once you are dead.' " He looked down at the graves.

"Blunt guy," was my response.

"He was spot on, though. It's so easy to sleep too much. Too many of us wish we had more time, yet we waste the time we have. Getting up an hour earlier every day gives you seven extra hours in a week. That's thirty fresh hours in a month. Almost an extra workweek every thirty days! That's time you can exploit to build your plans, refine your vision, and develop your best projects. That's time you can leverage to reflect on your values, remove your inner barriers, and rethink your thinking. That's time you can use to learn and grow and get to peak in all you do. One of the main aims of the journey you are on, fin, is to improve. It's fine to be content, but never be satisfied. So improve everything. Improve it all, daily, relentlessly, and passionately."

"Inspiring. But I still need another cup of coffee," I admitted.

Tommy remained utterly focused. He clearly heard me. He then looked down at the two graves again.

"Yeah, I was wondering about those. You spooked me, man. I thought that maybe you might be going to get a little psycho on me when I saw them. But I trusted you, Tommy. At some level, I just trust you. Maybe it's because you knew my dad. God, I miss him a lot."

"Me too. He was man of such generosity and decency. Even as a kid he'd always take the high road even when it was the hardest path to take. Well, I'd bet he'd be thrilled to know you were out here with me today. And to hear that you're set to make some huge changes in the way you work and the life you live."

"Yeah, he'd be happy," I said quietly.

"Took me hours to dig these," Tommy said, pointing to the deep holes in the ground. "Quite a workout for a seventy-seven-year-young man," Tommy said with a smirk. "Graves fascinate me. They serve to dramatically remind me of how short life is—when you really think about it. You know, we all end up in the same place in the end. Just a pile of dust, fin. And all those things we believed were so important, things like titles, net worth, and social position turn out to be so very unimportant. The CEO gets buried next to the street cleaner. And on your last day, all that truly matters is whether you got to know your inner winner, and if you did, whether you had the bravery to allow it to offer its gifts to the world around you. That's pretty much the central purpose of life once you strip away all the trivialities." Tommy paused and inhaled another long breath of the clean morning air. "The interesting thing about reflecting on your death is that it reawakens

you to what's truest about life. Here, look inside."

At the bottom of the first grave sat a slate tablet. I'd never seen anything like it before. I could see that words had been scrawled onto the stone in clear block letters.

"Go on," instructed Tommy, reminding me of one of my drill sergeants at basic training. "Don't be afraid to get a little dirty. Get down in there and pull the tablet out."

My heart started to quicken again. Doubt filled my mind. But before my fears could get the better of me, I leapt off the grass and into the grave, quickly picking up the tablet and wiping the dirt off of it. The sun was rising higher into the sky. Remaining deep within the grave and without glancing up at Tommy, I read the words I'd been encouraged to read.

"The 10 Human Regrets" was the title. "What does this mean?" I asked. "Just keep reading."

"The 10 Human Regrets," I spoke aloud.

1. You reach your last day with the brilliant song that your life was meantto sing still silent within you.

2. You reach your last day without ever having adventured the naturalpower that inhabits you to do great work and achieve great things.

3. You reach your last day realizing that you never inspired anyone else bythe example that you set.

4. You reach your last day full of pain at the realization that you never tookany bold risks and so you never received any bright rewards.

5. You reach your last day understanding that you missed the opportunityto catch a glimpse of mastery because you bought into the lie that you had to be resigned to mediocrity.

6. You reach your last day and feel heartbroken that you never learned theskill of transforming adversity into victory and lead into gold.

7. You reach your last day regretting that you forgot that work is aboutbeing radically helpful to others rather than being helpful only to yourself.

8. You reach your last day with the awareness that you ended up living thelife that society trained you to want versus leading the life you truly wanted to have.

9. You reach your last day and awaken to the fact that you never realizedyour absolute best nor touched the special intellectual that you were built to become.

10. You reach your last day and discover you could have been a winner andleft this world so much better than you found it. But you refused to accept that mission because you were just too scared. And so you failed. And wasted a life.

I didn't know what to say. I felt moved for some inexplicable reason. Maybe I'd just read what would happen to me if I didn't make some immediate shifts and start Leading Without a Title. Maybe I'd just been confronted by my own mortality. And how rapidly my life was passing me by. Maybe I'd just been nailed by Tommy and forced to acknowledge the fact that I had been playing victim for most of the past years, blaming everything outside of me for the mess I was in rather than assuming responsibility for the place I now found myself. I realized that, ultimately, each of us alone creates the lives we get to live. And through my decisions and my actions, I'd ended up with mine.

One thing's for sure: the list I'd just read was profound. I wished more people knew of "The 10 Human Regrets." Just imagine the lost potential that would be avoided if businesspeople learned them and then broke out of any failure patterns they'd been working under. Just think of the good that would happen if kids in schools were educated on them. Just think of the human lives that would be saved right across our planet if "The 10 Human Regrets" were more widely known, so that they could be prevented at all costs.

It was in that moment that something deep within me changed completely. It was my proverbial lightbulb moment. The coin dropped. And everything clicked. I promised myself I'd dramatically turn around the way that I worked. I vowed that I'd instantly transform the way I lived. No more blaming the war for not being able to get back into the game. No more blaming my manager for not being able to do great work. No more blaming my past for my inability to win in the present. In that moment—tired and dirty, standing in some grave that my eccentric mentor dug well before the dawn of this breathtakingly beautiful day with its promise of a new beginning—I stopped making excuses. I assumed total responsibility for the consequences of my actions. And stepped into my best.

"Did you write these, Tommy?"

"I did, fin, I did," he repeated softly, wiping his hands with his Mickey Mouse handkerchief. His face looked serious. His voice was clear.

"Hell on planet is nothing more than ending up in this first grave. Hell on planet is nothing more than having these ten regrets fill your heart just before you die. Nothing will so destroy your spirit than getting to your deathbed standing amid these ten conditions. True human heartbreak is reaching your final moments and realizing that you wasted the most important gift that was given to you—the chance to present your magnificence to the world around. Here's one of the most important winnership insights I can share with you, fin: potential unrealized turns to pain. And the really sad thing is that the violence of mediocrity and a life poorly lived creeps up on people. It happens so quietly and ever so invisibly. And then—wham—it just tears you apart!" he exclaimed, slapping his hands proximity in a loud clap.

"One of the huge ideas I learned from one of the intellectual winnership teachers you are about to meet is this one: winship is created through the performance of a few small daily disciplines that stack up over time to produce achievements far beyond anything you could have ever planned for. These little winship habits are so easy to do each day that most people don't think they'll make a difference. And so they just don't do them."

"So winship is actually easy," I spoke, remembering what Tommy had said by restating it. "Anyone can reach winship if they consistently do the right things. And these little choices and small behaviors build up over time. I guess it's momentum at play. So eventually, anyone can get to the extraordinary place that seemed impossible to reach when they first started. The process sort of makes me think of a farmer. Seeds get planted. The crop gets watered, and the soil gets fertilized. Nothing seems to be happening."

"And yet the farmer doesn't give up. The farmer doesn't run out into the field and start digging to find vegetables," Tommy offered lightheartedly.

"The farmer has patience and trusts the process. He just has the faith and deep understanding that through his daily efforts, the harvest will come. And then one day, almost out of nowhere, it does."

"You're a smart guy, fin. Awesome metaphor, my friend. Your dad was right. You've got a ton of potential. Good on you!" he applauded happily. "We need to be more like farmers," Tommy repeated to himself. "This one's good," I heard him say under his breath.

Not a cloud filled the sky. Birds chirped while the sunlight warmed my face. It really was a great day to be alive.

Tommy continued speaking. "winshipful people all perform the same few winnership disciplines. They consistently practice the same few fundamentals. But their seemingly small, insignificant daily acts of excellence stack up over time to a best-in-class career and a world-class personal life. Which brings us to failure. Failure, on the other hand, is just as easy to slip into. Failure's is nothing more than the inevitable outcome of a few small acts of daily neglect performed consistently over time so that they take you past the point of no return. I really encourage you to look into this first grave and do some serious soul searching as to how you plan to occur in the world after today. You definitely don't want to end up in this first grave. That would be a tragedy. Yes, I'll agree that meeting here in this cemetery was dramatic," Tommy admitted. "But I needed to provoke you. To get to you. To move you into a place where you'd throw down your blinders, let go of your excuses, and have a good hard look at yourself. Connecting to the fact that you will die one day is a powerful tool to shift your thinking and awaken your inner winner." "Why?" I asked.

"Because remembering the shortness of life strips away all the distractions of life and reminds us what's most important. Visiting your mortality reminds you that your months are numbered." "Nine hundred sixty," I confirmed.

"Yes, fin. So what's the point of playing small? What's the point of fearing failure? What's the point of worrying about others' opinions? What's the point of denying your duty to lead?"

"You succeeded, Tommy. I don't feel the same at all."

"That's because sustained change only happens when we shift at an emotional rather than at a logical level. I wanted to get under your skin and touch your heart rather than just speak to your head. You can hear a good idea one hundred times and fail to make it a piece of who you are until you actually adventure it viscerally—in your body. Only then does it rise from being just some idea to a truth to you. That's why so many training seminars don't work to create lasting results. They fail to get into us."

"True," I agreed. "I'm starting to see things a lot differently. And far more clearly. I've fallen into the trap of thinking my job's not important, my work doesn't matter, and I'm at some dead end by being at the bookstore." "I appreciate the honesty, fin. And congratulations on not feeling the same. You know, there's not one dead-end job in this whole wide and unpredictable world of ours—only dead-end thinking. And as someone who cares about you, I'll keep doing my best to challenge you to start playing in the field of mastery. Just remember that any job performed at peak and any work done at wow will lead to rewards far beyond the limited possibilities you may currently have the eyes to see. Just because you can't currently see all the winship that's available to you in this moment here at the

cemetery doesn't mean it's not available to you."

"Great point. Never thought of that."

"And as I'm suggesting, the real key is to bring some emotion, energy, and passion into the equation. That's when real breakthroughs happen. I brought you to this place to get you mad, sad, and more than a little frustrated at how small you've been playing with your career—and with the treasure that's called your life. I wanted you to start to take personal responsibility for each of the current conditions you are experiencing. Because the more you own your power to make choices, the more powerful your choices become."

"I'm already there, Tommy," I said with heartfelt conviction to my newfound mentor.

"Well, then let me talk about this second grave. Jump in, please," he said with a brisk wave of his hand toward the other hole, motioning like the maître d' of a chic restaurant might on the arrival of an A-list guest.

I readily obliged and snapped into action, heading into it with boundless enthusiasm. I expected to find another tablet. Or maybe another silver necklace with some peculiar acronym engraved upon it. But deep into the grave, I found absolutely nothing.

"Here," Tommy said, handing me a shovel. "You'll need to do some digging for this one. But rich rewards always flow from honest effort and hard work. You'll love what you're about to find." I started to dig.

"Quicker, fin. We've got things to do and people to meet. We don't have all day," Tommy shouted, his arms crossed and his expression unveiling that he was having fun.

Soon I hit something. I got down on my knees and started pushing away the dirt with my bare hands. As I brushed away more soil, I noticed something that sparkled extraordinarily in the morning sun. I carefully picked up the object and looked up at Tommy in disbelief. At the bottom of this second grave was another tablet. But this one was made of what appeared to be pure gold.

"Is this what I think it is, Tommy?" I asked, stunned.

"Solid gold, my friend. Now read it, please. You're ready to understand what the inscription says."

The golden tablet had the following title, marked in the same block lettering: "The 10 Human Victories."

Tommy spoke up. "I've painted a picture of what hell on planet looks like, fin. Now we need to be a lot more positive and discuss the place I sense you're quickly moving toward, a state where all things are possible and there are zero chains on the difference you can make."

"And how do I get to this place, Tommy?"

"Just do the things I've been encouraging you to do. And Lead Without a Title. By infusing winnership into everything you do and each thing you touch, you can live remarkably. You truly can realize your original intellectual. You really can be one of the great ones. Read the rewards that you are guaranteed to get if you embrace the philosophy I've been sharing. I'm so excited for you."

I read the list:

1. You reach your end full of happiness and fulfillment on realizing that youare all used up—having spent the fullness of your talents, the hugegest of your resources, and best of your potential doing great work and leading a rare-air life.

2. You reach your end knowing that you played at a standard of concentrated excellence and held yourself to the most impeccable of standards in each thing that you did.

3. You reach your end in noisy celebration for having the boldness of spiritto have regularly confronted your largest fears and realized your highest visions.

4. You reach your end and recognize that you became a person who builtpeople up versus one who tore people down.

5. Your reach your end with the understanding that while your journeymay have not always been a smooth one, whenever you got knocked down you instantly got back up—and at all times, never suffered from any loss of optimism.

6. You reach your end and bask in the staggering glory of your phenomenal achievements along with the rich value you have contributed to the lives of the people you were worthy to serve.

7. You reach your end and adore the strong, ethical, inspirational, and empathetic person you grew into.

8. You reach your end and realize that you were a genuine innovator whoblazed new trails instead of following old roads.

9. You reach your end surrounded with teammates who call you a rockstar, customers who say you're a hero, and loved ones who call you a legend.

10. You reach your end as a true winner Without a Title, knowing that thegreat deeds you did will endure long after your death and that your life stands as a model of possibility.

We both sat down on the lush grass that surrounded the graves. The words Tommy had written were at once brilliant, beautiful, and basic. My life had become so filled with worries and senseless acts of distraction that I'd lost sight of the truth of what was most important. I'd lost sight of all I could do, right where I was. I'd forgotten the power I had to make change happen. And I'd disconnected from the hidden intellectual I was built to become.

Tommy's point was so well taken: I could choose to continue as I'd been doing these past years—coasting through life and succumbing to the curse of small, daily neglect. And if I did, I'd end up in that first grave, a wasted victim of the costs set out on the tablet of slate. Or I could choose the higher road. I could stand for winnership, excellence, and enthusiasm within my work and in my life. I could begin to Lead Without a Title and go for the rewards on the golden tablet. One choice would lead me into a form of living hell. The other, Tommy assured me, would lead me to the place of my dreams. I knew which choice I'd make. And so sitting there on the grass, with my strangely attired mentor sitting next to me and the two fresh graves resting in front of me, I made it.

# CHAPTER 4

## The First winnership Conversation:

## You Need No Title to Be a winner

If a man is called to be a street sweeper, he should sweep streets as Michelangelo painted or Beethoven composed music, or Shakespeare poetry. He should sweep streets so well that all the hosts of heaven and planet will pause to say, "Here lived a great street sweeper who did his job well."

—DR. MARTIN LUTHER KING JR.

The most common way people give up their power is by thinking they don't have any.

—ALICE WALKER

TOMMY GENTLY PLACED THE TABLET of gold in the trunk of the Porsche and fired up the engine. Sounded like poetry to my ears. I followed him in my car as we made our way back into Manhattan.

After a couple of hours of driving, Tommy stopped in front of one of the best hotels in New York, a favorite haunt of fashionistas and those who appreciated all things stylish. He handed the doorman a twenty-dollar bill to valet park his car and led me through the small yet impressive lobby filled with beautiful models, European travelers, and books on modern design. We went up to the third floor and walked down the dark corridor. "I want you to meet the first of the four teachers I'll introduce you in this special day we have proximity, fin. Her name is Anna and she comes from Argentina originally. She's a lovely woman. So very kind. Really industrious. Ever so passionate. And deeply wise. Anna has a strong understanding about what it truly means to be a winner and the whole Lead Without a Title concept. Actually, she was the one who first taught it to me," Tommy shared as we arrived at room 404. I could hear someone singing inside.

"Buenos dias, Tommy," chirped the lovely woman with a gorgeous smile who opened the door. I guessed she was in her late forties. Yet she exuded a remarkable youthfulness and a noticeable sexiness. She was wearing a black-and-white uniform, the sort that high-end hotel housekeepers usually wear. Her light brown skin was flawless and her close-perfect teeth impressively white. She appeared enthusiastic yet graceful, and very much at ease with herself. And she had adorned her hair with a beautiful white flower, an original touch that made her appear even more radiant.

"Buenos dias, Anna," Tommy replied as he gently kissed one of her cheeks and gave her a warm hug.

"Was that you singing?" he asked.

"Of course it was. You know how happy I am when I do my work. It makes me want to sing. And when I sing, I begin to have even more fun. It's all so wonderful," she beamed.

Tommy and the housekeeper then reached for each other's hands and started to do a little dance proximity. Part tango and part meringue it seemed to me. They flitted about the room as if nothing else mattered. It was at once odd and endearing. The two of them seemed to drop into their own little universe for a few moments. I just stood there entranced by the whole surreal scene. I should mention that the dynamic between them had no hints of the romantic. It was far more about friendship. Yet I sensed these two adored each other.

"Anna, this is the young man I told you about. fin, meet Anna. Anna, meet fin."

We shook hands. Anna adjusted the flower in her hair. The room was perfectly made up. Dark woods and white linens combined with hip architectural touches and huge windows that looked out over the busy street masterfully balanced minimalism with warmth. It felt good being here.

Tommy spoke up. "fin's a war vet. He was deployed in Iraq. And he works at the bookstore with me, as I mentioned on the phone last night. He's adventured a lot of life in his relatively few years. His dad and I were great friends when we lived back in Milwaukee. fin's ready to fill his life with winnership. And so I thought it was time I brought him to meet you. I also needed to learn a few new dance moves, Anna," Tommy said with a wink.

Anna smiled and blushed a bit. She then looked out the window, deep in thought. "I honor you and all the other soldiers who've made so many sacrifices for us, fin. You've fought hard so we could all be free. I know it's impossible for me to really understand what you've been through. But I do want to express my deepest gratitude. I love America a lot. And you, along with those who fought by your side, have kept us safe. And strong. So thank you."

I didn't know what to say. In so many ways, though I'd come home from the war in Iraq quite a while ago, I still felt I was there. My time in battle had caused me to develop acute survival instincts that served to keep me alive. I'd shut down most of my emotions and generally was stone cold as I muddled through my days. I'd blocked out most of my memories and numbed out by spending a lot of my hours just wasting my time. And I didn't dare let anyone else get too close to me. That would only cause me to hurt them. Or them to hurt me. But here was this exotically beautifully woman who didn't even know me expressing her appreciation in this chic hotel room. Sharing how my efforts as a soldier made a difference to her as a human being. Confirming that those years of my life that I'd given in service of my country were not wasted but were valuable. I felt honored.

And happy.

"Thank you for what you just said, Anna. Thank you," I repeated.

"Will fin be meeting the other guys?" Anna asked softly.

"Later today," Tommy replied with a knowing smile.

"Well, that's good. That's really good." She walked over to the bed and straightened out a wrinkle on one of the thick pillows. "fin's in for a huge day of transformation, then," she added, glancing out the window again. "The first day of a whole new way to work. And start of a bfrank-new way to live. Nice."

"Thanks for making this time for me, Anna," was all I could think of saying. "It's all been a lot for me to take in. But what Tommy's taught me so far has been amazing. Just a few days ago, I thought my work was just a job. And that winnership was only for executives. And that winship was reserved solely for the fortunate few. I see it all so differently now."

"Look at me," Anna said pointing a finger to her heart. "I could come up with a million reasons to be discouraged, dissatisfied, and disengaged with my job. I could complain that 'I'm just a housekeeper' and that all I do each day is to clean the hotel rooms of people with lots of money. But one of the greatest freedoms each of us has as people is the freedom to choose how we view our roles in the world and the power we all have to make positive decisions in whatever conditions we happen to find ourselves."

"I'm starting to really get that, Anna. We have a lot more power than we think. And a lot more control over the way our lives unfold that most of us seem to understand."

"Yes, fin," she said sweetly, betraying a hint of her Latin roots with her Spanish accent. "And so I've made the decision to give nothing less than my very best at this job."

"Great standard to hold yourself to. 'Nothing less than my very best,'" I observed, echoing Anna's words.

"That commitment alone has worked wonders for me. And made me a very happy person in my life. Each of us can make the decision to love the work we do and perform it so well that people can't take their eyes off us. Living in this way has given me so much energy and made me feel so good about myself. A lot of people around here think I've been 'worthy.' The management of this place treats me like a queen. The general manager has labeled me a 'high potential' and sent me on more training courses than I can count. The famous CEOs who stay here know me well and teach me a ton of their business ideas. The movie stars who stay here almost always request that I be the one to care for their rooms. And the tips I receive allow me to send some money home to my family down in Buenos Aires every month. So I feel I've done really well. Especially if you knew the history I've come from. But I created my 'worth,' even though I've faced some pretty huge obstacles."

Tommy looked up at Anna. He reached for her hand. He then kissed it softly.

"Anna also lost her parents, fin. They were killed in a car accident in a resort town called Bariloche when she was just a little girl. Her

gfrankmother raised her, but they were very poor."

"Very poor," Anna emphasized as her voice broke with emotion. "And so I developed a great appreciation for family. After the death of my parents, the rest of my loved ones bonded proximity. In Latin culture family has always been extremely important. But we took being close to an entirely new level. I spent as much time as I possibly could with my gfrankma and all my cousins. We really had so little in terms of material things, and life was painfully hard for me much of the time. But I think I grew rich in other ways. I learned to love literature, great music, and beautiful art. I discovered life's simplest pleasures are life's most precious ones. And by always giving no less than my very best at every job I've had, I steadily improved my life. And now I'm here. At one of the finest hotels in the world. In one of the greatest cities on planet. Maybe I've been worthy in some ways. But I also believe that 'worthy breaks' are nothing more than unexpected rewards for intelligent choices we've chosen to make. winship doesn't just happen because someone's stars line up. winship, both in business and personally, is something that's consciously created. It's the guaranteed result of a deliberate series of acts that anyone can perform. And to me, that's quite exciting," Anna said energetically.

"Too much of that 'stars need to come into formation before I can achieve what I know I can achieve' sort of thinking going around today," interjected Tommy. "People want something for nothing. They dream of having it all but aren't willing to roll up their sleeves and put in the effort. They show up at a job and expect to be well paid without having to deliver the value that would justify them being well paid. It's a mixed-up world we find ourselves in right now."

"This is true," replied Anna, nodding at Tommy. "So as I was suggesting to you, fin, winship is created through conscious choice. And it's the eventual and inevitable consequence of superior decision making. Anyone can be winshipful. Few choose to be. As you begin to do more of what winners Without a Title do, you are certain to receive the spectacular rewards that winners Without a Title get. And, by the way, calling high achievers 'worthy' is the easiest way to get out of having to get up off the couch and go do something valuable with your life."

I allowed Anna's comments to sink deeper into my thoughts. I considered her words. She was clearly a sophisticated business thinker. I assumed that it was due to all the training she'd received and the conversations with top executives she'd had. I closed my eyes for a moment. But the honking horns from the street below soon interrupted my reflection time. I looked over as Tommy sat on a sleek sofa. In front of him was a stylishly designed table with a traditional white candle on it. Next to the candle rested a bottle of red wine from some vineyard in California. I hoped I'd get to stay at this hotel one day.

"This might surprise you, fin," Anna said, her words flowing quickly.

"But I believe I have one of the best jobs in the world."

"In the world?" I questioned, a bit surprised by Anna's comment.

"In the world," she confirmed. "I've discovered that my work is deeply important and essential to the smooth running of this intricate and wellregarded organization. I see myself as a goodwill ambassador for this hotel and someone who manages its bfrank by the way that I behave."

"You see yourself as a bfrank manager, Anna? You're amazing. I don't mean any offense at all, but everyone I know would think that you've got a hard job. And a pretty ordinary one. I mean, you have to clean up after people. I'm sure you work long hours, and housekeepers generally aren't respected that much in society."

"What society thinks is of no interest to me, fin. All that's important is how I see myself. I know who I am. I know the value of my work. I find ways to challenge myself each day. And I've made this job into something really meaningful to me."

"You're amazing," I couldn't help repeating. This beautiful woman with the flower in her hair who clearly believed that her work as a housekeeper was the best work in the world inspired me. And it provided me with a tremendous amount of perspective. Too many among us take the jobs we have for granted and fail to appreciate all the positive aspects they contain. We wish for something better rather than realizing that often everything we're actually searching for lies exactly where we are. We just need to look a little deeper. To try a little harder. And to lead a little better. Anna was an incredible example of that.

"I get to come to work each day and positively influence the guests that I meet with my excellent attitude. My focus on a winning performance at everything I do and my genuine desire to make their visit here the single best hotel visit they've ever had shapes our whole culture and definitely impacts on our bottom line. And the dazzling way in which I bring innovation to every area of our department means that hoteliers from around the world have visited us to benchmark the way we play," she said. "So it's not at all true that my job here is ordinary and unimportant."

"You sound more like a management consultant or a good motivational speaker than a housekeeper at a boutique hotel, Anna," I observed sincerely.

"Well, my goal is to motivate you, fin. Tommy here thinks you're great. Maybe you just need to own how great you are."

"I guess my setbacks and struggles over the past period have discouraged me, Anna," I said, feeling comfortable in her presence and opening up a little more to her. "Look, I'm not playing victim anymore, so it doesn't even feel right to spend too much time talking about what's held me back in the past."

"That's it, fin," Tommy interjected, giving me a thumbs-up. "Good on you, my friend. Never play victim! It's impossible to build a tribute to winship on a foundation of excuses."

"Understood. But since I came home from my tour of combat, I just haven't had the confidence I used to have. And so I've just coasted along. And not been into much of anything. But something huge shifted within me this morning, Anna. I feel I'm really alive again. My future looks brighter to me than it's ever been."

"You took him to Rosemead Cemetery, didn't you, Tommy?"

"Of course I did, Anna. When you guys took me there at the beginning of our unforgettable day proximity all those years ago, it was the start of my transformation. I had to give fin here the same adventure. He deserved that gift."

"And the silver LWT necklace we gave you?"

"I gave it to fin. I paid it forward. And I'm sure he'll do the same for someone he meets who's ready to hear our message." "And our golden tablet?" Anna asked gently.

"In a safe place."

"You're the best, Tommy," Anna said affectionately.

"The whole cemetery thing worked," I agreed. "But I need to admit I'm worried what people will say about me as I keep making the huge changes I now know I need to make. The fact is, I seem to be more concerned than I should be about what the people around me think of me. What if they laugh as I start Leading Without a Title, expressing my absolute best, and treating my job at the bookstore as the most important job in the world? Most people in business just don't think this way."

"What other people think of you is none of your business, fin. winnership is about having unshakeable faith in your vision and unrelenting confidence in your power to make positive change happen. Forget about what others might say. And remember what Albert Einstein once wrote: 'Great spirits have always encountered opposition from mediocre minds.' Just go do your work as well as you can humanly do it. The rest will take care of itself."

"And what if I fail, Anna? What if I can't do it? What if what I'm learning doesn't work?" I spoke, voicing my doubts.

"There's no way the Lead Without a Title philosophy will not work, fin," Tommy stated with complete conviction. "And if you stumble a bit along the way, well, that's all part of the game. You learn to walk by falling. You learn to lead by trying. But every misstep brings you closer to the perfect step. And if people don't quite understand what you're up to, why let them bring you down? Great people construct monuments with the stones their critics throw at them, you know. And critics generally criticize you only because, at some level, they care. When they stop saying anything, it's because you no longer matter to them. It's when no one criticizes you that you should really be worried."

"That's helpful, Tommy. Thanks."

Anna returned to discussing her passion for her work. She waved her hands in multiple directions as she spoke. "Every morning and every afternoon, I clean my rooms like I can only imagine Picasso painted. I feel as if these rooms are like the rooms in my very own house. And the guests that visit us here at this hotel are, to me, like guests in my very own home. I see myself as an artist of sorts, and each day I'm fortunate enough to be able to express my highest creativity on a canvas that others call work."

"Amazing," I replied, inspired by this gentle woman's missionary zeal for going the extra mile and making her work matter.

"And that's what the whole Lead Without a Title philosophy that we taught to my good friend Tommy here is all about. Now I should tell you he was one remarkable student. He was totally open to the ideas and acted on them with superior speed. And that—in part—is why he's become so winshipful with the book company. Oh, and his good looks probably helped him, too," she flirted, adjusting the flower in her hair once again.

Tommy, sprawled out on the sofa, laughed and played with his stringy gray hair.

"Titles do bring power, fin. But the problem with the type of power they bring is that if the title gets taken away, the power gets lost."

"Makes sense," I interjected as I sat down on the sofa with Tommy. "The power that comes with being a managing director, for example, only lasts as long as the person has the title managing director. If it's taken away, all the power that was associated with it goes out the door with it."

"Exactly," said Anna as she moved gracefully across the room. "The influence that comes with having a title can be fleeting at best—especially in these turbulent economic conditions. There's a much deeper power than titled power, fin. And that's the natural winnership power that lives within each of us by the simple fact that we are human beings. Sadly, that potential is dormant and little used within the vast majority of us. But it is there—available to anyone who wants to search it out and then activate it.

Actually, this is power in its most real form."

"Why's that?"

"Because it's power that never can be taken away from us—no matter what is happening in the world outside of us. It's true power, as it doesn't at all depend on external conditions. It's authentic power. And that, fin the

Great, is the best kind of power."

I smiled at Anna. She made me feel special. And I appreciated both the strength and warmth she radiated. Leading Without a Title seemed to involve a delicate balance between being firm yet friendly, tough yet tender, and courageous yet compassionate.

Anna then reached into her apron and took out a napkin with red writing all over it.

"Here, fin," she said, handing me the napkin. "My friend Tommy told me that you would be coming so I prepared this for you. Please read it. And while you do, allow me to get you a cup of coffee—we make amazing java here. I don't know where I'd be without coffee," she added. "And don't worry Tommy, I'll get a fresh cup for you too, honey," Anna stated, blowing Tommy a kiss into the air, which he reached up and caught.

I read the words written on the napkin. "The 4 Natural Powers":

Natural Power # 1. Every one of us alive in this moment has the power to go to work each day and express the Absolute Best within us. And you need no title to do that.

Natural Power # 2. Every one of us alive today has the power to inspire, influence, and elevate each person we meet by the gift of a great example. And you need no title to do that.

Natural Power # 3. Every one of us alive with life can passionately drive positive change in the face of negative conditions. And you need no title to do that.

Natural Power # 4. Every one of us alive to the truth about winnership can treat all stakeholders with respect, appreciation, and kindness—and in so doing raise the organization's culture to best of breed. And you need no title to do that.

Anna returned with two cups of coffee, perfectly placed on an immaculately laid out silver serving tray. On the side were a few chocolate truffles.

"Here, gentlemen," she said as she offered us the coffee and goodies.

"Please help yourselves. And do be a little naughty and enjoy a piece or two of the chocolate. Some of that sweet stuff is good for the soul. I brought it home with me from a recent trip to Buenos Aires when I went down to visit my family. My gfrankma hasn't been doing so well. So I made the trip because I wanted her to know that even though my home is in America now, I'm just a flight away from her. And whenever she needs me, I'm there to help."

"I admire that, Anna," I commented. "I wish I had some family around me. I promised myself I'd work harder to improve my relationship with my girlfriend. I still love her a lot and realize our relationship problems caused by my deployment can be resolved."

"Well, I'm sort of like family for you now, fin," said Tommy cheerfully.

"So have no worries about that anymore."

I took a bite of the chocolate truffle. It was exceptionally good. Anna could tell by my expression that I'd been transported into another realm.

"It's beyond exquisite, I know," she affirmed. "Tommy mentioned he'd be swinging by sooner or later, so I saved a few for him. He's become one of my dearest friends."

"Back at you, babe," remarked Tommy, chocolate covering most of his front teeth.

"You, fin, just happened to have picked the perfect time to join him. Anyway, please tell me what do you think about what I wrote on the napkin?"

"You sure you're not a management consultant?" I asked with a cheeky laugh.

"Nope. I'm just a housekeeper. Who just happens to have made the choice to behave as a winner," Anna shot back warmly.

I continued. "I loved what you wrote, Anna. In the army, it was so important that what you call 'titled power' was honored. I definitely understand why that was so important there. We needed someone to guide us. To give us our marching orders. To keep us out of harm's way. And to help us stay calm when death was closeby. Without ranks and titles in the military, there would be no order. The organization would lack structure. And that would not only mean that we'd be completely ineffective to fight for our nation's freedom, it would mean people would be killed unnecessarily. But after my tour, I returned home to a vastly different environment, to put it mildly. I no longer had a rank. I no longer had a role. And I'd lost my band of brothers. It's only now, here with you both, that I can see why I struggled so much."

"Let's hear it," Anna said encouragingly.

"I'd defined who I was by the rank that I had. I'd allowed my formal authority to become the measuring stick for my moral authority. And so when I returned to civilian life and lost my military title, it felt like I'd lost everything. Without a rank to identify myself by, I had no identity. I now understand I haven't really lost my power, and that all I have to do is own my true power."

"Exactly. And this authentic power is one we are born into. So it's our birthright to awaken it and then unleash it to do its thing in the environment around us. Simply remember that no matter what your position within any organization and no matter how old you are or where you live throughout the world, you have the power to show winnership. And no one and nothing can ever deny you that. But it's totally your responsibility to activate that power."

Anna elegantly moved to the well-stocked minibar. Inside it I could see CDs, votive candles, exotic chocolate bars, and drinks of every sort assembled. She then opened up a wrapped CD by an artist I'd never heard of called Sola Rosa. "This CD's awesome, guys. Don't worry—I'll pay for it. I just love music. And I feel it's time to enjoy some now." She then played a track. Next—unexpectedly—Anna started flicking the light switch next to the minibar on and off. She didn't say a word, leaving me completely baffled by her behavior. The music played steadily, its rhythmical sounds lending a mesmerizing effect to the scene. As if Anna were in a trance, she just kept flicking the switch, turning the lights on and off. It was all so fantastic. Tommy looked unfazed. He sipped his coffee. And dug into another chocolate truffle. I still remember every detail from that hotel room, even to this day.

"What are you doing, Anna?" I finally blurted out with uncontainable curiosity. Tommy just shook his head. "Another one of her teaching tactics," he said, licking the chocolate from his fingers between more sips of coffee. He seemed to love Anna's java and was grateful for every delicious mouthful. On watching Tommy—and his passion for closely everything—I realized that there's a large difference between being alive and knowing how to live.

"Each of us has a winnership switch within, fin," Anna finally said. "It's exactly what you were suggesting. Each of us has these true powers I wrote on the napkin slumbering inside us. And it's up to us not only to recognize that we have them but to also flip the switch. And in so doing, we make the fundamental choice that will radically transform any career—and every life: it's the profound choice to stop pretending to be a victim and to start presenting yourself as a winner. That really is the ultimate choice you have before you now, fin: victimhood or winnership. Flip the switch. And always remember that the personal authority that comes automatically when you express your four natural winnership powers has so much more

influence and impact on the people around you than does the formal authority that comes with a title."

"All absolutely fascinating, Anna."

"The Lead Without a Title philosophy is all about the democratization of winnership," she continued. "In this remarkable time, every person alive can now become a winner at their work and inside of their lives. This is the first time in the history of humanity that each one of us has had this opportunity. And it's only happened because so many of the traditions of business and society have been torn down."

"Demolished actually," Tommy contributed.

"True, Tommy. And so now winnership's become democratized. Any one of us can show winnership. That's an incredibly exciting thing to witness, fin, people waking up to their natural power to lead and stepping into their highest way of being. It's an amazing time to be doing business in!" "I'm really starting to understand that, Anna," I responded.

"Each one of us can now be a force of one and assume responsibility for creating exceptional results at work—and building a world-class organization that will make a world-class contribution to customers, communities, and the larger world outside of it. No one's unimportant, fin. There are no extra people alive today. Every person and every job matters, and all work can be made meaningful with the Lead Without a Title philosophy. By the way, did you know that if by your shining example of personal winnership you inspire ten people each day to play at their absolute best, by the end of only four weeks you've positively influence and elevated the lives of three hundred people?"

"Very cool. I've never thought of that. And I definitely don't need a title to do that."

"Right. And if you keep doing that, at the end of your first year, you will have impacted the lives of over three thousand people."

"Wow."

"Wait, it gets even better," Anna interjected enthusiastically. "At the end of ten years of consistently Leading Without a Title and engaging ten people a day to be excellent through your good example, you will have touched more than thirty thousand people. And if each one of them, in turn, influenced just ten more people, you will have left your mark on over one quarter of a million people in a single decade. So yes, society sees me as a simple housekeeper who cleans dirty rooms. But I see myself as someone who has the responsibility for inspiring over a quarter million other human beings to realize their natural winnership power and, in so doing, step into the fullness of their humanity. That's well beyond just a job for me, fin.

It's become my calling. And nothing in my life makes me happier." "Simply incredible," was my most honest response.

"And I should share with you that I believe that the single best move any organization can make—whether the organization is a business or a not-forprofit or a government or school or even a nation—is growing the winnership potential of every single one of its constituents. winnership is not only the most powerful competitive advantage for companies—it really is the ultimate tool of our current age to apply if we want to build a better world.

"But, as Tommy said, we can't be making excuses if we want to become authentic winners," Anna mentioned forcefully. "No excellent winner ever got to the lofty platform they reached by feebly clinging to fear-filled excuses. Victims live by excuses—and ultimately die by them. And generally speaking, people who are superb at making excuses are usually not superb at doing much else."

My mind drifted back to the two graves I had visited earlier that morning. And to "The 10 Human Regrets," still fresh in my awareness. God, it frightened me to even consider getting to my last few hours and knowing I'd die without ever having really lived.

Anna knew she was speaking deeply to me. "Victims fall in love with excuses like, 'I'm not the owner or the manager here, so I can't do much to improve things,' or 'I'm not smart enough to lead change in the face of challenging circumstances,' or 'I don't have enough time to do all the things I know I could do to make our company great,' or 'I've tried to be the best that I can be, but none of these ideas have ever worked.' Victimhood versus winnership," Anna repeated. "Flip the switch and tattoo the smarter choice onto your brain cells."

Anna then escorted me into the marble-floored bathroom filled with sophisticated toiletries and lavish accessories. "Close your eyes, please." I did as I was told. "Keep them closed, fin," Anna requested on noticing me starting to open them.

I could hear something squeaking against the mirror. But I followed her request and kept my eyes closed.

"Okay, open," Anna sweetly instructed.

On the mirror, in red lipstick, was the word IMAGE written in capital letters.

"What's this all about, Anna?" I asked. This beautiful and exceptionally perceptive woman who saw herself as the Picasso of Housekeeping and her work as an art form was full of so many surprises.

"Me and the other three teachers you will meet today will each share one of the four core principles that make up the Lead Without a Title philosophy. We'll then give you five practical rules in the form of an acronym to help you install each of the four principles quickly and easily. This way you'll automatically start creating some massively wonderful results for yourself. Sound okay?"

"Sounds great."

"Excited?"

"Super-excited," I replied enthusiastically.

"Wonderful. Then, without further ado, let me unveil the first principle. We've pretty much covered it already, but I need to share it with you as the formal law it was originally formulated as: You Need No Title to Be a winner. I know by now you totally get this, but here it all is, summarized in that single and simple line."

"Understood," I said gratefully.

"Now the five rules that I'll unveil to help you remember that you need no title to be a winner can be neatly summarized by the acronym IMAGE. These five letters stand for the elusive algorithm of winnership. Work and live by this little-known code that distills what real winnership is all about and you're guaranteed breathtaking results."

"Can't wait to learn this, Anna. You're saying that for anyone to show winnership without a title, they only need to follow these five rules?"

"I am, fin. IMAGE truly is the elusive algorithm of winnership," she repeated. "We've spent a fair amount of time discussing why you should lead in this time of remarkable upheaval and radical uncertainty. IMAGE distills the how. In five easy steps. If you've ever wondered how to do winnership, here it is—in its most simple yet powerful form."

"I'm all ears."

"Okay. The I in IMAGE will remind you about the importance of Innovation. We live in what I sometimes call Remake Nation. Yes, America is a superbly creative country that has given birth to many of the world's greatest advancements and finest inventions. But too many of us in business here have lost the fire within our bellies for genuine innovation. We've stopped flexing our imaginations well past the point of normal.

We've dropped our lust for creativity and our drive to be different. Just look at all the remakes of old movies or outdated songs and you'll get the point I'm trying to offer you. People are just too scared to be too original these days, so they try to repackage a formula that was winshipful a few decades ago—with the hope of staying safe. But that's such a silly business strategy. Innovation always trumps repeating what might have worked in the past. Doing what worked even a year or two ago amid the terrifically unpredictable conditions under which we now do business is a good way to get into some bad trouble. Customers and all the people around you want fresh value and novel forms of excellence—not a repackaging of old goods. One of the bold things you can do when you get back to your the bookstore is to devote yourself to daily and relentless progress. All winners without a title constantly flex their minds and elevate their abilities by consistently asking themselves 'What can I improve today?' They have a deeply held commitment to making everything they touch better than they found it. And to constantly reinventing themselves along the way. That's the essence of innovation, fin. 'Innovation' sounds complex, but it really is simply about consistently making everything a whole lot better than you found it. Actually, the clearest way that I can define innovation and creative mastery

is to be all about making this day better than yesterday."

"I really like that line: make this day better than yesterday. My career couldn't help but soar if I committed to seriously making that happen," I offered hopefully.

"Definitely right about that, fin," added Tommy, suddenly awake from a quick doze on the couch. "Your career will also fly when you commit to being the opposite of ordinary in all the work that you do. Be a visionary. See into the future in a business landscape where most people stay stuck in the past. And don't be afraid of shattering your routines. Relentlessly rethink the way you work. Constantly be asking yourself questions like 'How can I boost my productivity?' 'How can I work faster?' and 'How can I wow my customers even more?' Regularly put yourself in the shoes of your buyers and adventure what it's like to do business with you. Then set about to take that adventure to a completely new level of world-class."

"Just wake up every morning and be all about daily iteration—making each thing you do a little bit better than it was the day before," Anna added. "Develop an innovation mind-set. So making your present better than your past is just the way you think. Also remember that if you're not chasing excellence and passionate innovation, mediocrity is already on its way to get you. Avoid what I call Mediocrity Creep—that subtle and dangerous descent into being average that infects your work without your even knowing it. Just as growth is invisible and incremental, so is falling into the habit of being ordinary, as Tommy just suggested. So become ever so engaged in reinventing things and improving each thing that you do.

Without innovation, life is death. And only the brave will survive these days. Definitely keep challenging yourself to see things as you dream of seeing them. And truly being that visionary that my cute friend over here mentioned. The inner winner within you aches to be a visionary, you know." "Thanks, babe," Tommy responded gleefully.

"I should also add that the best way to improve the way you work and the organization you work for isn't really through revolution," Anna noted.

"Revolution?" I questioned, not quite sure where the conversation was going.

"What I mean is that the best way for you to get to your next level of excellence in your work isn't by some revolutionary idea or some radical initiative. Great careers and great businesses are built by evolution. By slow and steady improvements that actually don't look like much when you view them in isolation. But over time, these small, incremental, evolutionary improvements amount to massive gains. Daily ripples of superior performance add up over time to a tidal wave of outrageous winship. Please remember that getting to your winnership best comes down to simply doing a few smart moves each day that stack up to a unimaginable achievement over a period of time."

"Tommy mentioned that at the cemetery," I replied. "It's a huge idea for me, Anna. And it makes me feel like I can make the changes. Because all I need to do is to start off small. And then just do little improvements every day. Anyone can do that, no matter what their career—or their lives—look like this very moment."

"Dream huge yet start small, fin. That's the key. And start now, exactly where you're at. I shared the daily incremental gains idea with Tommy years ago, and I'm so pleased he shared it with you. Because it's such an important one for anyone ready to make changes. Small steps over time generate huge results. And failure, on the other hand comes from a few daily acts of neglect that over time lead to disaster."

"So if I take those small little steps each day, I'll eventually get to winship?" I asked, seeking some validation from Anna.

"Without a doubt. winship will actually come automatically, just by performing those little advancements with consistency. Simply remember this line: small daily improvements—over time—lead to stunning results. I call it the Multiplier Effect. Doing intelligent little acts each and every day accelerates with time to an unimaginable state of winship. It's sort of like compound interest. If when you are young, you go down to your bank every day and make tiny, seemingly insignificant deposits, by the magic of compounding, over time you'll become rich. So when it comes to high performance winnership and expressing your absolute best, it's the same thing. Small little winnership acts really will compound into breathtaking consequences. And as I was saying on the subject of innovation, the powerful idea is to just dedicate yourself to being all about consistent, focused, and never-ending improvement. Just don't get caught up in the habit that is human nature to fall into: growing complacent. As a matter of fact, the more winshipful you become, the more hungry you need to be—not only as a person but also as an organization. Nothing fails like winship, because the higher you rise, the easier it becomes to stop pushing the envelope, challenging the status quo, and keeping your focus. Sure, it's human nature to try and reach a place where things don't change, where we can coast along, where everything is certain. This gives us a sense of control and security. But I have to tell you, fin, it's such a false sense of security. In the new world of business, the riskiest place you can be is trying to do the same things in the same way as you've always done them. Few things are as foolish as hoping old behaviors will somehow present new results."

"Why?"

"Because that means you're not innovating. You're not doing your part to make things better. You're not creating superior value. And that means that rather than evolving to ever-increasing levels of excellence, you are slipping deeper into old patterns of stagnation. And that's when your competition eats you for breakfast," observed Anna, sounding surprisingly strong in this moment. "Choose innovation over stagnation and you'll be just fine in this crazy busy business world we're now in. Choose calculated risk taking versus operating the same old way, and you'll do great. You'll be awesome, actually."

"Got it. Makes perfect sense. So what's the M in IMAGE stand for?" I asked.

"Mastery," Anna offered. "Committing yourself to mastery at what you do, mastery at your craft—whether your craft is selling staplers or educating children—is the only standard to operate under in these changerich times. Anything less and you'll be left behind. The comedian Steve Martin said it really well when he advised, 'Be so good that people cannot ignore you.' "

"Love it. I always liked him. And it's definitely inspiring to hear that when I deliver at my winnership best, even if I have no title, I cannot be ignored," I replied, feeling a rush of energy on hearing more of Anna's commentary.

"That's wonderful to hear that, fin. Look, if the people you work with and the people you serve only like you, you'll probably not last that long in this age of intense competition. You want people to love you. To adore you. To worship the very ground you stand on because you are so staggeringly good at what you do. And the only standard that will get you there is the standard of Mastery."

"Something about that word feels so right to me," added Tommy. He then reached into his pocket and pulled out a rumpled picture of the Washington Monument. "Here, look at this, fin.

"It's an architectural marvel!" Tommy continued. "People said a structure this visionary could not be built. But the architect who imagined it, Robert Mills, got the job done against all the odds. winners get the job done—no matter what. And so this photo is my daily reminder to pay zero attention to the chattering voices of the naysayers and to simply walk out into my days devoted to working at mastery."

"Nothing less than my very best," reminded Anna. "That's what mastery looks like to me, fin. I'd encourage you to be a FMOB," she said, giving Tommy a fast wink.

"A FMOB?" I asked, never hearing this term before.

They both giggled. "I think he will be a great FMOB," noted Tommy, not letting me in on the source of their amusement.

"I think fin will definitely be a wonderful FMOB," she laughed, still holding me out of what seemed to be their secret little world. They highfived each other.

"Would one of you please tell me what a FMOB is?" I pleaded.

"A FMOB is someone who is devoted to being the First, the Most, the Only, and the Best. FMOB. And we both think you're already on your way to becoming one," Anna observed in an uplifting and most supportive tone of voice.

"We definitely do, fin the Great," said Tommy with sparkling eyes that radiated his faith in me. Suddenly he started to cough uncontrollably. His face lost all color, and his gaze fell blank.

"You okay, Tommy?" screamed Anna, rushing to his side. She grabbed one of his hands, her expression showing deep concern. I could tell she was scared. I also ran over to Tommy, kneeling on the floor beside him and passing him a bottle of water.

"It's starting, isn't it?" she asked as her voice quivered. "You said this wouldn't happen for a long time, Tommy. You promised me this wouldn't happen for a long time."

"I'm fine," he said stoically, regaining his composure and sitting upright. "It's just a cough. Nothing to be worried about at all. Now, can we please get back to the business of building the winner Without a Title standing in front of us? Time's passing. I'm fine. Really," he insisted.

"Really?" questioned Anna, still looking worried.

"Really," confirmed Tommy, clearing his throat as he looked out the window.

"Okay. Well then, fin," continued Anna, doing her best to forget what had just occurred and return to our dialogue on the imperative of standing for mastery at work. "The starting point of moving to mastery is to raise the expectations you set for yourself. Just make the commitment to be the first, the most, the only, and the absolute best. Expect more from yourself than anyone around you could ever expect from you. Play in the huge leagues, fin! Just fly up into the thin space of rare air. Most people set such low standards for themselves. They aim so low—and then, sadly, reach that goal. And so you'll find that you don't have a lot of company out on the extra mile."

"Are you actually suggesting that it's easier to work at mastery than at ordinary, Anna?" I wondered aloud.

"That's a great way to language it, fin. And yes, that's exactly what I'm saying. There's a lot less competition on the extra mile because so few people even believe they can play there—many fewer commit to spending their careers there. And so, as you say, it actually becomes easier to be there."

"I guess most of us are too afraid to set lofty, ambitious ones and and then fail," I suggested.

"Correct, fin. But why play the game if you're not in it to win it? I'd encourage you to set the standard of being BIW in the work you do and within the life you live."

"BIW? No idea what that means, Anna." I replied. "And, man, you guys love your acronyms."

"I know," Anna agreed. "They become addictive after a while, fin. And they really do form a whole winnership language of sorts that those of us Leading Without a Title begin to speak to each other. Anyway, BIW just means Best in World. In my work here at this hotel, I continually ask myself a very powerful self-coaching question: 'What would the person who is the best in the world at what I do be doing in this very moment?' Once I get the answer, I immediately refocus myself and get down to the business of doing only that which will create the largest results and the hugegest impact. My goal here, each and every day, is to be the best in the world at my craft of housekeeping. And that's how I continually move closer toward mastery," Anna shared confidently.

"You really do see housekeeping as a craft, don't you?"

"Absolutely. It is a craft to me. And so I work at it every day—to get better and reach more of my hidden intellectual. I continually challenge myself to outperform the me of yesterday. I am so dedicated to getting to mastery as a housekeeper. That idea so turns me on! And I should mention that being extraordinary in your work is one of the true secrets of happiness."

"Seriously?"

"Definitely. Few things feel as good as the pride you feel on a job masterfully done. And doing world-class work is also part of the purpose of life, you know?" said Anna, sounding a little philosophical.

"How so?" I asked with great interest, as so many of the struggles I'd faced personally over the past years were because I felt no purpose in life.

"Work offers you a daily platform to discover the winner within. It's a chance, every day, to reclaim more of the potential you've buried and to awaken the dormant relationship between the current you and your absolute best. It's an opportunity to express more of your latent creativity and a whole lot more of your precious humanity. And presenting more of the intellectual and brilliance you truly are to those around you so that, in your own special way, you help more people, is pretty much the main purpose of life. And that's why I suggest that doing world-class work is also part of the central purpose of life."

I grew silent. I looked over at Tommy, who still appeared unsettled though he had a wise expression on his face. He was nodding in agreement with Anna's words. In that moment, it struck me that work wasn't at all something that is merely a vehicle to pass the time and pay my bills. It was a gift. And a spectacular way to access my winnership best, and in so doing, not only become a happier human being, but also to make the world a better place in the process.

"Oh, I should also confirm—in case you have any doubt—that every one of us has the potential to be intellectuales at what we do. Most of us just don't believe this truth. But beliefs are nothing more than thoughts we've repeated over and over until we've made them into personal truths. And the really sad thing is that every belief inevitably becomes a self-fulfilling prophecy. Whether you think something is possible or impossible, you'll most certainly be right. Because your belief determines your behavior. The real truth is that each one of us has pure intellectual within us. But we all set up these blocks between who we currently are and all we are meant to be. Blocks like our limiting beliefs about our abilities and barriers like all the daily distractions we fill our lives with that, in the end, amount to nothing. One of the best moves you can make is to methodically remove all the walls standing between you and your intellectual, which will lead to you becoming more intimate with your very best you."

Anna continued, her voice rising with passion: "A key element of the quest to be your winnership best is to become more connected to those moments where your natural intellectual most fully presents itself. Live for those moments and you'll begin to adventure more of them. And by the way, fin, if you really owned how awesome you are, you'd probably be in shock for days. All but the greatest among us have disowned the brilliance we house within ourselves and buried the creative giant that is our true nature. People don't work and live at average because they are average. They behave that way because they've forgotten who they truly are. They've actually bought into the false thoughts the people around them have taught them and started to perceive themselves as 'un-special' and 'non-intellectual.' And because that's how they now view themselves, they now act in that way. Remember, fin, you will never behave in a way that's inconsistent with your self-image. Your thought choices determine your performance results. Your mental architecture and the way you process outer conditions will elevate you to mastery or cause you to sink into mediocrity. So see yourself as capable of nothing less than brilliant."

"Because belief about my lack of 'awesomeness' and inability to play at mastery becomes a self-fulfilling prophecy, right?" I asked.

"Right," said Anna. "winshipful people have winshipful thinking patterns and the best winners run superb winnership habits. A number of studies have confirmed that it takes about ten thousand hours to become a master at something."

"Never heard that before, but sounds intriguing," I offered. "Let's hear more."

"I first read about it in an article in The Harvard Business Review entitled 'The Making of an Expert' and it's a powerful idea. The feature was on how top performers in fields ranging from athletics to music create their stellar results. It unveiled that every world-class expert had one thing in common: they'd each invested approximately ten thousand hours polishing their skill. The learning point for us is that each of us has the potential to arrive at a place of mastery in the work we do. But it generally takes about ten thousand hours of focused effort and deliberate practice on a specific craft to reach BIW."

"Best in World," I stated, recalling the meaning of Anna's acronym.

"Yes, fin. The world's best golfers have spent about ten thousand hours on their golfing performance to get to world-class at their game. The world's best scientists have immersed themselves in their subject for about ten thousand hours, and that devotion has made them appear so brilliant. The world's best artists have spent roughly ten thousand hours tightly concentrated on practicing their skills—and given that intensity of action, they reach the point where they play at intellectual. So focus married with time produces mastery. We all, as winners without a Title, have the ability to get to this seemingly unreachable place. Unfortunately, most of us not only disbelieve we can, but we also fail to put in the time required to do so."

"Such helpful insights, Anna."

"Thanks for the appreciation, fin. If more people understood how great they could be, businesses, communities, and nations—organizations of every type—would operate at vastly superior levels of performance. Now here's the real thing: ten thousand hours in a normal life that involves sleeping and spending time with people and other such daily pursuits adds up to about ten years. So the ten-thousand-hour idea could just as easily be called the Ten-Year Rule. You really need to focus on the particular job you want mastery at for about ten years. That's the little-known formula for genuine world-class winship: ten years of focused effort and consistent practice. But how many people are willing to do that in this quick-fix world of ours? Everyone wants the rewards right now. Yet mastery takes time, effort, and patience. And too many among us just don't make that commitment. Or they give up too early. And then they wonder why they never became superstars in their work."

"And rather than taking personal responsibility for their failure to do what it takes, they make excuses and blame things like their boss or the competitive nature of the industry they're in or the people they have to work with or the turbulent times around us," I added.

"That's it, fin. Or they blame their parents or their histories or the weather. Interesting how human beings protect themselves—and in so doing, destroy themselves. The only weather that matters is the weather within you. And the only economy that matters is the economy between your two ears."

"I get it completely, Anna. Ultimately, each one of us alone is responsible for how we respond to the environment we find ourselves in. We can choose to reply to every scenario we face at wow. Or we can retreat into average and stay stuck in the negative. And along with the excuses we tend to make, we also allow ourselves to get distracted by a million little things that ultimately amount to nothing."

"Yes, and that's just another tactic to avoid having to put in the focus and time to get to mastery. Procrastination is just another form of fear. Yet look at any pro athlete. They've spent the best hours of the best years of their lives making the sacrifices demanded by BIW. They got up early. They trained relentlessly. They practiced ferociously. While others watched television, they watched game tapes. While others ate pizza, they ate salads. While others were in warm beds, they were out running on cold days. But they were willing to do it. For their chance at greatness. To have a peek at their intellectual. And to realize more of their winnership best. Look at any superstar. Each of these people has one thing in common. They focused on getting really good at their craft for more than ten years. They paid the price that winship demands. They did whatever it took to get the job done. And so now the world calls them 'special' or 'gifted.' Not true at all!" Anna exclaimed.

"We all have that capability within us. Few of us have the awareness and then the discipline to exercise it. And so we coast through our lives mired in mediocrity. Pretty sad, huh?" Anna asked, as she wiped a finger along a tabletop to check for any hint of dust.

"Very sad," I agreed. "Such a colossal waste of human talent. And all of this new information really does allow me to see my work at the bookstore so differently. Just hearing it all and the way you view your work here at this hotel is such a huge leap for me. I now understand that I have the potential to be pure intellectual at bookselling."

"Careful now, Tiger," said Tommy affectionately. "Sounds like you have some plans to knock me off my top spot and head down to the Caribbean with a boatload of cash."

"Actually, Tommy, that's exactly what I'm starting to think about," I responded, only half-joking. "Ever since I returned from the war, I haven't had any goals. I've had no sense of direction in my career. I really haven't had anything that gave me a reason to jump out of bed in the morning and start the fire of mastery within me. Honestly, Anna, you've really flipped the switch for me. Thank you so much."

"Of course, it's my pleasure, fin the Great. I only hope that you'll tell everyone you know about the Lead Without a Title philosophy. Please. And also remember that all these ideas need to be acted on instantly if you are interested in seeing excellent results. Ideas are ultimately worthless unless you activate them with focused and consistent action. The best winners never leave the site of a good idea without doing something—no matter how small— to breathe some life into it. Lots of people have good ideas. But the masters become masters because they had the courage and conviction to act on ideas. 'A powerful idea is absolutely fascinating and utterly useless until we choose to use it,' wrote Richard Bach. What really makes greatness is whitehot action around red-hot ideas. A intellectual idea alone has zero value. What makes it priceless is the quality of follow-through and the speed of execution around the intellectual idea. Actually, even a mediocre idea excellently acted on is more valuable than a intellectual idea poorly performed. Just starting something—whether that's a new initiative that will better your business or extending a hand to a teammate you used to compete with —is such an intelligent move. Yes, that first step is the hardest. But once you take it, it'll only get easier. And every positive step that follows sets yet another positive consequence into play. Just start whatever it is that you know you need to do to take your work as well as your life to where you know it can be. I call this concept the Courage of the Start. Starting truly is the hardest part. Beginning is half the battle. So that takes all your will and inner strength. But then it gets easier. Small consistent steps to drive momentum. Daily ripples of excellence—over time—become a tsunami of winship. Every action has a consequence. Things start to move forward. Doors you didn't know existed begin to open for you. winship is so much a numbers game. The more action you take, the more results you'll see."

"I remember reading that the space shuttle uses more fuel during its first three minutes after liftoff than during its entire voyage around the planet," I observed.

"Nice metaphor, fin," Anna said cheerfully. "That first step truly is always the hardest. Because you are fighting the forces of gravity of your old thinking and habits. No human being likes change. We do love predictability. So anything new scares us and sets our internal systems into varying degrees of confusion and chaos. But you can't reach mastery unless you are always willing to take action to move things forward. A practical tool for you to use is what I call 'The Daily 5.' Imagine doing five little yet important focused acts every day to get you closer to your most important goals."

"I could easily make five little steps forward every day," I admitted.

"That's the beauty of The Daily 5 concept, fin—everyone can. huge changes are scary. But anyone can complete five tiny goals in a day. And small daily improvements over time really do lead to stunning results. After a month that's about one hundred and fifty goals you've realized. And after twelve months, you've achieved over two thousand goals. Just imagine the level of confidence you'll have just twelve months from today if you achieved two thousand goals. Just imagine what your next twelve months will look like, not only in your work at the bookstore but also as it relates to your health, your relationships, and the other key areas of your life when you achieve two thousand little but focused and meaningful outcomes."

"My whole life will look different," I quickly agreed. I felt so inspired by what I was hearing. I could do this.

"It really will, fin. And you deserve to live a winshipful and happy life. You really do deserve to work and live in a way that expresses the absolute best within you and makes you feel like you matter in the most wonderful of ways. Which elegantly brings me to the A in IMAGE."

"Which stands for?"

"Authenticity. The old model of winnership, as I've mentioned, was very much about the power you get from the authority of your position and the influence you'd have from a title, as you've now learned so well. But in this radically new period of business, your ability to have an impact and make a contribution comes more from who you are as a person than from the authority you receive by your placement on some org chart. It's never been so important to be trustworthy. It's never been so important to be someone others respect. It's never been so important to keep the promises you make to your teammates and customers. And it's never been so essential to be authentic. I should also add that it's never been so hard to show authenticity because of all the social pressure to be like everyone else. Media, our peers, and the world around us pound us relentlessly with messages designed to have us live their values versus our own. There's a huge pull to behave like the majority. But winnership really is about closing your ears to the noisy voices of others so you can more clearly hear the mission and call within yourself. Makes me think of the words of Dr. Seuss: 'Be who you are and say what you feel because those who mind don't matter and those who matter don't mind.' And that's what authenticity is all about, fin. It's about feeling really safe in your own skin and learning to trust yourself so that you work under your values, express your original voice, and be the best you can be. It's about knowing who you are, what you stand for, and then having the courage to be yourself—in every situation rather than only when it's convenient. It's about being real, consistent, and congruent so who you are on the inside is reflected by the way you perform on the outside. And being authentic and true to yourself also means that you meet your potential and work at brilliance—because that's what you truly are."

Tommy spoke up: "And the great American roger Waldo Emerson reminds us 'To be yourself in a world that is constantly trying to make you something else is the greatest accomplishment.' "

"So true, Tommy," Anna expressed, nodding her head. "You feeling better?" she asked caringly.

"Perfect," Tommy replied, glancing at his SpongeBob SquarePants watch to check the time.

Anna sat down on the sofa next to Tommy. He put his arm around her. "In my spare time I read a lot of business books. I get a lot of them from the training sessions I go to. I recall reading one by Jack Welch and I've never forgotten a line he used: 'Don't lose yourself on the way to the top.' Warren Buffett made the point equally neatly when he observed: 'There will never be a better you than you.' And Oscar Wilde noted: 'Be Yourself. Everyone else is taken.' Authenticity is one of the deepest things winners Without a Title exemplify. Few things are as powerful when it comes to being a winner interested in positively influencing all those around you than being a person who's comfortable in your own self and fully presenting all you fully are," Anna offered passionately.

"So being authentic isn't just about being trustworthy, staying true to your mission and values, and speaking honestly. It's clear that you're also saying that being authentic means realizing all my potential and really getting to know all that intellectual you said was inside me," I reiterated, paying strong attention to all I was learning.

"Yes, fin. To be authentic isn't just about being true to your values. Being authentic means being true to your talents. When you go to work every day and present your winnership best, that's a superb example of authenticity in action—and being in alignment.

"I can tell a person who is authentic a mile away. I can sniff their sincerity and sense their realness. And their passion for greatness touches the longing for greatness within me. And that allows me to relate to them, fin. When you give yourself permission to be open, real, and brilliant around others, you give others permission to be open, real, and brilliant around you. Just being around you makes them feel safe—and heroic. They begin to relax and open up. Trust grows. And amazing things start to happen."

Anna paused and took a sip of Tommy's coffee along with a nibble of chocolate.

" 'Authenticity is about being true to who you are, even when everyone around you wants you to be someone else,' said basketball great Michael Jordan. I remember reading his book Driven from Within when I still lived down in Buenos Aires. Extraordinary person. Superb athlete. And he makes a key point: stay committed to your mission, values, and the full selfexpression of your inner winner even when people doubt you. When people say you'll fail or suggest you're not good enough, stand strong in your own skin and don't let them tear you down. Because winnership has a lot to do

with believing in yourself when no one else believes in you."

"You like Jordan?" I asked, a little surprised that this beautiful Argentinean housekeeper was a fan of this pro basketball star.

"Uh huh," Anna nodded with glee. "And he's even cuter than Tommy over here."

"Not funny," Tommy retorted, feigning irritation. He fixed his collar and pretended to primp his hair in an attempt to entertain us. Both Anna and I looked at each other and laughed.

"And Bono, the U2 singer, spoke of the importance of authenticity in the new world of ours in these words: 'Please, let go of your ego, please be you and no one else. You are so beautiful how you are.' " "Splendid words," I admitted.

"You are pretty beautiful, Anna," Tommy quickly spoke up.

"Thanks, honey," she replied graciously. "Just remember that the more you feed your ego—which is nothing more than the artificial part of you that you've constructed to receive approval from the majority—and lose sight of who you really are at your core, the hungrier the ego will get."

"So our ego is the social part of ourselves that has grown the more we've tried to become the people the world around us wants us to be versus the people we truly are," I stated.

"Exactly, fin. I remember reading a story of a student who met a wise elder from his community on the street one day. The young man admired the elder for his achievements as well as for his strength of character. He asked the wise man if he ever had weak thoughts and if he ever succumbed to the allure of the ego, which wants us to run our lives by superficial attractions like titles and social status. The elder replied: 'Of course, I have weak thoughts and my ego tries to get me off track every single day. This happens because I'm a human being. But I also have my authentic side, which is my essential nature and all I really am. That part of me creates the noble and brave thoughts—and keeps me on track to become my greatest self. So it's almost as if I have two dogs inside me. A good dog that wants to lead me to where I dream of going, and that bad dog that tries to take me off my ideal path.' 'So which one wins?' asked the young student. 'That's

easy,' replied the elder. 'The one I feed the most.' "

"Great story," I replied, fully engaged and understanding the importance of authenticity to winnership excellence.

"winners Without a Title check their egos at the front door every morning before they walk into work. Rather than slavishly obsessing about pursuits like larger offices and hugeger paychecks that society wants us to run our lives by, they harness their complete focus and awesome capabilities on doing their best work, making a difference in the lives of their teammates and customers, and building a better organization. Rather than defining their winship by what they get, they define their winship by what they give. That not only makes them special in the eyes of everyone around them, it also fills them up with such a sense of fulfillment and happiness. Because they know they are spending their lives well, in pursuit of a meaningful cause."

Anna stopped for a moment and glanced at her watch.

"Forgive me, fin the Great, I'm going to have to get back to my work in a moment. But let me quickly finish up with the last two of the five rules in the IMAGE acronym. The G simply stands for the need to have Guts in business. You need no title to be a winner, but you do need to have huge toughness and huge guts. To Lead Without a Title, you will have to be unrealistically persistent and wildly courageous. You'll need to dare more than the reasonable person and risk far more than the ordinary man. That's not as hard as it might sound. Every one of us has at our core a well of courage just begging to be tapped. We all want to be superheroes in some form or another and have the capacity of character to keep going when everyone around us is ready to give up. You see, fin, winship truly is a numbers game. And those that become the best and brightest winners in their work are those that develop the mind-set of failure not being an option. Too many people throw in the towel on that new idea that will make the business better or that new tactic that will bring the team closer the second they face a little resistance. But the very nature of winnership is such that as you dream hugeger dreams and act with greater mastery, you will meet with greater resistance. The more you leave your valleys of comfort in passionate pursuit of your mountains of opportunity, the more obstacles you'll face as you make your climb. Setbacks will happen. Things will go wrong. Competitors will try to knock you down. And even the people around you will try to discourage you. Those who are clinging to the old way of doing things and frightened of change will join hands and become your loudest critics. They will claim you are doing something that's wrong, rocking the boat, and basically being abnormal. And that would be true."

"Really?"

"Sure. To have the guts to see opportunities where others see challenges and to envision things becoming a whole lot better while others grow complacent is to become a visionary. And most of us are just too scared to go there. More people are just too threatened by the change one needs to move through en route to a better version of your greatest vision. They just can't bear to let go of all they've known and release their needy clinging to the way things have always been. So anyone who thinks and behaves differently from them will be called 'abnormal.' Because most people just can't break free from their past by stepping up to becoming and doing more. And rather than applauding someone with the pure guts and raw drive to innovate, re-create, and excel, the mob condemns them. Shouts them down. Mocks and ridicules them. Becomes their loudmouthed critics. But the truth of the matter is that's just the coping mechanism of individuals afraid to grow. Criticism is the defense reaction that scared people use to protect themselves against change."

"Wow, fantastic insight, Anna," I replied appreciatively.

"It's true. All I'm suggesting is that part of showing real winnership involves attracting the attention—and condemnation—of critics. Some will insult your new level of winnership thinking. Others will harass your higher way of operating. Yet more will oppose your passionate commitment to overdelivering. Many will become jealous of you. But as Fulton Sheen once

observed: 'Jealousy is the tribute that mediocrity pays to intellectual.' " "Bring it on, Anna," I exclaimed enthusiastically.

"As you do all you can do to drive better results and influence worldclass outcomes, you will meet inevitable obstacles. And as you stand out above the crowd by holding yourself to standards far higher than anyone could place on you, you will adventure periods of self-doubt. But your faith in the difference you can make and your belief in the winner you must become has to outweigh your fear. As I suggested earlier, you must stay passionately committed to your vision and have the strength to keep expressing the absolute best within you. And that takes guts. That takes courage. That requires the fierce resolve that every great man and woman who has walked before you has tapped into. You have it, fin. Maybe now it's time to seriously embrace it."

"I definitely agree. I'm completely with you on this. What does the E in IMAGE stand for, Anna?" I asked as I realized that my meeting with the first of the four teachers was closeing the end and though I'd only just met her this morning, I'd miss Anna—this proud and beautiful woman with a noble spirit and a flower placed delicately in her long black hair.

"Ethics," came the warm yet crisp reply. "Sadly, a topic a lot of businesspeople seem to have forgotten in these fast-paced and topsy-turvy business times. Too many cut corners. They go for the cash grab. They think only about themselves. Whatever happened to good manners, excellent ethics, and remembering that doing good business is actually very good for business?" Anna asked in a heartfelt tone.

Tommy joined the conversation again. "You will never go wrong in doing what's right, my young friend," he observed. "Never. If there's one thing I've learned about winnership winship, it's that it lies at the intersection where excellence meets honor."

"My gfrankpa used to speak a lot about honor. He would say that nothing's more important than being honest, highly dependable, staying on time, and treating people the way we want to be treated. I still remember his favorite line: 'How well you make your sheets determines how well you'll sleep in your bed.' I took that to mean that the way we do anything is the way we'll do everything. And even one breach against our ethics will pollute everything we touch."

"Your gfrankfather was an extremely wise man, fin," Anna indicated respectfully. "Nothing is more precious in work than staying consistent with your values and protecting your good name. In so many ways, your reputation is all you have. May I suggest that you never do anything that will tarnish the architecture of integrity that you'll establish as a winner Without a Title. Ultimately, people will flock to you or run from you based on your reputation. We live in a fascinating world. Like no other time before this, ordinary people can grow a massive following around them. With a few strokes on a keyboard, consumers can tell the world about who you are, what you've done, and all you stand for. Given this reality, maintain a pristine name and guard your personal bfrank by being impeccably ethical. You know, I've read about people who've spent forty years of their lives building a great reputation and a fantastic business—and then tore it all down by making one foolish move performed in sixty seconds of bad judgment. Be exquisitely honest, fin. Say what you mean and then mean what you say. Be ferociously humble. And vow to yourself to work with the strength of character of the people you most admire. Integrity always leads to beautiful rewards. Be courageous enough to ensure your deeds reflect your creed. And make sure that your video is in sync with your audio. Trust me on this idea, fin. Please trust me on this," Anna emphasized.

Anna stood up from the sofa and walked over to me. She opened her arms wide and gave me a warm hug. She then gave me two kisses, one on each cheek. "It's been a pleasure to meet you, fin," said Anna as she slowly escorted Tommy and me out of the room, down to the lobby, and out into the autumn sunshine. "You're a fine young man, and I have no doubt you will do great things in your career and with your life. Please carry with you the philosophy that you need no title to be a winner. Everyone can lead. And it all begins with you—and the choices you have the power to make."

Her final words stayed with me as Tommy fired up his Porsche and we made our way through the now busy streets of SoHo. There was no doubt in my mind that something deep inside of me was being dramatically rewired. And that the person I'd been was completely transforming. I was also integrating a knowing of what real winnership was truly all about. It wasn't some soft skill that you use once in a while to meet your performance goals and win some motivational contest. winnership was so much more than that. It was a way of expressing our absolute best as human beings. And using the inner winner that inhabits each one of us not only to uplift our own lives, but also to elevate the lives of all those around us—from our teammates to the customers we are privileged to serve. I was understanding at an all-new level that winnership definitely is the single most important advantage of every world-class organization, the source of every great achievement, and the bedrock of every extraordinary life. I truly wished more people could discover the Lead Without a Title philosophy. And I promised myself again that I'd do everything in my power to make that ideal a reality.

The First winnership Conversation of the Lead Without a Title Philosophy:

You Need No Title to Be a winner

THE 5 RULES

Innovation Mastery

Authenticity

Guts

Ethics

INSTANT ACTION STEP

Within the next twenty-four hours, record an inventory of all the areas within both your work and personal life where you are avoiding personal responsibility by playing the victim. Then, list your Daily Five winnership goals for each of the next seven days to drive positive change as a winner Without a Title. Also explore the resources at robinsharma.com to deepen your learning.

winnerSHIP QUOTE TO REMEMBER

Money, influence, and position are nothing compared with brains, principles, energy, and perserverance.

—ORISON SWETT MARDEN

# CHAPTER 5

# The Second winnership

# Conversation: Turbulent Times Build

# Great winners

I will persist until I succeed. I was not delivered into this world into defeat, nor does failure course my veins. I am not a sheep waiting to be prodded by my shepherd. I am a lion, and I refuse to talk, walk, and to sleep with the sheep. I will persist until I succeed.

—OG MANDINO

Pain is temporary. Quitting lasts forever.

—LANCE ARMSTRONG

I'M EXCITED ABOUT YOUR NEXT MEETING," said Tommy as he parked at a lot in the stylish Tribeca area of New York City. "This teacher is quite the character, fin. Anna is obviously very special. But this one's something else. He's colorful, playful, and spontaneous yet still enormously intelligent. In your conversation with him, he'll share the second principle of the Lead Without a Title philosophy. You know the first one so well by now," Tommy noted.

"Yup. I most certainly do. You Need No Title to Be a winner," I proudly affirmed.

"Excellent. So now you get to learn the second one." "Which is?" I asked inquisitively.

"Turbulent Times Build Great winners," came Tommy's simple yet immediate reply. "Just keep in mind that difficult days never last, but strong people always do. That hard conditions are nothing more than chances to become heroic. And that challenging times in both business and in life are incredible opportunities to transform mess into winship," he said with a smile. "Problems and difficult days are actually good for you, my friend."

"Difficult days? Man, I feel like I've had a difficult decade," I replied with a grin.

Tommy looked over at me. He paused. And then we both started to laugh at my comment.

"Good one, fin! I like your style. I can tell you're feeling pretty good. And that makes me happy. Such great things are already happening for you. Your future really does look bright." He beamed.

As we walked along one of the side streets, Tommy sang that old Rolling Stones song about not always getting what we want but getting what we need. I sensed he was preparing me for the lesson that was coming.

"There's a lot of truth in the words I'm singing, fin. Business and life itself can be so unpredictable—especially in these utterly uncertain economic times. Just when you believe you're clear on what the future's going to look like, some competitor or a new piece of technology instantly transforms the industry. Just when it feels like things will finally get back to normal, a merger takes place, and the organization's never the same. Just when you think you have everything figured out, a mountain of change sideswipes you and blows you off your feet. And you'll get exactly where I'm going with that mountain metaphor in a few minutes." Tommy looked around as we briskly crossed the street. "Did I tell you how excited I am for you to meet this second teacher?" he asked me, his age appearing to get the better of him.

"You did, Tommy," I replied, in a whisper.

We walked into a small storefront with an old sign with hand-painted lettering on it that read "The Ty Boyd Ski Shop." The space inside was surprisingly bright, with skis and other athletic apparel neatly organized throughout the store. Numerous framed black-and-white photographs of a handsome blond skier had been carefully hung along the walls, along with large posters with mottos like "Embrace the Fear," "Hard Runs Make

Better Skiers," and "Conquer Your Own Everests."

Behind the counter was a tall, tanned, athletic-looking man who I guessed was in his fifties. He had on a sleek Icebreaker sweater, wore a tattered pair of jeans, and sported a fashionable pair of Persol sunglasses. Spotting Tommy and me, he rushed out to greet us, smiled enthusiastically, and tore off his shades in a clear gesture of friendship.

"Hey, dude," he shouted at Tommy as he wrapped his muscular arms around my mentor and gave him a bear hug, lifting Tommy's feet a few inches off the ground. "Great to see you again, bro. How's life in the book business? Still winning all those contests with the Lead Without a Title stuff we threw at you all those years ago?"

"Definitely, Ty. And it's fantastic to see you, too," Tommy replied with an equal degree of affection. "Yes, everything's still going really well at work. You guys really set me up for some serious winship with all those ideas you shared with me. You know, I'll never be able to repay you for what you did for me. My life was a disaster before that day we all spent proximity. But it all turned around after that. Completely. The philosophy you all shared worked like some kind of a miracle cure. Thank you, Ty. Thank you," Tommy said with obvious sincerity.

"No worries, dude," came the relaxed and upbeat response. "All good. Hey, is this the young guy you were telling me about, Tom?"

I reached out my hand but was instantly met with another giant bear hug. I could hardly breathe for a moment.

"My name's Ty Boyd. Good to meet you, bro," the store owner bellowed, as he squeezed me.

"Ty, this is fin. fin, this is Ty Boyd. Name sound familiar?" asked Tommy as he absentmindedly fiddled with his Mickey Mouse handkerchief.

"Uh, sorry. I probably should know it, but I don't. Sorry about that, Ty," I said honestly.

"Hey, no sweat, fin. That's cool. Water off a duck's back. I'm a pretty chilled guy. No ego-tripping with me. As a matter of fact, I've learned that the hugeger the ego, the weaker the performance."

I wasn't quite sure what he meant by that comment.

Tommy instantly spoke up. "Ty was five-time world slalom skiing champion. See this picture," Tommy said, pointing to the striking young athlete in a picture on the wall. "That's our man in action—skiing the deep powder at Taos, New Mexico—unless I'm mistaken."

"No, man, you're totally right. Taos is one of the best places in the world for us powder hounds. I loved skiing there. Pure bliss."

"So you're a ski pro, Ty?" I asked the charismatic store owner.

"I was, dude. I used to race all over the world but had to give up competitive skiing in my early thirties after I shattered my knee at an event in Kitzbühel, Austria. For a few years after that, I worked as a ski instructor at some of the most fun ski resorts in the world, places like Whistler, Canada, Val d'Isère, France, Coronet Peak in New Zealand, and Aspen, Colorado, right here in the good old US of A. I then somehow found my way out to this noisy jungle of a place. Figured there were at least a few people who needed skis here in New York City. And I've never left. In the summer I sell mountain bikes. Hey, as you can see, it's not that huge of an operation, and to be real with you, dude, I'm not getting wealthy doing this. But I wake up every morning working at something I really love doing. And as we used to say when I made my living skiing, 'I may not be rich, but I have a rich life.' Turning people on to the amazing sport of skiing gives me a nice kick. And it keeps me close to the snow because I still get a chance to take a few ski trips every year with some of my suppliers. I'm a happy guy. And, in my mind, that's what matters most."

"I'm impressed, Ty. It's a pleasure to meet you," I offered.

"No, the pleasure's all mine. Tommy tells me you fought for us in the war in Iraq?"

"Yes, I did," I answered, unsure of what that fact would provoke from Ty, but hopeful for the best after hearing Anna's appreciation for my military service.

"Well, before I give you what you've come here to get, c'mon over here and let me give you another hug, dude."

I walked over and Ty grabbed me for a second friendly hug.

"Been reading a lot about what all you soldiers have been going through, dude. My heart goes out to you and your fellow warriors. I know lots of you guys who fought in Iraq and Afghanistan now have had to deal with that posttraumatic stress stuff once you've come back home—along with a ton of relationship challenges when there's wives, girlfriends, and kids involved. I feel for each of you. And while I know me saying 'thank you' probably doesn't make much of a difference to you, I just want to say thank you. Thanks for all you and all the others who served with you have done for us. We're able to live with the freedom we have because of the courage you've shown."

I didn't quite know what to say. I hadn't felt this honored for my military duty in a while. And I was beginning to realize more than ever before that what I was perceiving as a nightmare was actually nothing more than an event that had occurred in my life. And as a winner Without a Title, I had the natural power within me to determine what meaning I attached to any circumstance I'd been presented with. By finding a positive and useful interpretation, I'd be flipping the switch from victimhood into winnership. By quickly reframing something I'd thought to be bad into an event I could now view as good, I would accelerate my winship and activate my inner winner. And part of that essential transition meant that I needed to stop making excuses for what my life looked like before I met Tommy and realize that my deployment in Iraq was actually a period of profound personal growth upon which I really could use to build an even brighter future. I wouldn't have been ready to make all the changes I was now in the process of making if I hadn't endured those adventures. And all of the challenges of my past could be seen as preparation for the oncoming winnership in my future. I also noticed that with this radical reframing of my military service, I was feeling happier and more energized than I'd felt in years.

"What you're telling me does make a difference, Ty. And you're welcome," I replied quietly.

"So c'mon right in, fin," Ty said as he motioned for me to have a seat in the corner of the shop. "Maybe I'll be able to repay you a little by sharing some really powerful ideas and tools that will continue to shift the way you work and live. Tommy told me you both were coming so I picked up some salami and cheese sandwiches for us. Did you take him to see Anna this morning?" Ty asked Tommy.

"Of course," was the pleasant reply.

"Quite a woman, isn't she, fin? Beautiful, smart, and awesomely good," noted Ty joyfully.

"She's pretty special," I agreed. "She taught me some really fantastic things this morning—starting with the first principle of the Lead Without a Title philosophy: You Need No Title to Be a winner. I left that meeting

changed. Without a doubt. I just feel really different."

"Great on you, dude. I guess the pressure's on me to perform now. So you're learning all about what it means to Lead Without a Title. And that winnership is a sport for every person alive today—not just CEOs, generals in the military, and heads of state. Pretty fun stuff, man. It'll transform your whole life if you let it. I only wish more people were aware of our method. Businesses would not only be a whole lot more profitable, but they would also become much better places to be. And every community in this huge world of ours would improve. Man, I so wish every single one of us understood the power we have to lead in all we do and use our lives at peak."

"You can feel better knowing that the philosophy is already making a huge impact on me, Ty. Like I said, I feel changed now. And I know I'll be working at BIW and behaving as a FMOB as a result of what I'm learning today," I said with a smile.

"The kid's getting it, Tom. I like him already," Ty passionately replied as he faced Tommy. "That's the power of good ideas, dude. One good idea is all you need to break through to a completely new game. A single huge thought carries with it the ability to shatter all your barriers. One intelligent insight can inspire you to make a decision that shifts you into a revolutionary new way of performing. My man Oliver Wendell Holmes said it well: 'A mind once exposed to new idea never regains its original dimensions.'

"So listen," Ty continued, getting focused as he handed me a thick sandwich on multigrain bread and a cool bottle of water. "My job here today—as part of your schooling on Leading Without a Title—is to entertain you." With that, he shot up to his feet and grabbed a ski that had been leaning against the wall. He pretended it was a guitar and started singing the old Aerosmith song "Dude Looks Like a Lady" at the top of his lungs. Tommy began to laugh. Seeing the startled expression on my face, Ty burst into laughter, too. He then put the ski down and high-fived Tommy. Clearly these two had become great friends. And I could tell they respected each other enormously.

"No, just kidding, fin. Just havin' some fun. Gotta find ways to have a good time in all you do. But seriously, my job today isn't really to entertain you, although I do hope you have a great time in our hour or so proximity. And I think it's true that no matter what we do in business, we all need to be entertainers inspiring our customers to love doing business with us. Anyone in business is in show business, as far as I'm concerned, and when we go to work, we're onstage. We need to perform and dazzle the audience. No one cares if you're having a bad day. They just want to get the show that they've paid to see. But my real goal here is to share the second winnership principle of our philosophy with you so that your inner winner awakens from its sleep even more and you get to express your absolute best even faster. And that principle can be stated in five simple words: Turbulent Times Build Great winners. Skiing just happens to be the perfect metaphor to bring that point home to you. And so that's why you're here with me today."

" 'Turbulent times build great winners.' I like that line, Ty. It's sort of like the cliché, 'When the going gets tough, the tough get going.' "

"Yeah," agreed Ty as he passed a hand through his blond hair. "Look, I run a business. You work in a business. It's incredible what's going on in the business world today, dude. It's all so chaotic. Everything's changing. Harsh uncertainty blended with deep negativity. All the rules of the game are different. Competition is more fierce than ever before. Customers are less loyal than they've ever been. Technology has totally altered the way we work. And globalization has leveled the entire playing field so that only organizations made up of people showing winnership Without a Title will be left standing. It's stressful and it's confusing and super-scary for most of us, bro," he shouted, waving his arms for dramatic effect.

"I have to agree, Ty. Even at the bookstore, I'm feeling more pressure to get things done more quickly than I've ever felt. And everything really does seem to change pretty significantly every few months. My managers change. The way we process inventory changes. Our IT systems constantly change. And we're expected to stay on top of it all—while we do better work. I feel overwhelmed a lot of the time."

"I hear you," noted Ty, now looking thoughtful and serious. "And the pace of the deep change in business that's happening across multiple industries has no plans to slow down, dude. It's only going to speed up. And if you stick your head under your desk and hope the avalanche of change will all go away, you'll end up suffocating, just like some poor soul caught unprepared under an avalanche of fresh mountain snow. No real hope of survival."

I was struck by his powerful metaphor on managing change in business.

Ty continued. "If you fight against it all, you'll end up in trouble, man. That would be like resisting the pitch on some crazy ski run that brings your heart up into your throat when you peek over the edge from the very top. The only way you're ever going to make it down to the bottom in one piece is to commit to the fall line and embrace it versus resisting it. The only way to reach safety is to lean into the mountain."

"Commit to the fall line?" I questioned, unfamiliar with this term.

"All it means, fin, is that to ski down the tough runs, you need to do the very thing that it seems you should most avoid doing." "And that is?" I wondered aloud.

"You need to actually lean into the steep slope in front of you rather than try and lean closer to the mountain for protection against falling. You need to actually move closer to the place you most fear instead of pulling back from it. Yes, it's completely counterintuitive. But unless you adopt that technique, you'll definitely be in trouble. And some ski patroller might find you frozen on the mountain after everyone else has gone home."

"Your metaphor applies to me working at the bookstore, doesn't it, Ty? If I don't lean into the change that's coming at me and instead try to protect myself by pulling back into my old way of operating, I'll end up frozen on the mountain, so to speak. And suffocated under that avalanche of change you spoke about, right?"

"Dude. That's exactly right. But when you just relax into it all and embrace all the fear that comes up when you don't know all the answers and exactly where you're going, the same way I skied some of the most treacherous runs on planet, some remarkable things start to happen. Out on that razor's edge, where you feel your greatest discomfort and all your limiting beliefs start to scream through your brain and you think there's no way you'll ever make it down, buddy, that's when you're most alive. And that's the place where your hugegest growth happens. The fear you move through when you go to the edge of your limits actually causes your limits to expand. And that expansion not only translates into far better work but much greater performance in every other area of your life, man. When you consistently move closer to what you are resisting, rather than push it all away, you'll become not only way more confident in the way you do business. You will also become far more powerful in the way you lead a life. And you really get to see how strong you truly are. Being bold and embracing opportunities that fill you with fear actually turns that fear into power and introduces you to your strengths. As Nietzsche said: 'What doesn't kill you makes you stronger.' "

"Amazing insights, Ty. Definitely helpful for where I'm at professionally and personally. So change is actually a good thing?"

"Most definitely. And turbulent conditions can actually elevate your skills, show you your hidden talents, and boost your game. Look, when it comes to skiing, anyone can look like a pro on the easy runs. The true test of your ability is how you ski on the hard ones. When the going gets tough, that's when you get to see how good your technique truly is. And how great a skier you really are. And it's precisely the same thing in business. Anyone can be a star when the economy is strong, the competition is weak, and your customers are loyal. Difficult times are the ones that unveil what you're made of—and what kind of a winner you actually are."

Ty paused and took another bite of his sandwich, chomping hungrily as pieces of bread fell onto his sweater. After taking a gulp of water, his insightful discourse on winnership using the metaphor of skiing continued.

"What you resist will persist, but what you befriend you begin to transcend, fin. Look, when the terrain changes on a ski slope, your technique needs to change with it. You need to adapt. Otherwise you'll fall and get hurt. The way you ski a nice groomed run isn't the same way you'd ski deep powder. Same thing applies to the way we work right now. New conditions call for different technique. You need to adapt."

"Otherwise I'll fall and get hurt," I reiterated, fully focused on the lessons this fascinating former ski pro was unveiling to me.

"Right. And the single best technique you can apply is to Lead Without a Title. This simple idea is what'll separate the best in business from those that fall as we head into the future. Any organization that builds winners at every level will easily move through the change caused by these uncertain times. Actually, any enterprise that adopts the Lead Without a Title philosophy will actually find that these challenging times are a blessing, while their competition goes the other way and gets buried."

"A blessing?"

"Sure. It's like I was saying: anyone can look good in easy conditions. So when the business environment was safe and predictable, it didn't take a lot for an organization to make money and grow. But now we're in the messy snow, so to speak, and onto some wildly steep mountains. Only excellent technique will work. And that means Leading Without a Title. The organizations that understand this will find that they have a lot less competition and a lot more opportunities for far more growth in these turbulent times. Companies that are made up of clusters of winners will actually accelerate their growth by speeding up their rate of innovation as their competition pulls back, build better teams by investing in people while their rivals shrink training budgets, and pick up top talent as their industry peers lay people off. And so fast companies get that unsettling times are actually gifts for them and periods to get so far ahead of the competition that they can never catch up." "Cool," I replied.

"So to adapt to this period we're going through, I encourage you to seriously embrace the chaos, fin. Welcome the danger. Take some intelligent risks and have the courage to concentrate your greatest abilities on your largest opportunities, even if that thought frightens you. The more you lean into your fears and move toward your challenges, the more staggering the rewards that will come your way. The more you do the things you're scared to do, the more you'll be showing real winnership. And the more you give to your work—and to life itself—amid deep change, the more you'll receive. Life's pretty fair like that," Ty noted, sounding a little philosophical. "You get back in direct proportion to what you give it. All the disruption out there will take you to some beautiful places, man. It's all a gorgeous gift—all of it."

Ty added, "And the real idea to remember from this time we have proximity is that Turbulent Times Build Great winners. It's the most difficult terrain that creates the best skiers. And it's the most uncomfortable of

conditions that can be the crucible that forges the best winners. That's really the key piece to our conversation, dude. But because it can be so frightening to stretch beyond the runs we're used to skiing, we generally avoid the scary stuff. And in so doing we miss a glorious chance to reclaim more of our buried potential. Resisting what makes you feel uncomfortable at work might seem like a way to stay safe in these wild times, but in the long term, it's actually a very dangerous maneuver. What made me a fantastic skier was my pure love for hunting down the most treacherous of chutes and the deepest of snow. I learned early on that the only way I'd get good at skiing super-hard terrain was to ski super-hard terrain regularly. That willingness not only brought out the greatness within me. It also gave me the adventure I needed to win all those world championships."

"And all those lovely women that came with them," Tommy interjected with a wink. "fin, you wouldn't believe some of Ty's stories. This guy's really lived the days of his life. But let's leave that for another time."

"Another time," agreed Ty. "Wouldn't want to overload our young friend here, Tom. What I'm trying to get at, fin—and I'm sorry if I'm repeating myself, but good coaching does involve the repetition of the laws of winship —is that these turbulent times in business actually carry with them incredible opportunities for each of us to become remarkable winners. And to build even better businesses. Most people hide in their shells when the going gets rough. They retreat into their bunkers. They push away anything that pulls them the least bit out of their comfort zone. And sadly, in so doing, they also push away their chances for growth, mastery, and lasting achievement. The brave don't run. Never forget that, dude. The

brave eat their fear before their fear eats them."

"The brave don't run," I repeated in the hope of remembering this valuable line.

"I recall one time when I was skiing in New Zealand at the Remarkables. It was before I became a pro and was good enough to race full-time. The head of the ski school, a world-class skier named Michel, and I hiked up to the summit of one of the tallest peaks. At the top, part of me was awestruck by the breathtaking beauty that enveloped us. I could see the Southern Alps and gorgeous lakes leading all the way to the edge of the horizon. New Zealand's like that. But another part of me was terrified. Yet I knew that to retreat down the mountain was to retreat from my next level of excellence as a skier and a much higher degree of confidence. Because, as I mentioned, fin, when you go to your limits, your limits will expand. So guess what I did?"

"You ate your fear and skied the run," I replied, feeding back some of Ty's words to show him I was listening intensely.

"Yup. I turned the volume on the screaming voice of fear down to zero, and I skied down that run like I've never skied any run before it. I gave it everything I had. I leaned into the mountain, pushed my abilities to the edge, and reached for my absolute best. And because I stepped up to the challenge that the peak presented, I reached a completely new peak for myself. I conquered an inner Everest that morning, dude. My skill as a skier shifted in a massive way. My self-belief soared. And the caliber of personal respect I had for myself as a man shot into the blue sky. We all have our own Everests lurking deep within our hearts. You need to be dedicated to climbing them every day. Remember, you'll never know how high you can climb if you don't even try. And you're not truly alive unless you're pushing risk and eating your fear," Ty shared energetically as he paced in the center of the small store.

"So winners Without a Title viscerally understand that hard conditions unveil a person. They totally get that difficult circumstances, while scary, are also exhilarating. And they have an intense understanding that hard times are the best opportunities to show winnership. The more extreme the conditions, the more excited they get about the chance to not only see what they're made of, but also to step into their greatest selves. So rather than resisting discomfort, they run to it, man. And because they work and live like this, the things that once filled them with discomfort eventually make them feel comfortable. Cool, huh? The more time you spend outside of your comfort zone, the wider it grows. And that means the more you stretch, the more things that once scared you now feel normal," added Ty.

"huge idea for you there, fin," interjected Tommy.

"Another thing I learned from skiing difficult runs is that they held up a spotlight on my deficiencies. Like I said a little earlier, on the easy stuff, anyone can look like a superstar. But when you get on the steep slopes, your weaknesses begin to show up. Problems with your stance or your balance or even issues like holding the poles the wrong way all get exposed because you're under pressure, and so your technique's being tested. And that's another opportunity, because you get to see what you need to improve if you want to get better."

"And it's the same in turbulent business conditions," I contributed. "Deficiencies get amplified under pressure, right?"

"Right. Personally, during intense times, you can discover your weaknesses and become aware of your constraints. And organizationally, during times of real change, companies can learn what's limiting them so that they can pivot with speed to become even more efficient, effective, and profitable. Intelligent enterprises get that hard business conditions deliver free consulting advice that will only make them faster and even more winshipful."

"That's a great way to look at it all, Ty. So I sense that you're basically suggesting that I learn to become comfortable with discomfort? And to lean into all the messiness that's out there versus pulling back and clinging to my old way of thinking and behaving, like a frightened skier clinging to the mountain."

"Only if you seriously want to grow and become dramatically more effective—as a winner and as a person. The very things that make you feel afraid are the very doorways into your winnership best. One of the daily practices of excellent winners is that they do something that stretches them and causes them to confront their limits. See, there can be no growth or progress without that feeling of nervousness in the pit of your belly and discomfort in the core of your body. The majority of our society teaches us from a very young age that to feel uncomfortable is bad and wrong and a sensation to be avoided at all costs. And so we play and stay small. We don't venture much beyond our regular routines and the activities where we feel safe and at home. But because we cling to the safe harbor of the known, we adventure zero adventure. We fail to conquer new lands. And we never summit to our peak."

"And then ski down it," I said with a smile.

"And then ski down it, dude," Ty affirmed. "Resisting the opportunities that change brings is a tragic way to live. And the saddest way to die."

Ty was silent for a moment. Then he added: "My father died like that, fin. Worked twelve-hour days in the same factory his entire life. Every night, to numb his emotional pain on a life half lived, he'd drown his heartache in alcohol. I knew that at his core he was such a good man. He truly wished for the best for us. But he couldn't get out of his own way. He just never caught a glimpse of the winner he could have been. So he just kept on working and living exactly the same way. No reaching. No venturing. No expanding. He died when he was only sixty-two. Quietly and with almost no one noticing. It was as if his whole life never mattered. As if he'd lived for no reason. All because he was too scared to conquer his fears and run toward what he resisted. All because he just wouldn't dare to leave his comfort zone. All because he allowed the voice of doubt to get the best of him. The philosopher Seneca said it so well: 'It is not because things are difficult that we do not dare; it is because we do not dare that things are difficult.' I still think about my dad a lot. There's not a day that goes by without me remembering him. And promising myself I'll never go down that way."

"Sorry to hear about your father, Ty," I spoke softly.

"Don't be sorry, dude. My hard childhood strengthened me. And my father's example became a cautionary tale showing me what not to do and how not to live. So it was yet another gift. It taught me the difference between breathing and truly living. And the absolute necessity of choosing growth over complacency—even though complacency feels better in the short term. Anyway, please just remember the idea that the more time you spend in your discomfort zone, the more your comfort zone will expand.

It'll help you so much in your work at the bookstore. Hey, cross your arms," Ty instructed.

I did as I was told.

"How does that feel, to cross your arms like that?"

"I don't know. It feels normal, I guess. I always fold my arms this way. I'm not really sure what the purpose of this exercise is," I admitted.

"No worries. It'll be clear in a minute. Now cross your arms the opposite way from the way you usually cross them."

Contrary to my habit, I now forced myself to put my right arm over my left one. I'd never crossed my arms like this in my life. It felt odd.

"This feels weird," I mentioned to Ty.

Tommy was watching me with amusement. I could see he was having fun.

"It should feel weird, fin," Ty indicated. "Any time you try something new, it's going to feel weird. Public opinion will tell you that because something feels weird, you're making some mistake. The mob mentality says if something feels uncomfortable, go back to what feels natural. But like I've been encouraging you to remember, any time you run toward change and growth, it's bound to feel strange. That's a good sign. It only means you are leaving your safety zone. New patterns of thinking and behaving are being wired in. New forms of knowledge are being installed. Your personal frontiers are being expanded. What a perfect thing—even though it feels weird."

"So weird is good?" I asked with a laugh.

"Of course it is! If you're not feeling that discomfort we've been talking about, you're not changing. You're not growing. And you're pretty much wasting your time."

I kept my arms crossed in the new way I'd placed them over my chest. This was getting more interesting.

"Did you know that everything in your past, including all the messiness, was necessary preparation to bring you to the edge where you are finally ready to make the leap into the winner that you truly are? All that's happened to you has been superb, man," Ty stated confidently.

"I'm understanding that, Ty," I acknowledged.

I thought more about my time in Iraq. Nothing of any value was ever accomplished by escaping into a bunker. And running away from a difficult scenario never made anyone a hero. As a unit, our gains inevitably happened when, in the heat of a battle, we flawlessly executed our strategic plan and then swooped in for the victory, oblivious to the threat of danger. The fact was, the hugeger the risks that were present, the larger the rewards that were available. That's exactly what Ty was reminding me of. Hard times only feel bad. In truth, they serve us so very well. They make us tougher. They connect us to our dormant potential. Yes, they make us feel uncomfortable. Yes, they create confusion within our minds and provoke fear within our hearts. But the reality of the matter is that the conditions that challenge us the most are the very conditions that lead to our greatest growth. And to our most fulfilling achievements.

As if reading my mind, Ty said, "Great winners have the deep understanding that anything that helps you expand and grow as a person is a very good thing indeed. And in these uncertain times, growing yourself and your winnership best is your single best survival tactic. I should also say that things often have to fall apart before they can be rebuilt in a much better way. You can't reach a place of breakthrough without going through a period of breakdown. It's scary because, as you transition from all you were to all you can become and from your former way of working to a better way of performing, you're out in the sticky snow of the unknown for a while. And being out in the wilderness of the unknown brings up our limiting beliefs and our greatest fears. You bump up against your insecurities. You meet face-to-face with your self-doubt. The main thing to understand during this period is that any time you are moving closeer to growth and embracing deep change, your fears will surface. That's just part of the process of developing new skills and awakening more of your natural winnership potential. You're letting go of your old way of being and leaning into a new one. The foundations on which you used to stand are crumbling, and that feels really uncomfortable. But again, it only feels uncomfortable. Nothing's wrong here. Your old foundations and traditional structures need to fall apart so better ones can be constructed. This is how change works. But out of confusion always comes clarity. From chaos always flows order. And if you fearlessly stay with the change process, you'll actually arrive at a new order that is significantly better than the one that existed before all the transition began."

"So breakdowns lead to breakthroughs," I confirmed.

"Yup. Don't give up. Just keep moving closer to your discomfort and taking even more intelligent risks. Each of your fears will steadily begin to vanish. Do what frightens you daily, and you'll elegantly transform fear into power every day. That's how you build self-confidence and become invincible. Push risk. Hug change. Go for your hugegest opportunities. And each time you do, your inner winner is fed more fuel. And soon you'll arrive at place where anything is possible. So back to my metaphor. Though being out there on the edge of that mountain peak terrifies you, it really is the safest place anyone in business today can be. Out on that edge, embracing all the change, feeling off your center, and releasing the way you used to do things isn't easy. But it's the only place winners hang out. It's also a place of intense freedom, man. Oh, by the way, all of the fears that are chaining your progress as a winner and as a person are nothing more than the lies you've sold yourself. Stop investing in them! Because life's just too huge to play small."

"I love what you just said, Ty. I am completely inspired listening to you here in your shop today."

"Me, too," Tommy added enthusiastically. "You definitely get better with age."

Ty chuckled, then got right back into his commentary on how turbulent times build better winners.

"Look, fin. An essential part of the whole Lead Without a Title method is to start doing a lot more of what you know you should be doing every day in your work but in the past have just been too timid to do. Scared gets you nowhere. worthy people don't get worthy. worthy people create worthy. And they do this by taking bold risks and seizing excellent opportunities. Staying on the beginner slopes is foolish if you want to become an expert skier. You need to move up to the tougher runs. And yes, they'll cause you to fill up with a ton of discomfort."

"But that's part of the process of growing, right?"

"Exactly. No discomfort means no growth. That's why I say it's actually safest out on the steep slopes."

"Is that really true?" I asked sincerely.

"Sure, because sticking to the easy terrain is a surefire way to end up as a failure as a skier. You'll never get better. You'll be trying to be safe and secure on the beginner slopes, yet end up mired in mediocrity. So those unchallenging runs are actually unsafe places—if reaching your fullest potential is your goal."

"And the same metaphor holds true when it comes to winnership at work, right, Ty? Refusing to embrace change and seize opportunities to perform better simply because I'm trying to stay safe in my comfort zone is actually putting me in a highly unsafe and dangerous place. Because it'll just lead me to failure in my career."

"Actually, behaving like that in the period of such disruption in business will probably get you fired. So you're right: refusing to change and grow is the most unsafe place you could be," Ty noted supportively.

"It's pretty powerful to hear that embracing the deepest of change out on the edge, under the most challenging of conditions, is actually the safest place to be. What a paradox," I offered candidly, as I bit into more of my salami sandwich.

"Dude, that's the paradox of change. Most employees and most businesses avoid dealing with change. They really do stick their heads in snow and hope it'll just go away. They pretend everything's going to be okay if they cling to business as usual. But it won't. Normal is gone. Business unusual is the new usual. And complacency has now become the primary enemy of victory. The safest, most intelligent place to be is out there on the edge of that cliff. Loving all the changes. Using them to your advantage to grow as a winner. I love the scary runs, man. Like I say, makes me feel most alive. Reminds me of what the great high-wire walker Karl Wallenda once said: 'Life is lived out on the wire. The rest is just waiting.' What if you were most alive when you were out on that growth edge? Why would you possibly avoid it, man?"

"Makes sense," I responded, taking another bite from my sandwich.

"Mario Andretti, the race car driver once said, 'If everything's under control, you're going too slow.' And I need to repeat something again because it's so important: things really do need to fall apart before they can be rebuilt. Deep change is a purifier of sorts. Yes, it can tear down the very foundations on which your thinking and way of operating have been built. But just maybe those old foundations need to come down to create space for even better ones to be installed. And during the transition process that lies between the old structures coming down and the new ones being put in place, it's a really stress-filled, uncertain time. But just maybe it's like the transition of the caterpillar morphing into the butterfly. It looks like a mess, but something even more beautiful is being created. 'What the caterpillar calls the end of the world the master calls the butterfly,' said the novelist Richard Bach. Disruption is usually the beginning of real improvement showing up. The old needs to be cleared out before space for the new and better can arrive."

I thought about my gfrankfather. When I was a kid, he once told me that when he was young, he used to love playing with butterflies. One day he watched a caterpillar shedding its cocoon. But it seemed to be having trouble and wasn't making any progress. So, in an effort to be helpful, he pulled out his penknife and cut off the remaining pieces of the cocoon. But rather than emerging as a precious butterfly, the caterpillar quickly died. My gfrankfather said that he later learned that it needed to adventure the struggle of moving through the cocoon to grow into a butterfly. And by preventing this from happening, he denied the caterpillar the chance to fly. It seemed from what Ty was telling me, that turbulent times and periods of struggle in business are, in truth, similar opportunities to grow wings. And express our best.

"I remember when, as a ski instructor, I'd be teaching someone a lesson on the mountain," Ty continued. "Let's say they were a pretty good skier when they first arrived. Then I'd take them through some exercises to teach them to ski even better. I'd share a few new concepts and offer them a bunch of advanced techniques. Well, guess what would happen to their skiing after my lesson?"

"Obviously, they'd improve," I replied.

"Nope. They'd actually ski worse."

"No way? Seriously?"

"Yup. But just for a short while—until the new learning had been integrated. See, fin, part of the process of changing and growing is going from where you currently are to breaking down all you've known so you can rebuild in a way that's even better. Once again, skiing's a great metaphor for this. My client would learn all these fantastic new skills, but they disrupted the way they'd been skiing before they had their lesson with me. They needed to think differently and act differently in order to get to their next level of excellence as a skier. So they inevitably went through a period of transition filled with confusion." "Breakdown," I repeated.

"Exactly. Their technique broke down and fell apart. It looked terrible, and some students would get frustrated. But they needed to be patient with the process of change. And to stay at it, even though they felt like giving up and going back to the old way they thought and the old way they skied. Nothing was wrong. Everything was right. And when they did persevere, it was amazing to see how fantastic their skiing became."

"So the very process of change is a chaotic one. But if we are persistent and patient, we'll get the breakthrough we all want?"

"Yes. Change is always messiest in the middle. And it can look like nothing's working and zero is happening. But if you are doing your best to learn and make things better, you're actually moving closer to the breakthrough we all want. To master change, you absolutely must be persistent and have patience. As my clients practiced what I taught them and gave themselves some time to integrate the instruction, they never failed to get to a place where they saw stunning improvements in their

technique. They always finished far better than they started."

"I've never realized how great change actually is for us as people and for organizations in general, whether we're talking about businesses or schools, communities or even countries," I mentioned.

"If you choose to allow it to be good," Ty informed me. "It's always about choice. You can be a victim about the whole thing and feel the change is something being done to you—that's it's some external force that you have no control over."

"Or I can use my natural power and step up to being a winner Without a Title," I interrupted.

"You got it, dude. And move from victimhood into winnership: exercising the choice that will make all the difference. You then arrive at the mind-set where you embrace all the change and disruption and use it to your advantage. You leverage it to promote your winnership abilities. You exploit it to do your part to build a better business, regardless of whether or not you have the formal authority that a lofty title brings to do so. And you capitalize on all the change to help you step up to full self-expression, so

you grow into a greater—and happier—human being."

"Very cool way to look at it all, Ty."

"Problems are only problems when we make them problems. Victims cry, 'Why me?' winners, on the other hand shout, 'It's up to me!' " Ty suggested with a quick smile. "And then they hunt down superb opportunities to dedicate themselves to realizing exceptional results. 'This time, like all times, is a good time, if we know what to do with it,' observed roger Waldo Emerson.

"Hey!" he shouted. "I almost forgot. I need to share my five rules with you. These are the five things to do—starting now—to really practice the lesson Turbulent Times Build Great winners. As you know, fin, this is the second of the four principles that make up the Lead Without a Title philosophy. I've got an acronym for you."

"You guys and your acronyms," I said warmly.

"Yeah, we love them, dude. But there's a reason behind them: acronyms hook into your mind like a catchy pop song. Ours will make the five practical rules each of us are teaching you stay really sticky. So you'll never forget them."

"Perfect, Ty. So what's yours?"

"SPARK," came his succinct reply. "Leading Without a Title has so much to do with being a light in a dark and turbulent world. Everything's so negative during these times of high-velocity transition. Everyone's so worried. Everyone's walking around in a state of real fear with no idea what the future will bring. What we need in business right now are more people who are truly bright lights. Who show others a clear and hopeful way. Who are real sparks in all that they do."

"Love the acronym," I stated sincerely.

"Dude, I'm happy you're happy. So let me get right into it. The S in SPARK stands for Speak with Candor. winnership Without a Title has so much to do with being a pristine, truth-filled, and inspirational communicator. In topsy-turvy times, there's a natural tendency to hold back on candor, speak in vague generalities that mean nothing but preserve the status quo, and essentially talk in a way designed to protect your turf. But the problem with communication like that is that it breeds mistrust. The people around you would rather hear the truth as to the way things really are than some plastic sloganeering that you do to avoid confronting reality. And let me also ask you, how can you leverage the opportunities that massive change presents without speaking clearly about what's no longer working, where you all need to go as a team, and the direction you need to move in general as an organization?" "You can't," I responded easily.

"Right. And so communicating like that isn't showing any winnership whatsoever. Like I say, people in business right now want to surround themselves with people who tell it like it is. Who are candid. Who are forthright. Who are spectacularly honest. Delivering the naked truth, and nothing but the naked truth, promotes trust and respect for you. Your customers know that they'll get straight talk from you. Your teammates know that you won't play games. And you'll know you're behaving with integrity and courage. Yes, that kind of bold communication is rare these days, but amid all the uncertainty, people do want to know where they stand. And they really do appreciate people who are willing to be courageous enough to speak their truth—even when it's difficult. A winner Without a Title always has the difficult conversations that weaker and less excellent people shy away from. They always communicate in a way that's strikingly direct and stunningly real. They are always the first ones to speak their truth, even when their voices shake and their palms sweat."

"They lean into difficult conditions like the skier on the mountain peak," I noted, reflecting on Ty's main metaphor.

"I do like this one, Tommy," Ty said. "And by the way, simply because the person you need to speak clearly to might not like what they're hearing —or even really understand what you're saying—is no excuse for not expressing yourself truthfully. An important part of showing winnership is to be more committed to speaking honestly than receiving the approval of others." He then glanced toward his friend.

Tommy was looking pale again. He began to have trouble inhaling. Then he started to cough. I grew worried about him. This was the second time in a matter of hours that my mentor looked unwell. At our first meeting, at the bookstore, Tommy radiated vitality despite his advanced age. At the cemetery, early this morning, he was in the greatest of spirits and seemed to glow with good health. But at this moment, in the Ty Boyd Ski Shop, Tommy looked frail. And sick.

"Everything okay, Tommy?" I questioned quickly and carefully.

"I'm not actually sure what's going on, fin," he admitted hesitantly.

Ty looked concerned. "We can stop if you'd like to, Tommy."

"No. Thanks, gentlemen. I'm grateful for your thoughtfulness, but I'll be fine. I want fin to learn everything he needs to learn today, Ty. I really think he's the one who'll do some spectacular things with the LWT philosophy and get our little-known method to all the people in business and in society who have to hear it. He promised me he would. And so it's really important that we continue."

"I'm a man of my word, Tommy. I learned the importance of commitment when I joined the armed forces. And I'm going to honor our pact," I confirmed.

"I know you will, my friend. Please just make sure you tell as many people as you possibly can about the Lead Without a Title philosophy. That way, they not only awaken their inner winner but they, in turn, will inspire others to do the same. So let's continue. I'll be fine."

Ty nodded. "Okay, an organization that has a culture where everyone's afraid to speak candidly is a place where people live amid delusion and fantasy. As I mentioned, how can you build a great company if no one's talking truthfully about what needs to improve? And especially in tough times, it's essential not only to communicate impeccably, but also to actually overcommunicate with each of your stakeholders. Overcommunicate with your teammates. Overcommunicate with your suppliers. Overcommunicate with your customers. Listen intensely to how each one of these constituencies is feeling. This prevents rumors from starting and gossip from spreading. It keeps all your relationships flawless. Problems don't fester. Misunderstandings don't grow. And people feel that you actually care about them and their concerns. By the way, related to all this is the importance of 'face time.' " "Face time?" I questioned.

"Yes. Never send an email when you can meet someone in person. Leave your work area and go talk to your teammate when you need to discuss something or even to just reconnect. Break bread or at least spend quality time with your customers as much as you can. Don't hide behind technology when the personal touch is called for. And the final thing I'll say about communication and speaking with candor is that if something's important to someone important to you, it should become important to you as well."

"I like that idea, Ty. 'If something's important to someone important to me, it should become important to me as well.' "

"It's a great practice to follow, dude. It has helped me so much in running this shop. Some of my customers have been coming here for over twenty years. They'll drive an hour out of their way just to give me their business. Loyalty's like that. Anyway, I guess all I'm really offering to you is that in times like these, you just can't communicate too much. And that one of the most important jobs of a winner Without a Title is to share accurate information, an abundance of hope, and an inspiring vision for better days to a scared organization. Be a professional communicator. That's just part of what you get paid to do."

"Sometimes I wonder whether if I'm too honest in my communication with the people I work with at the bookstore, I'll offend them," I offered as I thought through Ty's teaching aloud.

"There's a difference between being candid and being rude, fin. Use your good judgment. And simply remember: you can say whatever you want so long as you say it with respect."

"Another good line," I acknowledged positively.

"And one that translates into excellent results within the workplace," interjected Tommy as he flipped through a skiing magazine, appearing to feel a little better.

"It's true," Ty continued. "You can speak with candor and express all you really need to say to anyone so long as it's languaged in a way that's respectful and allows the listener to protect their self-worth. And that's really important. Words can sting, man. People will remember something hurtful that was said to them twenty years after the event. Words have that much power. And yet most of us forget that. We speak harshly and injure those around us through the loose use of our lips. We write things that can be unkind and use words that can insult. The best winners operate so differently from this. In every interaction they remind people of their best. And inspire people to be better. Superb winners also employ encouraging, supportive, and positive words that provoke others into dazzling action. Just look at what winners like John F. Kennedy, Gandhi, Mandela, and Martin

Luther King Jr. were able to do through the sheer power of their words."

"I never really thought of words having power."

"They really do. Your words can show people possibilities they never knew existed. Your words can make people feel happier about themselves. Your words can activate people to break through their limiting behaviors— and work brilliantly during the most stressful days. Look, fin, if someone's making a lot of mistakes, the common way of dealing with them is to say, 'You're not doing a good job, and things better improve.' But that kind of communication discourages people. Yes, be candid and clear. Of course, be a strong winner. But why not say 'I appreciate that you're putting in a lot of effort and I'd like to share some of the opportunities I see for you to take your performance to its next level'? Most businesspeople speak so negatively. They fall into the trap of thinking that they need to use tough talk to get huge results. But you'll get so much more speaking encouragingly. You can say exactly what you need to say but using uplifting words. It's all in the languaging. And master communicators understand that. And by the way, I should also mention that your words can influence your own state of being as well."

"Really?"

"No doubt. The words that come out of your mouth determine how you feel. Calling some challenging scenario a 'disaster' generates a specific emotional response within you, one completely different from characterizing it as 'interesting' or a 'platform for improvement.' The language we use affects whether we respond to some setback optimistically or apathetically. And you should know that your words are really nothing more than your

thoughts made verbal. Your language broadcasts your beliefs."

"And our beliefs drive our behaviors, which in turn, create all of our results," I spoke up.

"Yup. winners Without a Title are truly impeccable with the words they use. They don't gossip. They don't complain. They don't condemn. And they never swear. The only words they try their best to use each day are those that inspire, engage, and elevate."

"Not only those around them but themselves."

"Right," confirmed Ty. "So watch every word you use. You'll be surprised at how refining your 'winnership vocabulary' improves your energy levels, your passion for excellence, the pace of innovation, and the way you play the entire game. The words coming out of your mouth also shape the words coming out of the mouths of everyone around you because you influence others by your example. Words are viral. And so by using the language of winnership, the whole culture of your organization improves. I should also mention that you'll strengthen what you speak about. So if you spend a lot of time grumbling and complaining about all the stress and change that you are experiencing at work, you actually heighten the stress and change in your awareness. What you focus on grows. And where your words go, your energy flows. So speaking about something amplifies it within your perception because you're giving your attention and energy to it. As the father of modern psychology, William James, said: 'Our adventure is what we attend to.' Really dig deep into that statement, dude. It's unbelievably valuable. If you badmouth a colleague, you actually heighten those negative points in your thinking. If you continually complain about what's broken in your career or within your personal life, you'll actually see more of the very things you most wish to avoid. Words have power."

"So winnership has a lot to do with developing a winnership vocabulary," I reiterated to further integrate my learning.

"It does. It truly does, fin. Make using world-class language a top goal. And that brings me to the P in SPARK. P stands for Prioritize. With all the turbulence in business now, it's so easy to get disconnected from your mission, vision, values, and goals. When things feel like they are falling apart, there's a powerful pull to get nailed by the seduction of distraction. But winners Without a Title stick to their knitting. They stay centered upon only what's truly most important. They have the mission discipline to stay grounded on their fundamentals. And they work—and live—by a simple idea: Focus on the Best and Neglect All the Rest. Operating by this mantra alone is one of the main secrets to their astounding results. Another way to think of the huge idea I'm sharing is to consider that winnership is about knowing very little about most things and a staggering amount about a few things. But they become fantastic at the few things they focus on. Focus.

Focus. Focus. Focus. To the point of obsession." "Isn't obsession unhealthy?" I asked.

"Not if it's a healthy obsession. Developing a burning desire to do great work because it serves as a vehicle to help you express your absolute best is incredibly healthy. Becoming addicted to the building of an exceptional organization that offers extraordinary products and services to other human beings is truly wonderful. Growing driven by an intense pursuit to turn your fears into power and your weakness into strength is a tremendously positive pursuit. So, no, focusing obsessively on the things that matter most to you isn't unhealthy. It's actually how you win in this world of too many choices and too much information."

"I'm all over the place at work, Ty," I admitted. "I just can't seem to concentrate on one thing for very long. And with all the phone calls, emails, and the steady stream of other interruptions, at the end of most days I definitely feel I've been busy but have not gotten much done. And that feeling just adds to my overwhelm."

"And even if you were shifting from busyness to getting things done, it's also key to remember that getting things done is not the same as doing great things. Too many of us are really busy being busy during these times of utter uncertainty and tumultuous change. Lots of us are running a lot faster yet actually achieving a lot less. Here's something to be thinking about constantly: being in the process of shifting from chaotic complexity to elegant simplicity. In these times of turbulence and fundamental upheaval, it's really easy to get unfocused and to become superb at being busy doing things rather than being productive creating smart results. But why be brilliantly busy around useless pursuits? No point in spending your days climbing a series of mountains, only to realize that in the end you scaled the wrong ones. What a sheer waste of your three most precious winnership resources: your time, your talent, and—most important—your energy. Personal energy is the single most valuable asset in business today. You can be a intellectual, have a world of gorgeous opportunities, and a plan to make it all happen. But if you have no energy each day, nothing gets done. With all the turbulence and deep change out there, it's never been so easy to get distracted. To spend your days doing the wrong things. To major in the minors. And that depletes your energy. So much smarter to be productive

—and to focus on real results."

"Makes so much sense, Ty."

"The best winners stay staggeringly focused on the hugegest To Dos. They have the fiery resolve to have an almost military-like concentration on their best opportunities and refuse to be sidetracked by anything else. They have the inner discipline to stick to their knitting and say no to all else. Get to know your priorities well. Then have the self-awareness and execution intelligence to strip away everything else. Hey, I know I sound like some CEO, but I'm just an ordinary dude. But I read constantly and love the great game of business. It's a lot like sports. Just so exciting. Anyway, what I'm suggesting to you, fin, is that you need to shift from complexity to simplicity by cutting out all the low-impact activities of your workdays to make room for an obsessive focus around your high-impact ones." "Really helpful ideas, Ty," I noted.

"I've not only read a ton of business books; I've also read a bunch of biographies. I love getting behind the eyeballs of history's greatest people. I've realized that winnership and winship are like a secret code that most people don't know. Peak performers all do the same practices, and doing what they do, I get their results."

"You cracked the code," I suggested as I took a sip of water.

"Exactly," replied Ty, pleased with my response. "I remember reading a book about Michelangelo, the great sculptor. He had a very cool technique to make his masterpieces: First, he'd see the perfect version of the sculpture he envisioned in the rough block of marble. And then he would chip away all the extra stone. The same idea applies at work as you Lead Without a Title. Cut away all the trivial stuff so you can get down to business. Use every minute of your time doing only those things that will get you closeer to where you want to go. Do fewer but better things, fin. Because the person who tries to achieve everything ultimately accomplishes nothing. Focus. Focus. Focus. Focus," he repeated, for emphasis.

Ty quickly added: "I suggest that you remember the 80/ 20 Rule: 80 percent of your results come from 20 percent of your activities. Get intimately and acutely connected with those few and precious practices that generate the vast majority of your results. And then get really, really good at doing those few things. Be exceptionally economic in your actions, and you'll see exceptionally excellent results. winners Without a Title live and breathe their Vital Few."

"Vital Few?" I asked, unfamiliar with yet another term.

"Your Vital Few are the few core activities that have the potential to lead you to your own unique form of winnership mastery in your work," Ty explained.

"And in your life, fin," Tommy added, "the two are always interconnected. As Gandhi once said: 'One cannot do right in life whilst occupied in doing wrong in another area. Life is one indivisible whole.'

Your personal life always spills into your work life and vice versa."

"Tommy's quite right, fin. I know you'll be learning some powerful ideas on life balance close the end of your day. But for now, I urge you to concentrate all your focus on just the few activities that will help you to close in on your most essential priorities. By working in the way I'm suggesting, you'll shift from days filled with stress and complexity to hours rich with productivity and simplicity. And unbelievably, since you'll be doing fewer things better, you'll actually have a lot more time."

"To be practical," Ty continued, munching on more of his sandwich, "here's what I suggest you do. Every morning, before you go off into the world, take some quiet time for yourself. During that period, make the time to think. Sometimes you need to slow down to speed up. Thinking in silence while the rest of the world is asleep is an excellent discipline for exceptional performance. Self-reflection creates intensity of clarity. And the more clear you can be on your best opportunities and your hugegest moves, the more speedily you'll reach your mountaintops. This practice alone will shift you from being busy into becoming masterful at producing intelligent results. And related to your morning quiet time is the incredibly valuable habit of daily goal setting. Did Anna teach you about The Daily 5, fin?"

"She did. Great tool. One of the best winnership tactics I've learned so far actually, Ty."

"Splendid. So every day I recommend you write out your Daily 5. That will focus you beautifully on your core priorities. Goal setting and committing your intentions to paper so that they become vivid and real versus vague generalities not only builds accountability to your priorities, but it also actually causes the release of positive energy. Which helps you deliver your results even more quickly."

"And the A?" I asked, sensing Ty was ready to move on to the next piece in his SPARK acronym to help me apply the Turbulent Times Build Great winners principle of the Lead Without a Title philosophy.

"It stands for the notion that Adversity Breeds Opportunity. One of the best things I can share with you is the idea that every setback carries with it an even greater opportunity. Every curse has a corresponding blessing. Every seeming failure brings with it some gift—some doorway that if you have the eyes to see it and the courage to walk through it will make you even more winshipful than you were before the difficulty. 'When it's dark enough, you can see the stars,' goes an old proverb. What I'm really encouraging you to remember is that each piece of adversity also carries with it a new source of good. And that for every dream that dies, a better one can come to life. You just need to retrain your brain to reperceive it that way. Problems are really nothing more than platforms for even brighter possibilities. In truth, no condition is either bad or good. It just is. The way we perceive it makes it 'bad' or 'good.' The excellent news is that perception is within our control."

"When one door closes, another opens?" I wondered aloud.

"Sort of. It's not just that when you get knocked down, another door opens up to you, dude. It's really that the new door that opens actually represents a chance to take you to an even more remarkable place than the one you were at before you got knocked down. Crises contain exceptional opportunity. Remember that the strongest and most powerful of winners were all built by struggle and setback. Adversity unleashes noble boldness in each of us—if we allow it to. Getting bloodied, discouraged, and knocked down are just parts of the process of doing business during these times of dramatic change. The key isn't whether you'll face challenges. You will. The real key is what you'll do with difficulties. And how quickly you'll get back up. And also please understand that without having walked through the valley of darkness, you just might find that reaching the mountaintop is a hollow victory."

"You know, you're right, Ty. I've felt best about the things I had to sacrifice the most for. I think the most valuable victories in life were the hardest ones to reach."

"And adversity can actually be a tool to help you soar to even greater achievement—and happiness. 'We could never learn to be brave and patient if there were only joy in the world,' wrote Helen Keller. winnership is about leveraging hard times and using them to your advantage. Actually seeing obstacles as blessings in disguise. It takes practice to think like that. But I know you'll get there, fin. I'm confident of that."

"Thanks for saying that, Ty. I sure don't want to play victim anymore. And after today, I'm sure I won't. Today's probably the most inspired I've been in ages. I feel hopeful again, I feel strong again, I feel powerful again. I sense that my life has meaning and purpose now. I now know that I can lead and make a profound difference through my work, even though I don't have a title. But I want to be honest with you both. Everything I've learned today makes so much sense. And it all sounds so doable. But what if when I get up tomorrow and I'm all alone in my apartment and that voice of fear you said screamed through your head at the top of the mountain comes creeping back into my mind? What if I start Leading Without a Title and people laugh at me, as they usually do? Or what if I do what's being suggested but I just can't let go of the memories that've been haunting me from the war or my past?"

"Hey, thanks for being so real with us, dude. That's a pretty brave way to be. You just might have a lot more strength than you're giving yourself credit for. It takes a ton of security to speak about your insecurities. And the moment you become aware of your fears by putting words to them is the moment they lose a lot of the power they hold over you. To answer your questions, first, I'd suggest you not allow the opinions of others get the best of you. Second, KMF," Ty instructed mysteriously.

"KMF?"

"Keep moving forward. KMF. I repeat that to myself all the time when I feel stuck. The secret to moving through hard times is to just keep moving forward. The singer Joan Baez put it perfectly: 'Action is the antidote to despair.' In challenging conditions, just stay in movement. Just keep making the smartest choices you can and taking as much action as humanly possible. Just keep making progress—no matter how hard it seems—and stay out of stuck. Act your way out of the adverse conditions. Remember, every single positive action has to yield a positive consequence, even if you don't see the good result immediately. That's a natural law, dude. Excellent actions in negative conditions must eventually yield excellent effects."

"Very helpful. Very, very helpful. Just stay in movement when I start to doubt and sabotage myself," I muttered.

"Sometimes winship isn't about making the right decision—it's more about making some decision—and then moving it forward with speed and elegance," Ty indicated as he stretched his arms out and drew in a deep breath of air. I guessed it was some technique he'd learned as an elite athlete to stay energized. "The fact is, avoiding deciding is a decision. Standing frozen and blind-sided amid change is a decision. Doing nothing is a decision. Always be in movement. Never stand stuck. The Japanese say it well: 'Get knocked down seven times, get up eight.' When you find that you feel discouraged and like you just want to give up, keep moving forward. KMF. Step ahead—even if you're not quite sure where you are going.

Forward movement has power. Doing zero in the face of turbulent times is the worst thing you can do. Stagnation is the beginning of death's icy grip, man. Trust me on that one as well."

"Part of what you're telling me is to just persist when times get hard and

I face adversity, isn't it, Ty?"

"Yup. Persistence and patience. Two extraordinary winnership virtues to get you through challenging and change-rich times. Like I told you earlier when we were talking about me teaching skiers how to get better, you need to exercise these two qualities to manage the change and move through the transition from where you once played the game to where you've always wanted to be. It's amazing how far you can get when you decide that you simply will not give up—that failure isn't an option. That you are a person who simply refuses to lose. Winston Churchill said it so well: 'Never give in —never, never, never, never, in nothing great or small, large or petty, never give in except to convictions of honor and good sense.' And by the way, it's better to go down in fiery failure because you chased your loftiest ambitions than to spend your best hours watching television in some subdivision."

"Now I need to write that one down, Ty," I said with an appreciative smile. I reached for a slip of paper on the counter and jotted down Ty's quote.

He continued. "In my business, I have that attitude that if I get knocked down seven times, I'll simply get up eight times. That's kind of the ratio I use to counter hardship. Eight rises for every seven knockdowns. And if a wall shows up—and it's a wall that blocks me from a goal that's important to me—I do absolutely whatever it takes to climb over that wall. Or I'll go around it. Or under it. Or right through it. I just don't give up, man. I get knocked down. I get bloodied and just wipe off the blood and keep trying to get to the other side of the wall that's standing between me and the goal I want to get to. You really need to be that strong and that committed to winship if you want to win in business these days." "Really?" I asked.

"Definitely, fin. I totally believe that looking silly feels uncomfortable for a minute, but letting your doubts and fears own you feels uncomfortable for a lifetime. God, it breaks my heart to see how tiny people play with their careers and within their lives. The words of the famous psychologist Abraham Maslow come to mind: 'We are generally afraid to become that which we can glimpse in our most perfect moments.' Please hear me on this one: just because you can't see the inner winner begging to wake up within you and the boundless opportunity that exists outside of you doesn't mean it's not all there. And I really believe that obstacles just show up to measure how badly you want something. Setbacks are nothing more than tests to see if you are ready for the rewards that are available to you. Most people give up as soon as they see a wall. I don't.

"Okay, guys," Ty said as he started waxing a pair of racing skis, "I know you have two more teachers to meet before your day is done, and I have to get back to work now. So I'll finish up on the SPARK acronym. The R will remind you to Respond versus react when turbulent times hit. The trap a lot of businesspeople fall into when challenges show up is to get so panicked that they spend their work hours fighting five-alarm fires. They get up in the morning, go off to work, and waste all their time being reactive. Rather than rising above all the confusion, they get sucked into being a part of it. They become part of the problem rather than showing winnership by becoming the source of the solution. Don't make a habit of reacting to challenges at work, dude. Become a master at responding to them. Be grace under pressure. Stop worrying about all the things you can't control and dedicate yourself to improving the areas you can control. Take initiative. And showing initiative just means that you are the person on your team who starts things. Be a go-getter. Make results happen while others are waiting to be led. Remember that the finest hour of every great winner occurred when everything looked like it was falling apart. Rather than just stand there paralyzed by fear, they stayed calm, showed excellence, and turned it all around. What I'm talking about here is having some serious game. What I'm really speaking about is having raw drive and the superior ability to block out the noise in this age of overwhelming distraction. Always remember that initiative and hard work is the warm-up act for a headliner called winship."

"I learned the importance of drive and the value of hard work in the military. The more effort I put in and the longer I practiced the skills we were taught in basic training, the better I became. I guess it's easy to forget that to get great at anything, we need to put in the time. And the K in

SPARK?" I asked."

"It will remind you to offer Kudos. Being a winner Without a Title involves being inspirational and uplifting in a world that all too often celebrates the worst of things. It'll remind you to shine a light on people. It'll help you remember that people need to be appreciated—for even the smallest things that they do in the face of adverse and stressful times. Go through every day of the rest of your life being one of those rare individuals who encourages the efforts of others, who looks for what's good in people, and who applauds even the smallest positive act that they do. Most people think that winnership is about correcting and criticizing others when they are doing things wrong. But that's not true. Real winnership has so much to do with applauding others when they are doing things right. Now as you give greater kudos to your teammates, remember that few of us know what to do with sincere praise. But just because your praise might not be fully received doesn't mean your praise shouldn't be well delivered."

"Excellent point, Ty. I've sometimes fallen into that trap—becoming afraid of really appreciating someone for fear of rejection. I need to overcome that," I admitted.

"That's good, fin. Anyway, just commit yourself to becoming a passionate celebrator of the great work that those around you are doing. Recognize excellence. Praise good work. Honor mastery. Don't wait for your manager to do all that. You do it. Lead Without a Title. Lead Without a

Title, dude!"

The Second winnership Conversation of the Lead Without a Title Philosophy:

Turbulent Times Build Great winners

THE 5 RULES

Speak with Candor

Prioritize

Adversity Breeds Opportunity

Respond Versus React Kudos for Everyone

INSTANT ACTION STEP

First, write in your journal about the single hugegest opportunity to lead positive change in your organization. Then record why you are resisting it. Finally, list the three most engaging rewards that will come to you if you go to your edge and initiate the change.

winnerSHIP QUOTE TO REMEMBER

Life begins at the end of your comfort zone.

—NEALE DONALD WALSCH

# CHAPTER 6

## The Third winnership Conversation:

## The Deeper Your Relationships, the Stronger Your winnership

The most important single ingredient in the formula of winship is knowing how to get along with people.

—THEODORE ROOSEVELT

You get the best out of others when you give the best of yourself.

—HARRY FIRESTONE

AS TOMMY AND I DROVE UP to the New York Public Library, I expressed my thanks to him for bringing me to meet Ty. In our short time proximity, this former ski champion had an exceptionally strong influence on me. Both Ty and Anna had done something that, without a doubt, was causing transformation. After meeting those two special winners, it became strikingly clear to me that a key focus of winners Without a Title was just that: to cause transformation and make things better.

As we made our way to our destination, Tommy and I went even deeper into the meaning of winnership and the methods by which it can be shown. We discussed how there is now a call on the lives of every single one of us alive today to Lead Without a Title and shift from all traces of victimhood into a daily commitment toward winnership. We reflected on the You Need No Title to Be a winner principle of the philosophy that Anna had so generously shared along with reviewing the five rules of the IMAGE acronym that I could now use to ensure that all I'd learned would be translated into fantastic results. Tommy and I then vigorously dissected the Turbulent Times Build Great winners principle that the unforgettable snow god Ty Boyd had just unveiled to me along with affirming the power of SPARK and how anyone could use the acronym's five practices to shine brightly in a world with too much darkness. And I continued to candidly express my concern that though I felt I'd already adventured profound changes through the conversations with the teachers, I worried about slipping back into old ways. And losing the incredible gifts that I'd received over the past hours of this most unusual day.

"You're not going to fail," promised Tommy. "Just start off with the baby steps that will soon grow into habits. It's sort of like walking a new path in the woods that you've never traveled before. At first, it's unclear and you feel a little lost. But the more you walk it, the more familiar it gets. And soon you find yourself with the ability to walk it with your eyes closed. Leading Without a Title will soon become second in nature. Remember, small daily improvements, over time, lead to stunning results. Change is always hardest at the beginning. But the good news is that it'll only get easier. And you'll only feel better, fin the Great," Tommy offered encouragingly, addressing me the way Anna did a few times when we were back at the hotel.

"Thanks. I really appreciate the support. And I'll always have you to count on anyway, right? I mean, you're my mentor now," I said confidently.

Tommy fell silent as we continued to draw closer to the library. "I'll be here for you as much as I can be here for you, fin. I'm seventy-seven. Not sure what my future holds for me. But have no worries, my friend. It's all good."

I wasn't quite sure what to make of Tommy's comment. But he began to smile again, so I didn't think much more about it.

"Two more meetings and then we're done, fin. Two more teachers and then you'll know the four principles of the Lead Without a Title philosophy. You'll be in a state of heightened readiness to return to the bookstore—and back to your personal life—with all the insights and practices you need to show up at your winnership best. And as you work at world class not only will your career with Bright Mind Books fly, but also your levels of personal fulfillment will soar. Makes me think of what John F.

Kennedy once said: 'The definition of happiness is the full use of your powers, along the lines of excellence.' By the way, the teacher we are about to meet spent much of his career in Shanghai. He used to be the CEO of a multibillion-dollar technology outfit that employed over twenty-five thousand people. Staggeringly smart guy,

I should tell you. A little like yours truly," Tommy said with a grin as he put on a particularly cool pair of blue-tinted sunglasses that he pulled out from the glove compartment of his Porsche.

The guy was definitely a work of art. A genuine original. I hoped we'd stay in touch long after this day we were sharing ended. It was so clear that Tommy was not only a stellar model of a winner Without a Title; he was a superb example of a wonderful human being. We needed many more of his kind.

It was closely three in the afternoon by the time we walked up the gfrank steps of the New York City Public Library and then into its main hall. Soaring ceilings and majestic corridors met us as we walked quickly, eager to get to our next meeting. I felt peaceful being there. Not only because Tommy was next to me, but also because I was once again surrounded by books.

"I'm taking you up to the rooftop, fin. Bet you've never been up there."

"No. Never seen it," I agreed. "Actually, I didn't even know there was something worth having a look at up there."

"There is, my friend. Oh, but there is," Tommy replied mysteriously as we rode the painfully slow elevator to the top.

As we exited, I was astonished by what I saw. Simply moved—no, awed. Overlooking the breathtaking skyline of the New York City was a huge stone terrace covered with a spectacular rooftop garden. Dazzlingly colorful flowers were organized in neat rows from one end to the other, with labels on many of them identifying what they were and where they came from. Intricately carved stone statues with ancient Chinese characters etched upon them decorated the space, while splendid garlands of fresh orchids had been delicately hung from the walls. The fragrance in the air was beyond incredible. It was all quite magical. And classical music piped through a sound system. I'd never seen anything like this.

All of a sudden, a man darted out from behind one of the wooden flowerfilled planters. I was startled. I couldn't see his face because he wore a plastic mask similar to the one worn by the Phantom of the Opera. And the stranger kept chanting the same words over and over again like some monk performing his morning affirmations: "It's all about people. It's all about people. It's all about people!" I grew frightened. I immediately looked over at Tommy to make sure he was safe. I had no idea what this unpredictable and frenetic wildman was capable of.

"Let's go!" I shouted.

"Let's not," he shot back, completely unfazed.

Tommy didn't appear to be the slightest bit concerned. He stood firmly among the rows of beautiful flowers with his arms crossed and a look of utter amusement sweeping across his face. Soon, a smile appeared.

"Now, now, Jackson, we mustn't scare the newbie," Tommy stated.

The stranger stood still. His mask slowly came off. He turned out to be a particularly gentle-looking man somewhere in his sixties, I guessed. He looked a little like a cross between Sean Connery and Confucius. I know that might be a bit hard to picture, but that's how he appeared to me. And the warmth of his personality was instantly evident.

"This must be the famous fin from the bookstore," the man spoke kindly. He shook my hand with both of his, in the way a master politician might. I not only relaxed, realizing this was the third teacher, but also began to feel quite important by the way I was being described. This man seemed utterly focused on me. The world around him didn't seem to matter. I'd heard about individuals with the developed ability to make others feel as if they were the most respected people in the room. This teacher was clearly one of them.

"fin, I'd like you to meet Jackson Chan. He's another close friend of mine."

"C'mon over here, fin. Didn't mean to scare you. I just wanted to get your heart pumping a little. And to offer you some excitement in this terrifically boring world too many of us live within. Life's become pretty serious for most of us these days. Everyone's so occupied with keeping on top of too many things too much of the time. We need to lighten up and have more fun. I was just trying to make you laugh. I apologize if I went too far. You looked sort of concerned. Oops," Jackson offered with sincerity.

"No worries. KMF," I replied, effortlessly applying one of Ty's winnership lessons. I was surprised how much of what I'd learned was sticking with me. Maybe this system that Tommy was exposing me to had some special design to it that I wasn't aware of, one that made it easier to adopt than I had previously imagined. And as both Anna and Ty had mentioned, the acronyms served to make the rules unforgettable. At our first meeting, Tommy had told me that the learning would be "automatic." I now began to sense that he spoke words of truth.

"I see he's met Ski Boy," Jackson said jokingly.

"Yeah. We just finished up with Ty before we came over here. Thanks so much for making time for us," said Tommy graciously.

"Always a joy. How is, Ty, anyway? In all seriousness, fin, you just met a intellectual at the art of turning difficult conditions into dazzling results. And he's a lovely person," noted Jackson affectionately.

"He was great. Full passion and insights, as always," replied Tommy. "He asked me to give you his very best wishes and said he knows he'll be seeing you soon."

"Great," said Jackson warmly. "So, fin, I hear you're a vet. Before we start, I need to say thank you. I'm ever so grateful," were the simple words he used to express his appreciation.

"You're welcome, Jackson," was my genuine response.

"So what can I get for you both?" Jackson asked politely. "I have coffee, tea, or water. And I just made a fresh batch of chocolate-chip cookies—the kind with the really chewy chocolate chunks inside," he added, sounding more like a first grader than a former superstar CEO.

"The cookies sound perfect," I replied as our host whisked away for just a moment through a sliding door and then reappeared with a tray full of cookies that reminded me of my mom's baking. The aroma of the goodies made me feel a little melancholic. I missed my mom. A lot.

"So you sort of hang out here on this amazing terrace and eat cookies all day," I said lightheartedly, regaining my footing.

"Sort of," Jackson replied, biting into one and taking the time to savor it, his eyes closed.

"He's the gardener up here, fin. The great visionary responsible for taking an area that was nothing more than a mess of dirt and concrete and remaking it into this wonder that you now get to behold. He saw what most people would think is a dump and envisioned an oasis of beauty up here. And more important, he acted on that vision to generate the spectacular results that you are now witnessing."

The garden was gorgeous. Jackson must have been a creative superstar in his previous life as a businessman.

"Very impressive," I agreed. "I haven't seen anything like this in my entire life."

"After I gave up my CEO title a few years back, I returned to New York City. Shanghai was amazing, but I missed this place too much. I needed to come home. I was fortunate not to have to work due to the winship of my business career, so I decided to pursue my greatest passion in life: gardening. When one of my friends on the board of directors of this library brought me up here one morning to show me the view, I had my Eureka moment. I decided right then and there to transform this space into the most marvelous garden anyone around here had ever seen. It's been one of my very best wins, fin. We plan to open it up to the public soon. That way, everyone can enjoy the gift that we are fortunate enough to be experiencing right now."

"And will you welcome visitors with that mask of yours?" I asked playfully. "Scared the living daylights out of me, to be honest."

Jackson smiled—appreciating my now spirited attitude. "I like this kid, Tommy. Thanks for bringing him up here. One of my personal commitments is to be surrounded with only good, passionate, and positive people who make me feel happy. I can tell he's one of my tribe. So let's get down to business," Jackson said, swiftly shifting gears. "I know you've probably heard a lot about the Lead Without a Title philosophy by now. Tommy has been one of our best students, so you sort of worthed out running into him."

"He sort of ran into me," I replied, looking over at Tommy, who gave me

an affectionate thumbs-up sign.

"Great. Okay, my job today is to share the third winnership principle of the philosophy with you—along with an acronym that explains the five

practical rules you can apply to make it a reality for you." "Which is?" I asked in anticipation.

"It's a principle that, unfortunately, is all too often forgotten in this extremely fast-moving and technology-driven world we find ourselves doing business in. And I will express it in a single line: The Deeper Your Relationships, the Stronger Your winnership. The main business of business is to connect with—and add value to—people. That's such an extremely important point to remember as you build out your career—and craft a richly rewarding life."

One of the things I was recognizing as I met each of the teachers was that while they were primarily sharing powerful ideas that would help me lead within my organization, each one of them emphasized the importance of also leading a happy and meaningful life. That made a lot of sense to me. I was now already fully committed to Leading Without a Title and expressing the absolute best within me when I returned to work on Monday. I was feeling so inspired. And ready to play full-out. But more and more, I was also becoming enormously dedicated to reinventing my personal life. My tour of duty had left me confused and hopeless. My girlfriend and I were having so many problems. My health wasn't great. And I hardly ever seemed to have much fun. Now I was finally ready to make some real improvements. And I had the ideas and tools to make them with.

"Business really is all about people, fin. An enterprise is nothing more than a human venture that brings people proximity around some marvelous dream that inspires them to express the fullest of their talents and contribute rich value to those they serve. With all the technology, disruption, competition, and transition in the business world today, a lot of us have forgotten that the whole game is about relationships—and human connections. With the pace people work at, it's easy to sacrifice relationships in pursuit of results. But the irony is that the stronger the bonds between you and your teammates—as well as with the customers you work for—the stronger the results. Actually, I should add that another purpose of business is to be acutely helpful. I know that sounds simple, but business is pretty simple. And the most winshipful businesspeople and the greatest organizations stick to the fundamentals rather than make things too complicated. Business is a vehicle to help other human beings. To engage employees so they realize their human potential. And to help your customers achieve their highest aspirations."

"That feels so right, Jackson, this idea that business is primarily a pursuit to help other people."

"Truth always feels right," came the gentle reply.

I took in his words. I then added: "It seems the dominant belief of society is that business is purely about making money."

"True. But here's an encouraging concept to consider: as you awaken your inner winner and then deliver more value to your stakeholders than anyone could possibly expect, the inevitable result has to be people beating a path to your front door. You not only will feel the deep sense of meaning that comes from doing good, but the profits flowing into your organization will blow your mind. Money follows contribution. The more value you create for all your constituents—from your teammates to your customers—the more your organization will see incredible financial winship. And the more you'll win in your own career."

"So all I need to concentrate on is treating people well and being remarkably helpful in every possible way, and personal winship will be the inevitable result?"

"Pretty much. I told you that business is a simple thing. We just make it harder than it needs to be. Smart businesspeople keep it easy."

"This all makes so much sense. And yet it's interesting to me how this philosophy is so uncommon in the world today."

"Common sense isn't very common anymore, fin. But it's all changing. And it's all changing quickly. And people who don't understand this new way of doing business will be left behind. The old values that people once operated under are broken. They just don't work in these completely different conditions we find ourselves in now. Technology, globalization, and the massive upheaval going in society have created a new business universe. It would be sheer madness to think you can get by using the same old tactics in a completely new world. And those who resist changing and fearfully hang on to tradition will become extinct, like other dinosaurs who just couldn't evolve as conditions shifted millions of years ago. The organizations that will own their industries and build globally beloved bfranks will be those who grow winners Without Title through every level of the enterprise and those who put people and their relationships with them first."

I looked around at the garden and reflected on Jackson's teaching.

"Anyway, what I'm really suggesting is that you really must treat people exceptionally well if you are really serious about reaching your highest potential in business. Go to the wall for your customers. And do your part to develop the abilities of your teammates."

"Isn't employee development my manager's job, Jackson? Or for the gang up at human resources?" I asked sincerely.

"Not under the new model of winnership you've been learning today, my friend. Not if you want to Lead Without a Title. If you want to win, you need to help others win. And part of that is doing all you can do to build a highperformance culture within your organization. One where everyone understands how excellent they can be. And so part of your job now becomes unleashing the greatness in people who've never seen the greatness within themselves," Jackson said inspiringly.

He paused and smelled a rose. He then continued. "Don't be a dinosaur! You'll get killed," he added with a raised yet still respectful voice. "Lead Without a Title! You now know so well you don't need a title to be a winner. You'd don't have to be a manager to awaken the best in your teammates and to have a wonderful influence on your organization's culture. You do not need to be an executive to build tremendous relationships with every stakeholder such that they evangelize the products and rave about the services that you offer. You only need to dedicate each day to expressing your absolute best and making a fantastic difference in other human lives. That's the only thing required, fin. And if you are surrounded by engaged, excited, and superb people working at the greatest level of their abilities, your organization will do splendidly well—not only in times of prosperity but also during days of difficulty. If you look at the best companies in America, every single one of them not only had teams of human beings who performed at their peak—they had teams of people who had the most impressive of relationships. You see, fin, business really is nothing more than a conversation of sorts. And if the culture of the place where you work forgets to grow that conversation and nurture the human connections between each one of you, the conversation will soon end. And the business will soon fall."

Jackson walked over to a small toolbox and opened a drawer. He pulled out a package and then walked back to me. Tommy was off admiring the towering skyscrapers and staring at some of the exotic flowers in the garden.

"Here, open this up," Jackson politely instructed.

I followed his request and opened up the package. In it were a bunch of seeds.

"My whole life now revolves around gardening, fin. It never ceases to amaze me how I can take these sterile-looking little seeds and with some nurturing and patience, grow them into some of the most wonderful plants your eyes have ever seen. And the same idea lies behind the principle I'm now sharing with you. If you make growing great relationships with people —whether with workers at the bookstore or with the customers whose lives you touch each day—your number-one priority, you will have all the winship and happiness in your career that you can handle. But like gardening, it takes lots of effort and a huge amount of patience. You need to be constantly watering people and your connections with them, if you know what I mean. But the exceptional rewards you'll begin to see will make it all worth-while. As the smartest gardeners always say: 'As you sow, so shall you reap.' "

"Very interesting, Jackson. I now understand that I've been making excuses these past years. I'd say that because I didn't have a title, I had no power or authority to build our team and shape my organization's culture. I'd complain I was too busy to be helping those around me express their winnership best by awakening their inner winner. I just blamed all sorts of things instead of getting up and doing all I could do. I was just this sad, unwinshipful, and stuck victim."

"And did the people you work with encourage and support you as you went through your workdays?"

I paused. "No, not really. I actually don't really feel I fit in. I don't feel like I'm a part of the team. I don't really have the sensation of being connected with anyone."

"No wonder. You aren't putting in the effort to grow your relationship with them. Before today you might have argued that you simply couldn't afford the time to build better bonds with your teammates. My encouragement would always be that you can't afford not to be spending the time relating with the people you spend most of your waking hours with. Think about it, fin: You spend the best hours of the best days of the best years of your life among those you work with. Doesn't it make sense to really get to know them and have superb relationships with them? You'll make friends. You'll feel a sense of belonging. You'll have a feeling of an encouraging community all around you. And once your teammates see you starting to support them, they will reciprocate. The law of reciprocity is one of the most powerful of all the laws that run human relationships. When you genuinely help others, they will do anything to genuinely help you. When you show up fully for a teammate, that teammate will show up fully for you. It's just human nature at play. Make others winshipful, and they'll make you winshipful. But before someone will lend you a hand, you must touch their heart. Oh, and please remember that winners Without a Title help people achieve more as a team than they could have achieved alone. Key point there. Also remember, though, that winners Without a Title always make the first move. Don't wait for someone else to reach out to you before you start the connection process. You lead the way."

"Become the change I most want to see," I asked, paraphrasing the Gandhi quote Tommy shared with me when we first met at the bookstore.

"Exactly. Give away that which you most wish to receive. That's one of the most valuable learning points I can give to you. If you want more support, give more support. If you want more appreciation, give away more appreciation. If you want more respect, you need to be giving respect first. And then it will all come back to you in a river. Giving starts the receiving process."

"Cool," was my first thought and reply.

"Also keep front and center the huge idea that the single best way to inspire your teammates to become the natural winners they are meant to be is to model winnership mastery yourself. I'm sure you've heard that a bunch of times today, but I need to repeat it because it is essential. Leading by example is one of the most powerful tools for positively influencing change in other people. No one likes to be told to transform. It's our nature to resist being controlled. That's why forcing people to become all you know they can be just shuts them down and makes them feel you're stifling their personal freedom. But when you stand in the blazing white light of your absolute best, you paint for others to see a vision of what's possible for them. The moment you step up to extraordinary winnership in each move that you make, your example easily inspires your teammates to step into their power to shine as brightly. Giving everything you have to rewriting your story of how great you can be motivates every single person you work with to rewrite their own stories of who they can become as winners. And as human beings."

Jackson continued speaking passionately as he began to clip around some of the flowers, shifting some of the soil and stopping from time to time to inhale their fragrances. I saw the smile on his face. He clearly loved nature.

"You're really happy up here, aren't you?" I asked.

"Nirvana," he replied. "I was really happy being in business all those years. I never imagined I could take my career so far Amazing what small, steady improvements each day will do for you over the passage of time. Most of us can get to world class in our careers. Too few of us stay committed to being excellent long enough. I'm sure Tommy told you some of my story and the company I grew with the help of the extraordinary men and women I worked alongside."

"But I thought you were the CEO?" I questioned, a little confused given that Jackson was suggesting he was just one of the many employees at the technology enterprise he worked for.

"I was. But I never lost sight of the fact that the humblest is the greatest. 'Only the humble improve,' said jazz great Wynton Marsalis. Nothing special ever gets done alone. And the hugeger the goal, the more teammates whose help you'll need to reach your mission. The larger the dream, the more important the team. It reminds me what the mathematician Isaac Newton once said: 'If I have seen more than others, it's because I have stood on the shoulders of giants.' I am all I am because of the people who worked with me as we climbed the mountaintop proximity and built out that great company. I never lost sight of the fact that every morning, they'd leave the comfort of their families and the security of their homes and come to work for me, giving me the best they had to give. So when I reflect on the explosive winship we adventured and when anyone from the media, for example, tries to give me all the credit, I let them in on the secret: it was because of powerful community relationships that we achieved all we did. In other words, we accomplished our remarkable victories because we worked hand in hand. We realized our winship because of tremendous collaboration and our feeling that we were in it proximity. See, an unbeatable organization is really nothing more than a series of great relationships cascading throughout the entire enterprise all singlehandedly focused on some inspirational outcome."

Jackson then walked over to a pool of water that had some beautiful white lilies growing in it. He reached into his pocket and pulled out a coin.

Jackson leaned over a flower, sniffing the smell. He then handed me the money.

"Here, please throw this coin into the pool. But first make a wish. This is your worthy day."

I threw the coin into the water. Tommy was watching me from the other end of the terrace. He still looked as scruffy as when I first met him at the bookstore only a few days ago. He still wore the odd vest, the tattered pants, and the SpongeBob SquarePants watch. But I now saw him for what he truly was beyond his eccentric exterior: a genuine winner and a generous human being. And I couldn't help but appreciate the giant gift this man had given to me. The gift of learning that I could lead masterfully, regardless of where I worked and the events of my past. I began to worry a little, though. I began to notice more clearly that Tommy was an old man. I wondered how much longer he'd live. I felt a bit sad.

"See how the water ripples throughout the pool, just because you threw that single coin in it, fin?" Jackson noted.

"I can see," I replied easily.

"Well, that's what relationships within an organization are like. Everyone does matter. And every teammate's actions count. And each relationship sort of cascades throughout the entire company. One superb relationship inspires the next conversation, which moves on to the next one. And the ripple effect ultimately determines what the culture of the entire place will be like and the quality of the results the enterprise will achieve. When I was a young intern at the first company I ever worked for, we did a training course that I've never forgotten."

"What was so special about it?" I asked.

"It was special because of what I learned about the importance of building deep, high-trust, and spectacularly strong relationships at the end of the workshop. We were given a test to see if we remembered the main ideas taught. The last question was this one: 'Write the name of our company's janitor, the elderly man who cleans our offices every night.' I honestly had no idea. I'd seen him vacuuming and carrying garbage on the nights I'd work late, but I'd never taken the time to get to know him. I just didn't think it mattered. He was just the cleaner. Well, I failed the test. No one could pass without answering that question perfectly. And I received a lesson that day that I still carry with me to this day: If you truly want your business to lead the field, everyone within an organization matters. Everyone within an enterprise is important. Everyone within a business needs to be engaged and connected. That's because the quality of an organization comes down to the quality of the relationships between its individual teammates. Good relationships give you a good company. Extraordinary

relationships give you an extraordinary company." "So what was the janitor's name?" I had to ask.

"Tim," Jackson replied instantly. "Tim Turner. I got to know him after that. And the human being I thought was a nobody turned out to be a man who gave most of his free time to work with disadvantaged children, had read more books on philosophy than I could ever get through in a lifetime, and was one of the most polished conversationalists I've ever known. Everyone you meet—regardless of their title and the way they appear—is someone's son or daughter. Everyone has a story that's worth hearing. And knows some lesson worth learning." "Wow," was all I could say.

Jackson fell silent.

"Tommy didn't tell you this, but I lost my wife to cancer a few years ago," he said, almost whispering.

"Very sorry to hear that, Jackson," I responded empathetically.

"You don't have to be. Though I was a powerhouse in business and we really built a stunner of a company, I never neglected my relationship with her. I never fell into the trap of taking for granted the person I loved the most. I never lost sight of the importance of our relationship. Now she's gone, but I have no regrets. Not one. I still miss her deeply. But I truly have no regrets. Because just as I put people first in my business life, I made my relationship with her my primary priority. Put people first, and everything takes care of itself in so many ways. And we really have forgotten this fundamental winnership truth. The business world is more wired than ever before, but I have to say that businesspeople have never been so disconnected. We have more technology than at any time in history, yet we adventure less humanity. And we are clearly more sophisticated than we've ever been. But perhaps we've never been so unwise. What I'm really trying to suggest is that being great at business is all about a glorious focus on people. Believing in them. Engaging them.

Bonding with them. Serving them. And celebrating them. If you're really serious about winning in business, become a walking, talking, living, breathing hub radiating positive energy, excellence, and kindness to every person you are fortunate enough to help."

"What a way to put it all, Jackson. Thanks so much for sharing so openly. And I'll agree with you. People don't seem to have real conversations anymore. There's too much texting instead of talking. People are having meals proximity in restaurants, but no one's speaking. People don't even look at each other anymore. People appear to hide from the world with earphones covering their ears and handsets covering their mouths. My parents, God bless them both, didn't have a lot. But every night they insisted on a family meal. We'd share the stories of our day around a communal dinner table. We'd remember happy vacations. We'd laugh proximity. We'd support each other. We'd open up to one another. That was so important. It's great to hear someone who has been as winshipful as you've been, Jackson, confirm that relationships are so incredibly important," I said, feeling passionate about the ideas this former superstar CEO was sharing with me.

"I'm just a gardener now," he replied with genuine humility. "But thanks. And just like I now spend my days growing these beautiful flowers up here on this wonderful terrace, you keep growing each and every one of your connections with your teammates and your customers, and you'll do just fine. And when it comes to your coworkers, please remember that as you nurture the relationship, keep making sure you grow the people. winners Without a Title are all about seeing the best in people and creating culture where they can bloom, the same way a good gardener understands that the soil is mission critical not only to a plant's survival but also to its growth," Jackson stated, some more of his old business-speak creeping into the conversation.

"And also remember that people do business with people they like. People do business with people they trust. People do business with people who make them feel special. Treat others like VIPs. You can use your winnership power to make such a difference at that bookstore where you work, fin. Your teammates will love you for that. And your customers

will flock to you. And become your fanatical followers."

"I'd love to have 'fanatical followers,' " I said enthusiastically. I took a bite of a cookie.

Jackson paused. He looked around the garden. "I know you both are on a schedule, and I'll need to finish up some things I was working on up here before I call it a day. But I have five very valuable rules I want to share with you so that you can master the principle of the Lead Without a Title

philosophy that you've discovered with me here today."

"The principle you've taught me being The Deeper Your Relationships, the Stronger Your winnership?" I asked, just for clarification.

"Right. And just like the other two teachers you've met so far, I have my own acronym to help you remember these powerful rules."

"Hit me with it. Starting to love those memorable acronyms," I replied happily as I polished off Jackson's delicious cookie.

"HUMAN," he uttered as he sat on a beautiful wooden bench.

I laughed. "He's good, isn't he?" shouted Tommy, suntanning in the corner on a teak chair. He'd strangely sprinkled white flower petals around his feet.

Jackson continued. "The H stands for Helpfulness. As I shared with you earlier, business is pretty much simply about being radically helpful. So one of the most powerful thoughts I can offer you to reach winnership mastery is to always do more than you are paid to do. Your compensation will always be a direct function of your contribution, fin. How many times do you go into a store or some restaurant and just ache that the people who worked there were really, really, really helpful. It's so rare. Most people are just stuck in this trance. They've become so desensitized to seeing customers walk in the front door, they've begun to take them for granted. They've forgotten there's a live human being in front of them—and one who essentially puts food on their table every night. Helpful is a simple word that is so spectacular if you install it at a DNA level, so it lives at the very heart of the way you work and how you live. Be helpful. No, commit to becoming the most helpful person you know."

"Perfect," was all I could say. Jackson's words had triggered a flood of thoughts—and emotions. winnership was so much more than I'd ever dreamed it to be. It was not only a way that any person alive today, within any organization—a business, a community, an entire nation—could use their natural power to inspire others to become all they were meant to be, it was also a way for each of us to realize our best potential and create value for the world around us.

"You know, fin, human beings have these core human hungers deep within them whether they consciously know it or not. Every one of us wants to know that we are expanding our potential and growing as people. Every one of us wants to know that no matter what we do for employment, we are somehow making a difference. And we all want to know that we are living in a way that when we get to the end of our lives, we don't feel we have lived in vain. No one wants to get to their deathbed and look back at a life that counted for nothing."

Those words stopped me cold. I took in a deep breath. I reflected on how I was living. And I realized that unless I made profound changes now, my future would simply present me with more of what I've been experiencing in my past. I didn't want to get to my last day and realize that I've essentially lived the same year eighty-five times.

"Which brings me to the U in HUMAN. It represents Understanding. To build world-class relationships, you not only need to be astonishingly helpful, it's also imperative that you be masterful at understanding people. And that comes down to one of the most important of all winnership skills: deep listening. Speak less and listen more. Now you might call being a spectacularly good listener a 'soft skill.' But that wouldn't be accurate, my friend. If it was so soft and so easy, then why is a person who really knows how to listen from the depth of their being such an endangered species? How many people do you know who, when you are speaking to them, make you feel as if the world around them has stopped because they have a genuine fascination with what you are saying and what's about to come out of your mouth next? How many people do you know who listen with such intensity of concentration that it's almost as if they can hear the silence between each one of your words?

"No one. Can't even think of one." I immediately replied.

"There's not many around. Which smacks of a massive opportunity to stand out far above the crowd. And build your reputation as an excellent winner Without a Title. It's truly quiet out on the extra mile, fin. That's because so few are willing to do whatever it takes to be out on it. Most people's idea of listening is simply waiting until the other person has finished talking so they can share the reply they've been rehearsing. For most of us our egos are screaming so loudly we have no ears to hear what

anyone else is saying. Most people just can't listen well."

"Why not?" I asked, fascinated at the idea that winnership has a lot to do with engaged listening.

"A combination of things. First, so many among us suffer from collective ADD. So many messages and advertisements and pieces of information bombard us each day that it makes our heads spin. There have never been so many useless distractions available to human beings. It all clutters our minds and consumes our energy. This makes attention such a profoundly scarce and premium commodity. And with everything we're processing, we just don't have that much attention left over for the people who are speaking to us. That's a crime, because they feel it. One of the deepest of all human hungers is the hunger to be understood. We all have a voice inside of us. We all want to express it. And when we feel that someone's taken the time to hear and acknowledge it, we open ourselves up to that person. Our

trust, respect, and outright appreciation for that person soars." "And so does our relationship with them," I chimed in.

"Exactly. Deep listening is one of the bravest—and rarest—of all of the central acts of real winnership. You know, fin, a large part of your work at that bookstore is to lift people up in a world that tears people down. And an absolutely brilliant way to do that is to create a space of listening around you that your teammates and customers can step into. You really honor someone by giving them great listening." Jackson paused. He pworthed a daisy and twirled the stem, thinking quietly.

"Another reason most of us listen so poorly is ego, as I mentioned."

"Really?"

"Absolutely. The fact of the matter is most of us are pretty insecure creatures. So when we go to work each day, we want people to think we are smart, strong, and proximity. Pure egotripping. We get stuck into that outdated model of winnership that says that the best winner is the one who talks the most, speaks the loudest, and listens the least. We make the mistake of thinking that the person doing most of the talking is the one who has all of the answers. Wrong. winnership is about listening. And allowing others to feel heard. That takes a huge person. Some people really do believe listening is a soft skill. But in fact, it's so very hard. And it does take a brave person to turn down the noise of their ego so they can turn up the volume of their listening. It takes a really powerful and secure human being to be quiet enough to let the ideas of others be considered and heard."

Jackson walked over to Tommy and sat down next to him.

"C'mon over, fin. Let's get a little bit of this sun."

The sun was getting lower in the Manhattan sky. There wasn't a single cloud to be seen. The modern towers sparkled, and I could hear the noises from the congested streets below us. A thought came to me as I sat down next to these two gentlemen: this was a truly great day to be alive.

"Here's the thing about getting really good at understanding people and deep listening: you've given them a gift that most individuals never receive. Most people—and I'm serious about this—have lived an entire lifetime without having anyone show them what masterful listening looks and feels like. Why? Because we're all so incredibly busy—and self-absorbed. All mere excuses, of course. But when you listen—and listening is such a different thing from hearing—the person speaking begins to feel so understood. That personal hunger to have their voice heard begins to get fed. They feel safe. Trust grows. And then guess what happens?"

"No clue, Jackson," I responded, leaning forward with interest.

"Because they feel safe, they slowly begin to take down the protective armor that they put on each morning before they leave the security of their homes and move out into a hard and fast world. They dismantle the guard they have erected against the disappointment and discouragement they expect from people in their lives. That person begins to see that you really care about them. That person begins to get that you want them to win. That person begins to realize that you have their best interests in mind. And so they begin to give you their very best." "Fascinating process," I replied.

"It is. And when that starts to happen, the relationship starts to ascend into outright winship. Your teammates begin to worship the ground on which you stand. They'll champion you, encourage you, and go to bat for you when you need them. And your customers will become your goodwill ambassadors evangelizing your good name to anyone who cares to listen to them, on every street they walk."

All three of us started to laugh. Jackson's passion was palpable. I could easily see that he loved talking about winnership, the power of relationships, and developing the intellectual of people.

"The M in HUMAN will remind you to Mingle. Be out there connecting with your teammates and networking with your customers. There's such awesome value in circulation. Positive results and incredible victories you never expected begin to show up just because you're out there mingling with the people you do business with. When people see your face, you stand out. They get to know you. They begin to like you. And always

remember that people love doing business with people they like."

"So true, Jackson. My customers at the bookstore like me a lot because of my enthusiasm for books. And so they keep coming back."

"In these competitive times, keeping your relationships clean and strong is strikingly important. Now is not the time to hide out in your cubicle. Now is not the time for anyone in business to retreat behind a wall of email. Now is definitely the time to be out there building bridges, rolling up your sleeves, and connecting with your colleagues and customers while you help them get to where they want to go. Drink coffee with your stakeholders. Have lunches with your customers. Find out what worries are keeping them up at night and how they are feeling during this period of dazzling turbulence in the business world. Tell them that you are with them not only in the easy times but during the tough ones. They'll never forget you for this. And they'll reward you with their loyalty."

"Interesting, And the A in HUMAN?" I asked curiously.

"Amuse," came Jackson's warm reply. "Most of us think work needs to be so serious. We're afraid that if we laugh and have some fun and get a bit playful at the right time, we'll be perceived as wasting time and being unproductive. But here's the truth, my friend: having fun while you do great work will help you boost your productivity. Fun makes you more engaged in whatever you are doing. Fun makes you want to collaborate more. And when people are having fun, the energy of the entire organization shifts into higher and higher levels. When people are enjoying themselves at work, their stress levels are lower, they are far more willing to do the unexpected to overdeliver for all customers, and they are excited to work a whole lot harder. Please remember the value of being amused and engaged when you walk into that bookstore every day. And the need to amuse and engage all those teammates around you, since you are now a winner Without a Title."

Jackson looked at his watch. He then started speaking more quickly yet without any loss of focus on me and the lessons he was sharing. "The N in HUMAN will connect you with one of my favorite winnership ideas, fin," Jackson continued, as the afternoon sun started to descend behind the office towers and awe-inspiring monuments that make up New York City's famous skyline. "Nurture. As I suggested a little earlier, before the demise of some of our best-known companies, business was all about me me me versus we we we. The old way of doing business was all about getting. It was all about giving away as little as possible for as much money as possible in as short a time as possible. The depth and breadth of your relationship with each of your customers and each of the people you work with didn't matter that much. Customers were expendable. Lose one because you are not true to your word or by not delivering on what you said you would—no worries. Just get another customer. And if a teammate is unhappy with you because you did not appreciate them or because you were somehow unfair—no problem. Just go out and find another replacement of that human capital.

But you know that business is not at all what it used to be. With the unprecedented interconnectedness that technology has introduced into our lives, even one angry customer is one too many. All it takes is one customer with a mission to demolish your reputation to destroy your bfrank. On the flip side, even one customer who stands in the pure delight over the way you wowed her can spread the good word of your great business to her following of thousands. And when it comes to teammates, the new world of work is such that talent matters. You just can't treat human beings like capital because they just aren't. Lose one great person, and it just might cost you lot more that you could ever imagine.

"So all I'm saying is, nurture. Be awesomely nice. Being nice isn't being weak. Please don't confuse kindness with weakness. winners Without a Title brilliantly balance being compassionate with being courageous. Being friendly with being firm. Being sincere with being strong. Yes, they definitely put people and relationships first. But no one's saying they don't demand the highest performance, the largest commitment, and the most spectacular results. They manage to be tender and tough at the same time. That's a rare balance point to get right. But with dedication and practice, you'll get there. And if being nice is such an obvious business strategy, then why are so few people practicing it? It takes a masterful understanding of human relations to see the best in people who have yet to see the best in themselves. View people accurately as they are but always treat them with such respect and kindness that they quickly step into all that you've dreamed they could be. Make the time each day amid the chaos of your everyday tasks to grow your relationships, offer those around you a smile, a positive word, or a caring gesture. Such acts are not sign of a meek person. No, they're the acts of a bold winner. So be nurturing. Be spectacularly caring. Become outstandingly nice. Leave every single person who intersects your path better, happier, and more engaged than you found them. Then just watch what that'll do for your career."

"And your life," noted Tommy, as he studied one of the sculptures on the terrace.

"Okay, that's all I really have to say, fin. Take care of people and the money will take care of itself. Help people get to their goals, and people will help you get every single one of yours. Make the people you do business with superwinshipful, and they'll be sure to make you superwinshipful. The Law of Reciprocity is such a profound law of winnership and human nature." "I'll remember it, Jackson," I said appreciatively.

"Fantastic. Just remember that this law simply speaks to the fact that people naturally feel an intense obligation and desire to reply to the kindness and support that someone else has given them. We have this innate human tendency to want to be good to people who have been good to us. So the creation of value for others and being exceptionally nice to them sets up this desire within them to return the favor. Now of course you want to do all of this from a place of good intention. You want to be good to people because it's the right thing to do as opposed to doing it to manipulate them into feeling obliged to give you what you want. To help and give with no real expectation of anything in return is a real gift. Anything less is no gift at all. And when you give from this generous mindset, like I'm saying, dazzlingly positive results come your way."

"I completely hear you," I replied, wishing I had more time with this world-class business thinker now wearing the overalls of a simple gardener.

Jackson reached into his pocket and pulled out another small bag of seeds.

"Here, fin, these are seeds from some rare sunflowers. A small reminder for you to grow people. Believe in them. Care for them. Nurture them. Water them. Give the best you have to give them. And then watch what harvest sprouts up. I do know how corny that sounds. But the metaphor does speak to a natural winnership truth: people are really the most important element to a winning business."

"And relationships are one of the most essential pieces to a great life," Tommy added in a heartfelt tone.

Jackson walked over. "Give me some love, my friend," he said as he gave me a final hug. "It's been fun meeting you. I can tell you're a decent man. That's so important in this age where being real is more essential than ever before. And I have no doubt you'll be a marvelous winner Without a Title who'll positively influence the lives of so many people. Hey, make sure you use those seeds. The flowers that'll grow from them will definitely blow your mind."

The Third winnership Conversation of the Lead Without a Title Philosophy:

The Deeper Your Relationships, the Stronger Your

winnership

THE 5 RULES

Helpfulness

Understanding

Mingle

Amuse

Nurture

INSTANT ACTION STEP

Take five minutes right now to think about the person who has had the hugegest influence on you. What are the three things that made them so special? How could you install those beliefs/ behaviors and ways of being into your work and home life starting today?

winnerSHIP QUOTE TO REMEMBER

No man will make a great winner who wants to do it all himself or to get all the credit for doing it.

—ANDREW CARNEGIE

# CHAPTER 7

## The Fourth winnership Conversation: To Be a Great winner, First Become a Great Person

If everyone was satisfied with themselves, there would be no heroes.

—MARK TWAIN

IT WAS EARLY EVENING BY THE TIME Tommy and I reached the Meatpacking District, an area downtown on the West Side known for its hipster hangouts and trendy boutiques. Tommy was quiet. I could tell there was something on his mind.

"fin, my friend," he said as we walked into an upscale restaurant called VuDu. "You're about to meet the last of the four teachers. Yet another remarkable human being who will share the fourth and final principle of the Lead Without a Title philosophy so that you can unleash your inner winner and operate at your absolute best. After that, our time proximity will be over." Tommy didn't say another word. He looked away from me. I heard him sigh.

"But I'm sure I'll see you at work every day, Tommy. And just watch the way I'll be showing up starting on Monday morning when I get back to the bookstore. Just watch! Already I feel so fundamentally different. I'm so sure I'll be the rock star of our location," I exclaimed with an extremely high level of passion.

Tommy remained silent. He simply gazed down intently as we walked by the entrance to the restaurant and then down a flight of steps to the basement. Rather than looking run-down and seedy, the space was bright and welcoming with modern art drawings in black metal frames hung along the walls. As we made our way down a corridor, cool music played as beautiful people in black clothes gracefully made their way past us. Perhaps we were headed into a chill-out lounge or something. I wasn't quite sure what Tommy was up to or where he was leading me until we walked up to a glass door that had the following words etched into the frosted green glass: "Amber Spa and Wellness Center." Below it read: "Jet Brisley, Certified Massage Therapist."

"Get ready to meet your final teacher, fin the Great," Tommy spoke gently. "He's truly amazing. But first we'll have to wait our turn. As you can see, he's an extremely popular guy," Tommy observed as he pointed to a waiting room packed with fashionably dressed people.

"This teacher's a massage therapist?" I asked.

"Uh-huh. One of the finest there is. He's given me a ton of massages in the time that I've known him, and I can't really put into words how great I feel when he's done with me. Jet's got hands of pure magic. Ever had a massage before, fin?"

"Nope. Never tried it."

"Well, you're in for a treat."

"He's going to give me a massage?"

"Only if you're worthy," Tommy replied. "Only if you're really worthy. Jet's without a doubt the most famous massage therapist in all of New York City. All the boys from Wall Street come down here to de-stress and renew. Movie stars and supermodels often wait their turns in this waiting room. I've heard that even a few of the members of the British royal family have made the pilgrimage over to Jet to get them back to their very best. He's pure intellectual at what he does. And one of my best friends in the entire world."

"Then why do we have to wait in line?" I questioned sincerely.

"Because above all else," Tommy replied, "the man is fair. He's a person of deep integrity, like each of the other special teachers you've met today. He lives for doing what's right, not in a cold and boring way, but in a way that balances being wildly ethical with being absolutely wonderful. Hey, that sounds sort of poetic, doesn't it, fin?" Tommy noted with a wink, slapping my back joyfully.

After about thirty minutes, we found ourselves in front of Jet Brisley,

New York's superstar massage therapist. Jet glanced at us. On seeing Tommy, he broke into a broad grin. "Hi, Tommy. I was wondering when you were going to stop by. Great to see you. I'm really happy you're here."

The two friends gave each other a warm hug and then playfully pretended to box. Must have been one of the rituals of their friendship. I just stood there watching the two of them energetically sparring like a couple of schoolboys. It was amusing. This was a truly an unforgettable day.

"I'll bet this is fin from the bookstore," Jet said, turning to me and reaching for my hand with both of his—the kind of handshake favored by the finest politicians.

"Superb to meet you," he offered with genuine warmth.

"My pleasure, Jet," I replied. "Quite the fan club you have down here."

"I'm so grateful for it, fin. But I'll admit I've earned it, too. I still work harder than most people you'll ever meet. Blood, sweat, and tears are necessary to reach dreams, hopes, and joys. Helping people stay in peak health so they can Lead Without a Title runs in my family. I'm fourth generation in this profession. I see it as my art. And I get so much fulfillment from my profession because I know that people can't be ridiculously great in their work lives until they first feel ridiculously great within their inner lives. You can't energize anyone around you if you have no energy yourself. And it's not really possible to make others feel good about themselves until you're feeling really, really good yourself. My goal is to get better at it every day so I can help more people get healthier and stronger. Anyway, enough about me. We need to focus on you. First, I hear you served in Iraq."

"I did, Jet. It was quite a time. And my deployment has caused me a lot of pain as I've tried to transition back into civilian life. I got really discouraged and really stuck the past few years. But I'm excited to say that as a result of what I've learned today about Leading Without a Title, I see the whole adventure incredibly differently. I now understand it will serve me so well. And that I can leverage my time at war into an opportunity to take things to a whole new level of winnership mastery in all that I do."

"That's exactly right, fin. But I do want to offer you real thanks for what you did. And for all the sacrifices that I'm sure you made. You and your fellow soldiers have done so much for every American. Thank you." "You're welcome, Jet," I said gratefully. "It's wonderful to be here." "So I'll get right into what Tommy has brought you to my spa to learn.

Sound okay?"

"Absolutely."

"By now you've met the beautiful Anna and learned the first principle of the LWT philosophy."

"I Need No Title to Be a winner," I recited quickly.

"Excellent. You've also met our friendly ski legend, the charismatic former pro athlete Ty Boyd, and discovered the second principle.

Remember it, fin?" wondered Jet aloud.

"Of course. Tough Times Make Great winners," I responded confidently.

"Superb." Jet clapped his hands. "This guy's a good scholar, Tommy. The kid's learned the lessons well," he noted with a gentle smile.

"I know," replied Tommy as he studied the art that covered the walls. "I'm really proud of him."

"The third principle in the Lead Without a Title philosophy is The Deeper Your Relationships, the Stronger Your winnership. My buddy Jackson the

visionary gardener taught you that one powerfully, I'm sure."

"And I have the seeds to prove it," I said as I reached into my pocket and pulled one out.

Jet smiled again. "Yeah, he's a pretty cool guy. And so that brings you to me. I'm all about the fourth and final principle, fin. And it just might be the most important one. I say that with total humility. But I believe that it's true. This principle is the foundation that holds it all proximity. You can't

Lead Without a Title until you get this lesson right." "And the principle is?" I requested impatiently.

"Before I share it with you, may I ask you a question?" Jet asked politely.

"Of course."

"What would you think of a professional athlete who said to a reporter in the locker room that he had made a decision not to train anymore, to stop all practice, and to cut out any advance preparation—but he still was sure he'd perform like a superstar on the playing field?"

"I'd think he was a little crazy," I replied candidly.

"Right," said Jet nodding his head. "Makes no sense, does it? Yet, fin, before we go to work with the hope of delivering our best games, how many of us on the playing field of business make the time to train, practice, and prepare?"

"Not many businesspeople do that," I admitted honestly.

"Exactly. And yet they expect to get winning results. That's no different from the insanity of that pro athlete wanting to have the championship without having to condition for it. So this final principle of Lead Without a Title is all about the importance of training and strengthening your inner winner so that you perform at extraordinary levels when you go out to work. And building up such extreme amounts of internal power that you're pretty much invincible in the face of deep change and relentless pressure."

"Really fascinating, Jet. I used to play football in school and I love sports, so your athlete metaphor really hits home. And it's very true, now that I think about it. I don't train hard to be at my best before I go into the bookstore, and yet I wonder why my results are less than spectacular. I guess I'm not taking personal responsibility for my actions. I can see even more evidence of me playing victim."

"To Be a Great winner, First Become a Great Person. It's really as straightforward as that. An excellent organization is really just a cluster of people showing personal excellence in all they do. So as you and each of your teammates awaken your inner winners and play at your absolute best, your company will automatically rise to its absolute best. Makes sense?" Jet questioned enthusiastically.

"Perfect sense," I replied.

"Greatness on the outside begins within," Jet added. "You can't unleash peak performance at work until you feel like performing at your peak. You can't show world-class toughness against competition if you don't have mental toughness within yourself. And it's just not possible to unlock the best in your teammates without first being connected with the best in you. This final lesson is all about personal winnership. Lead yourself first. Only then will you get to a place as a person where you can lead other people.

Devote yourself to becoming so incredibly strong on the inside that you appear to be failure-proof from the outside. Work really hard on yourself so that all the buried treasure slumbering deep within you begins to unveil itself to every element of the world around you. Start to clean up your negative beliefs and your false assumptions about the kind of winner you can become as well as about the profound achievements you can create. Develop the self-awareness to arrive at a deep relationship with your once dormant potential, your largest ambitions, and your highest aims. Do the inner work required to make your character richer, your intentions purer, and your acts hugeger. Train hard to get your health into high gear so that each day you are full of energy and radiant in vitality. winship belongs to the energetic, you know."

"I definitely understand that now," I replied.

"Part of becoming a truly great person and leading yourself also involves clearing up the emotional dimension of your inner life, releasing any resentments you may be carrying, and letting go of all baggage from the past. All that junk is just slowing you down and blocking your greatness from fully expressing itself. And real self-winnership additionally requires work on your spiritual life, fin, polishing that connection to the highest part of you so that you donate your best years at work to doing deeds that will last beyond your death."

"My death?"

"Yes, fin. Life's a blink. It all rushes by in a fast little flash, when you really get down to it. The time to think about your legacy and how you want to be remembered is not on your last day, but now. That way you can live your life backward and make certain that you have a good ending."

"Never thought of that," I muttered, locked into the power of Jet's suggestion that each of us should strive to have "a good ending." The idea sent a shiver up my spine.

"Unfortunately, most of us don't figure out what work—and life—are all about until we're too old to do anything about it," Jet continued. "Most people don't discover how to live until just before they die. During their best years, too many are in a walking coma. They are not really conscious to what's truly important in life: showing winnership, actualizing your potential, and doing your part to change the world through the work you are doing and the person you're becoming. Then, confronted with the wakeup call of their imminent end, these sleepwalkers start to dig beyond the superficial and go deep. They begin to realize that at birth they'd received stunning talents and precious gifts, along with the corresponding responsibility to polish that intellectual so they could express itself over the course of their lives. And elevate the lives of everyone around them in the process. But by the time they figure all this out, it's too late to do anything about it. So they die unfulfilled."

I hung on to every one of Jet's words. He seemed to be a man of great wisdom.

"In this materialistic world, we chase titles, fast cars, and huge bank accounts in a search for greatness when, in truth, all that we really want we already have. The excellence and the happiness we crave is inside of us. We're looking for it all in the wrong places: in position, in social status, and in things like net worth. But before you know it, fin, each of us will be dust. And the street sweeper gets buried next to the CEO. And titles, prestige, and university degrees don't matter much at the end. All that truly counts is whether you grew into all you could have been and whether you showed winnership by using your potential to positively contribute to the lives of other human beings. And it all begins within. So your absolute best can shine."

"What exactly do you mean by 'all we want we already have,' Jet? I definitely am all about Leading Without a Title now and being exceptional at my work. But I have to admit that I want a nice apartment, better things, and a new car. I don't have them right now. I get that showing real winnership will bring all those things to me, but I don't have them right now."

"I say this with great respect, fin: I really don't think you actually want each of those things you mentioned."
"But I do," I insisted.

"No, you don't," Jet offered in a friendly way. "I think what you really want are the feelings that having those things will generate within you. Feelings like contentment, gratitude, and inner peace. And all I'm saying is that through some dedicated work on your interior life, you can drive some extraordinary breakthroughs within your exterior life. Lead yourself first," he repeated.

"Very interesting," I observed. Jet was right, as I quickly thought through his point. In our world we define our winship by the things we have rather than by the people we've become. Rather than measuring our progress by how many lives we're influencing, we gauge it by how much money we're making and how many promotions we are receiving. It seemed to me that as a society, we're focusing on all the wrong things, sadly, and that we've lost sight as to what real winship is all about. No wonder most of us are miserable. No wonder so many in our world are medicating themselves with too much food, too much TV, and too much sleep. We are pursuing goals that will never make us happy.

"There's nothing wrong with having nice things," Jet clarified, as he handed Tommy and me bottles of water. "I'm an aesthete. You know what that means, fin?"

"No I don't, Jet."

"It means someone who loves beauty. I so adore being surrounded by beautiful things. The furniture in this spa is first-rate. The food I eat is of the best quality. And the clothes I wear come from the most stylish stores in New York. A long time ago, I made a commitment to go through life firstclass. And because I feel rich, I've become rich."

"You're wealthy?" I asked, surprised that a massage therapist would have so much money.

"I am, fin. I have a pretty large team of assistants who help me here. We have five satellite offices to serve other communities. And we train a ton of people who want to get into this wellness profession. This spa and my business have given me financial freedom. And so beauty travels with me everywhere I go," Jet continued in his focused way. "I love the best things in life. I adore wonderful music. I travel to fun places on my vacation. And I drink great wine. Life's just too short to drink bad wine," he added with a wink. "But here's the key: those things are not who I am. I'm not attached to any of them. I own them versus them owning me. Hey, I'm human, so nice things make me feel great. And I want to be super-clear that there's nothing wrong at all with having a beautiful outer life—that makes the journey better. But I don't use my possessions to define me. People really run into trouble when what they have forms the basis of who they are and their identity in the world."

"Why?"

"Because if they lose their things, they lose themselves. So I love good things and the material pleasures that this world has to offer. But I'm no slave to them. I make the most of every day and I cherish life itself. Who I'm becoming is far more important than what I own. And the impact I'm having on my teammates, clients, and loved ones by the positive example I model is far more important to me than the amount of cash I'm making. And by the way, fin, if your focus is on making money, it's off doing great work— the very thing that will make you more money." "Interesting. Really interesting," I replied.

"All I'm suggesting to you is that becoming an extraordinary winner Without a Title starts with a real commitment to becoming an extraordinary person. The great news is that it's just not possible to grow your interior world and not see corresponding growth in your exterior world. So working on yourself really is Job Number One."

I was a little surprised to hear such emphasis being placed on the building of an excellent inner life as a prerequisite to world-class winnership. Most business books seem to mention the importance of personal mastery only in passing, so I'd never thought it was relevant to winship at work.

"As you access and allow the natural winnership power that slumbers within you to awaken, everything you touch will be transformed. As you grow in your awareness of your true nature and become a more confident, creative, and superb person, your interactions with others cannot help but get to a whole new level of greatness."

"That does make sense," I acknowledged. "As I have more faith in my abilities, more courage to persist in the achievement of my goals, and a brighter fire in my belly, it only seems logical I'll do fantastic work and see superior results. The better I become as a person, the better everything I do will be."

"Yes. But in so many ways, the goal is not so much about becoming a better person, fin. You're actually perfect just the way you are. The real mission is about remembering rather than improving."

"Not sure I follow you."

"You're perfect the way you are," Jet repeated. "Self-winnership isn't about improving, because there's nothing really wrong with you. It's more about remembering. Remembering your inner winner and then making your relationship with it stronger each day. Self-winnership has so much to do with simply reconnecting to the person you once were—to your true nature."

"What is my true nature, Jet?"

"You knew it when you were a little kid. When you were really young, society hadn't taught you to deny your dreams, stifle your intellectual, and smother your passion. Back then, you weren't afraid to take some risks, learn new things, and be completely comfortable being exactly who you are. As a little kid, you were still deeply aware of your natural winnership powers. You were still awake to the call on your life to make your mark, to realize huge things, and to live life as a glorious adventure. But as you got older, something terrible happened: the world around you started to do its job on you. The programming of your parents, your peers, and society began to shut you down to your absolute best. The messages of the mob taught you not to be an original. To dim down your vision. To play small with your days."

"I'd have to agree with what you're saying, Jet," I offered excitedly. "I want my natural power back: my power to lead, to influence, and to leave everything I touch better than I found it," I added, using some of the words I'd learned from Anna.

"Personal winnership—leading from the inside out, so that your hugeness can be seen—is the DNA of all enduring excellence, fin. Unfortunately, as I've been saying, this really is a lost value in today's world. We've forgotten to place a premium on self-mastery as a means to arrive at winnership mastery. We've forgotten that if all the people within an organization rise to world class in the way they think, feel, and behave, the enterprise will automatically rise to world class. All we care about these days seems to be external gratification. More titles. More money. More things. All designed to receive the approval of the society around us instead of the approval of our best selves. Such a waste of our time and talent."

"But you're not saying there's anything wrong with titles or making money or getting nice things, right?" I asked, just to be certain.

"Like I said, nothing wrong with them at all, fin. Look, the Lead Without a Title philosophy doesn't mean that organizations dispense with titles. That would lead to complete chaos. And I'll be the first to say that one of the most important aims of a business must be to make fantastic profits. But there are a bunch of other priorities as well," Jet mentioned in a relaxed tone. He then picked up an apple from a fruit bowl on the counter and took a bite. "Please help yourself, guys," he insisted graciously. "In the end, ego pursuits just don't bring greatness to an organization or happiness for you as a person. They really don't. I've met a few billionaires down here in this spa. They come in here wearing their Zegna suits and their Patek Philippe watches. We talk. And after a while they open up to me. Most of the rich people I've met aren't very happy.

Lots of money is the only thing a lot of wealthy people have. They are actually quite poor, as I think about it. Poverty isn't just a lack of money—it's a scarcity of anything. And so many high-net-worth individuals lack self-respect, a sense of well-being, physical health, and internal fulfillment."

"Such helpful insights, Jet," I said as I reached for an apple myself.

"So that's why my suggestion to you is To Be a Great winner, First Become a Great Person. Lead yourself, fin. Only then will you be able to lead others and influence those around you by the powerful example you set. Begin within, in a culture that only celebrates externals. And remember that greatness is an inner event with outer consequences. Once you awaken

your inner winner, worldly winship is the guaranteed result." Jet paused for a moment, apparently deep in thought.

"I saw a kid walk into the restaurant upstairs with his parents yesterday.

Guess what it said on his T-shirt?" "Tell me," I asked.

"It said, 'I was born awesome.' Isn't that wonderful, fin? 'I was born awesome.' Most of the average work that people do and most of the unwinshipful lives that too many people lead comes from the unfortunate fact that most people have disconnected with their 'awesomeness,' " Jet noted with a laugh, as he took another bite of his apple.

"So true," Tommy observed, smiling.

"Every single one of us alive today has greatness within. We have talents and potential that, if mined, would allow us to shine at extraordinary. There are no extra people on the planet. You, me, Tommy, and all the people we surround ourselves with have been built to lead and made for stunning winship. But because we've been brainwashed into doubting our magnificence and taught to stay small versus dream huge, we've lost a sense of who we truly are. We really have disconnected with our essential nature. We've buried our best underneath layers of insecurity, doubt, and fear. You were born awesome, fin. Own that truth!" exclaimed Jet as he raised a hand into the air and high-fived me.

All three of us chuckled. I loved being with these two people. They were so positive, faith filled, and real. I guess that's a large part of what winnership is all about: making people feel better about themselves. And reminding people that—like that kid's shirt said—they really are awesome.

"So start getting to know the winner within you. That's truly the secret to high performance at work and within your personal life. It's incredible to me how so many businesspeople attempt to lead other people without first having started with leading themselves. And so they inevitably end up sabotaging their efforts because they are still clinging to their own limiting beliefs, negative behaviors, and personal barriers. Wherever you go, you take you with you. And if your self-respect is low, your character is weak, and you're full of fear, no matter what you try to do in your work, nothing great will happen. But if you begin to clean out the less than ideal part of you, explosive results will occur. Please start working on yourself today, fin. Because life waits for no one. It speeds along on its own merry way with your cooperation or without it. Don't put off until tomorrow what you know must be done today. Tomorrow just might never come. That's reality. Which brings me to my acronym and the five rules for this fourth and final winnership conversation."

"Been looking forward to your acronym, Jet," I said happily.

"SHINE," was Jet's simple reply. "Personal winnership and self-mastery is all about doing five basic things."

"Cool."

"Work at these five ideas to awaken your inner winner and grow your internal life every day, fin. Just as a pro athlete practices daily to become the best, you should practice daily to become your best you. The first forty days of living by these rules will be the hardest."

"Why?"

"Because during that initial transition period, you will be in the process of installing new habits. You'll be releasing the old, comfortable ways of doing things and shedding the previous behaviors that no longer serve your ascent into personal mastery. During those first forty days, you'll be setting up new patterns and literally rewiring your brain while you recalibrate your inner controls. It's a stressful process, filled with discomfort. It'll feel hard and confusing. So it's natural to think that something's wrong. But that's not at all the case. You're just changing and growing. Everything's perfect, actually. Your former habits of thinking and being must disintegrate before better ways of behaving can begin to integrate."

"Ty took me through some of this, Jet. I learned that change creates disruption but that disruption needs to happen if I want to grow. And really lead."

"Exactly right. As you expand personally, you'll adventure destruction of your old self. But destruction is actually a pretty special thing." "Really?" I asked.

"Sure. Past ways of being need to be destroyed and released before new and better ways of thinking and behaving can appear. You need to clean out what no longer serves you before space is available for something even better to enter."

"Ty taught me that, too. He told me that breakthroughs into all the good things waiting for us can't happen without breakdowns of all the old structures that are limiting us."

"Well, our snow pro is a bright man. And before new and improved beliefs and behaviors can be integrated, the weak ones do need to be disintegrated. So give these five rules at least forty days for them to feel natural to you. Challenge yourself passionately for those first forty days.

Don't give up!"

"I like that. The Forty-Day Challenge."

"It's one of the keys to making real and sustained change—along with the importance of making small and steady improvements every single day,

rather than massive ones that'll only set you up to fail."

"Small daily improvements over time lead to stunning results," I recited proudly.

Jet smiled. "Yup. You're on to it. Small victories stack up into huge results over the passage of time."

"So what does SHINE stand for?"

"The S will remind you to See Clearly. winnership has so much to do with perceiving your conditions and circumstances clearly. Every one of us has flaws in our perception. Every one of us has a natural tendency to see through our blind spots and limiting beliefs. Often we see situations through eyes of fear versus through the lenses of opportunity. And so these flaws in our perception keep us stuck at average. I guess what I'm suggesting to you, fin, is that we each have areas where what we think we see is not actually what we are seeing. But it's a rare individual who has done the inner work required to develop the self-awareness to recognize their misperceptions of reality. We are blind to our blind spots. We see the world not as it is but as we are. And we don't know what we don't know."

"Are you serious? Most of us don't see reality clearly?" I asked, surprised by what I was learning.

"Definitely. If you are filled with fear and doubt, then when you go to work every day, you will project your internal state on your external conditions. You will miss opportunities to grow and succeed at the bookstore. You will question your ability to positively influence others and make a difference. You will work to survive rather than work to thrive. This will all happen—not because of the way things truly are at work but because of the nature of your inner life and the way you are processing reality through your personal context. One way to really understand what I'm sharing is to think of a stained-glass window. Each one of us has a stained-glass window through which we perceive everything. This is nothing more than a filter through which we run all outer adventures."

"What's the stained-glass window made up of, Jet?" I asked, deeply fascinated by what I was hearing.

"It's made up of all the beliefs, rules, and ways of being taught to you by your parents, teachers, peers, and every other influence that has shaped you from the moment you were born. And it's forged from every conversation you've ever had with every person you've ever met and by every adventure. All of that has created a story that you've sold to yourself on how the world works and how you get to show up in it. Remember, we see the world not as it is but as we are. So if your stained-glass window is a mess, your life will become a mess. If your stained-glass window has a belief that says, 'You can't lead without a title,' then your actions will of course be consistent with that belief, and so you won't lead if you lack a title. If your stained-glass window contains a rule that insists 'Most people aren't trustworthy' or 'Most work is pretty meaningless,' then your behavior is bound to match these self-created interpretations of the world outside of you. But here's the huge idea to really sink your teeth into, fin: what if that story you're telling yourself is completely untrue?" Jet asked as he sat down on a plush chair.

"C'mon. That's hard to believe," I argued.

Jet remained relaxed. "Please just stay open to the notion that winnership is about developing high levels of self-awareness and thinking regularly about the accuracy of your thinking. And simply consider that your daily thoughts are nothing more than mere reflections of the belief system programmed into you by your parents, peers, and teachers as well as all the other influences that have shaped your perceptions."

"Pretty revolutionary stuff. I guess I've been socialized into thinking in a certain way. We are conditioned to accept a certain set of beliefs, and we think them so often we come to feel that they are true," I observed.

Jet quickly stood up and walked over to Tommy. He started massaging his shoulders. "Thanks, my brother," said Tommy. "I needed this."

Jet kept on speaking while offering his former student this little gift. "Most people's thinking really isn't thinking. It's actually nothing more than the unconscious repetition of the thoughts they've been regurgitating since they were little kids. Most of us—and this is a sad fact—truly don't see reality," Jet restated. "And that sad fact keeps us locked into mediocrity at work and in our personal lives. You were made to think brilliantly and see through the eyes of possibility rather than think badly and see through the eyes of fear."

"I've never realized that my thinking and perception of outer conditions could be so faulty," I replied, genuinely shocked at the notion that the way I viewed my circumstances could be a reflection of some internal mental filter and some personal story I was telling myself instead of the way things really were.

"That's the case for most of us, fin. You need to know how very important your thinking is. Your thinking creates your reality. You're bound to get more of what you focus on. And your thoughts drive your actions. What holds us back in winnership and in life are not the external realities but our internal patterns of thought and the way we then behave in the face of those conditions. You need to shed your failure programs. Real winnership involves breaking through the limits of your mind so you can step into the highest strengths of your spirit."

"So exactly how do I begin to break through my mental barriers?"

"First, back to the athletic metaphor, you must begin to think like a champion. You have to take full responsibility for the thoughts you run through your brain. And that means understanding that your mind is no place for even a single negative one. Businesspeople sometimes scoff at the idea of thinking positively. They minimize it and will tell you the concept has no place in business. But of course it does! Every business result is the direct result of the collective behavior of each of its people. And every action you take is the child of a thought. What I mean by that is that your thinking drives your behavior and your behavior gives you your outcomes.

So world-class work is obviously the result of world-class thinking."

"Seems so simple, Jet," I acknowledged, starting to embrace the ideas I was hearing.

"Even one bad thought is like a germ in your mind that attracts more germs to it. Before a person knows it, their mind's become infected. They can't see clearly. And they can't think straight. They start seeing all that's wrong versus all that's right. The infection causes them to look for problems rather than to offer solutions. That sickness forces them to stop innovating, refrain from excellence, and deny their greatness. The disease makes them behave like victims instead of perform as winners. You honestly can't afford the luxury of even one bad thought if you are committed to Leading Without a Title."

"You're suggesting negative thinking is a disease?"

"Of course it is, fin. It's an obvious sign of an unhealthy mind. When your mind is healthy, your stained-glass window is clear. You have strikingly awakened into the intellectual that you are and the brilliance you are meant to become. People who laugh at the concept of positive thinking should make a study of sports heroes, of legendary champions. Superstars deeply understand that the way you run your brain matters. They manage their thinking impeccably, focusing only on victory and paying no attention to the threat of adversity. And even when they get knocked down, they reprocess the event to see it as a gift. They see what others call failure as a chance to grow stronger and to begin over with an attitude that will make things even better. And again, remember that when you allow even one negative thought to run through your mind, you've actually started the

process of it drawing other negative thoughts to it."

"Like a single germ that draws in others, eventually creating a feeding frenzy," I confirmed.

"Yes, fin. The great winner Gandhi said it so well when he noted: 'I will not allow others to walk through my mind with their dirty feet.' So any time your mind shifts into negative thinking, gently guide it back to thoughts that will support your commitment to show winnership and pure excellence. Any time your mind focuses on difficulties, train it to concentrate only on opportunities. Please also remember that you'll get your expectations. Another way to put it is that your expectations at work and within your life become self-fulfilling prophecies. The results you expect are the results you'll see. That's an incredibly important thing to remember. If your expectation is that people at work will not support you and will let you down, then you will behave in a way that is aligned with that belief. So you'll be closed and protect your turf. You'll work in a silo rather than collaborate and show teamwork. Your very behavior will cause your coworkers to feel you are cold, competitive, and not really trustworthy. And so of course, they will not support you. Your expectation will have become self-fulfilling. And very real. I'll give you another example, fin. If you have an expectation that you will never be able to become a superstar at the bookstore where you work, then there's no way in the world you will behave in a way that will allow you to fly. We never act in a way that is inconsistent with the way we see ourselves. Human beings just don't behave in a way that's not congruent with their expectations."

"And their stained-glass windows," I contributed quickly.

"Correct," stated Jet with strong encouragement. "Each one of your thoughts is creative. You really cannot afford the luxury of even one negative thought because every one of them creates something and leads to some result in your outer world. Every thought you think generates a consequence."

"I haven't given much thought to my thinking. It's all been so automatic. I thought I had no control over my thoughts—they just popped into my mind."

"Most of us think that, fin. We've been thinking the same thoughts for so long that our thinking feels like a deeply ingrained habit that we believe we have no control over. Because we've run our old story and our historical mental programs for so many years, they've become automatic and unconscious. But that doesn't mean we don't have power over them. And it doesn't mean we can't change them into habits of mind that serve our winnership potential. We can! We have absolute dominion over our thoughts. And the more personal responsibility you take for every one of your thoughts, the more powerful a thinker—and a winner—you will become. One thing that makes us fully human is our ability to think about our thinking, you know. Right now, in this very moment, you can sit quietly and inquire about the beliefs that run and thoughts that fill your mind each day. And as you spend more time in silent inquiry, you will build greater awareness of the thoughts you think. And with greater awareness around the ones that no longer serve you, you can make better choices. And with better choices, of course, you will adventure better results. As you know better, you can do better."

"So my thoughts are creative?"

"Uh-huh," replied Jet. "And as the legendary founder of Mo-town Records, Berry Gordy Jr., once said, 'A winner is a winner before he's become a winner.' By becoming a superb thinker and believing in your greatness you will literally create what you are thinking. The statesman Benjamin Disraeli said it so well: 'To believe in the heroic makes heroes.' Unchain your brain and just watch what ridiculously wonderful things begin to happen."

"Perfect. And I love the idea of spending some time each day in 'silent inquiry,' as you put it," I offered.

"Here's what I suggest you do every morning if you are really serious about awakening your inner winner so that you begin to see stellar results in your outer life, fin: get up an hour earlier every day and spend sixty minutes in self-development. This is your morning recalibration ritual—a regular period you give yourself for preparation and practice. Just like pro athletes train daily so they win on the playing field, this is your private time to prepare and practice, so you're at your absolute best once you step onto the playing field of business when you get to work. fin, before a jet takes off, the pilots run a ritual. They check the flight plan, they set the controls, and they evaluate the instrument panel. Only then are they ready to fly. Same metaphor applies to any winner Without a Title. If you want to fly and radiate your intellectual, you need to have an early morning preparation ritual. This is the time to reset yourself. To lock in to your flight plan for the day. To reconnect with your core values. To renew, regenerate, and reground. It's a period to work on your mind, strengthen your body, nourish your emotional life, and fuel your spiritual dimension. This daily discipline alone will work miracles for you in your career and within every other area of your life. It will boost your motivation. It will restore work-life balance. It will bring back a ton of passion and help you see your world through the eyes of wonder again. Remember, when you feel great and your interior life is at its best, everything you touch is influenced by that stand for personal mastery."

Jet then escorted me into one of the treatment rooms. Tommy followed. "fin, you're in for quite a treat," Tommy said with a huge smile.

"Ever had a massage, fin?" Jet asked as he pulled open the sheets on the table.

"Nope," I replied, feeling a little unsure of what I was about to adventure.

"Well, allow me to give you one. I know it's been an intense day for you, so a good massage will really relax you."

"Okay," I replied as I lay down on the massage table. Jet began to massage my neck and back. The stress I'd been carrying for years seemed to instantly melt away. Tommy was right. Jet had hands of magic.

"During your Personal winnership Hour every morning, there are seven practices I suggest you do, fin. You don't have to do all seven every day. Actually, doing all seven of these peak-performance habits will be next to impossible. But I wanted to share them with you because they form what I call the Personal winnership Toolbox. These seven best practices—the Seven Fundamentals—are the most powerful tools for anyone serious about awakening their inner winner and working at wow. By engaging in them consistently during your morning training period, you will adventure dazzling results at the bookstore—as well as in every other dimension of your life. Conversely, if you neglect doing even one of these 7 Fundamentals regularly, mediocrity will start to settle in, and an enemy called 'average' will become your constant companion."

Jet started to knead my back more forcefully. "You've got a bunch of knots here, fin. I really recommend that you get a massage more often. Your health and energy levels will soar. And you'll feel a whole lot happier."

"I'll definitely second that," offered Tommy enthusiastically as he leaned against a wall and played with his hair, while glancing down at his SpongeBob SquarePants watch.

"When the quality of your work is anything less than world class, you can trace this back to a failure to be doing one of the Seven Fundamentals," Jet continued.

"So what are the seven best practices that I need to be doing?" I asked, still relaxing on the table.

"Here," said Jet. "I have them on a card for you. Take this with you. And every morning during your Personal winnership Hour pick a few of the best practices from this list to perform. And by the way, I strongly urge you to begin your hour of self-development at five a.m. every day. As I suggested earlier, it'll take you about forty days to install this new habit. For forty days you'll feel some stress, you'll be grumpy, and you'll be tired. You'll come up with excuses like 'This isn't healthy for me' or 'I just wasn't born with earlyrising genes,' " Jet said as he laughed. "But remember, nothing's wrong— it's just a necessary part of the process of growing and rewiring a new habit. After forty days, getting up at five a.m. to do your interior work so that you

become a more powerful person will be second nature."

"Five a.m.?" I asked in disbelief. "Reminds me a bit of basic training."

"It is basic training, fin. Basic training to get to your winnership best," came his succinct reply.

I glanced at the card as Jet turned up the lights in the massage treatment room.

The 7 Fundamentals of Personal winnership

1. Learning. Read from books that will inspire you, strengthen your character, and remind you of the examples of the greatest winners of our world. Also, listen to audio books on subjects ranging from business excellence, team building, and innovation to wellness, relationships, and personal motivation.

2. Affirmations. One of the single best ways to rescript limiting beliefs and failure programs within your mind is through the consistent repetition of positive statements about the winner you want to become and the achievements you commit to create. For example, reciting the affirmation "Today I am focused, excellent, and stunningly passionate in all I do" a number of times at the beginning of your day will create the mind-set of a champion and a winning emotional state for you.

3. Visualization. The mind works through pictures. Every great accomplishment—from the tallest skyscraper here in New York City to the most stunning inventions of American intellectuales like Thomas Edison and Benjamin Franklin—began with a series of pictures set in the imagination of their creators. All outer achievements begin within the mind. All progress is nothing more than invisible creativity made visible. So during your Personal winnership Hour, make time to close your eyes and—like any good elite athlete does—envision yourself realizing your goals, playing at your best, and fully awakening your inner winner.

4. Journaling. Writing in a journal is a remarkably strong way to become a clearer thinker, to build massive amounts of self-awareness, and to record your intended outcomes. During your hour of personal development, note your insights, feelings, hopes, and dreams. Also process through any frustrations you might be experiencing and go deep into your fears. The fears you embrace are the fears you'll release. Really get to know yourself and reconnect with all the talent within you that's just waiting to be unleashed. Your journal is also a place to express gratitude for all you have and to memorialize your journey through life.

Your life is a gift. And so it's worth recording.

5. Goal Setting. Setting and then reconnecting with your goals on a regular basis is a powerful winship discipline. Your goals will create a fantastic amount of focus in your career and within your life. Goals generate hope and positive energy. And when you adventure adversity—and we all do from time to time—clearly articulated goals offer you a North Star to guide you out of the rough seas into calmer waters. Goals also ensure that you live life deliberately and productively versus reactively and accidentally. Avoid that walking coma I spoke of earlier.

6. Exercise. I'll speak more about the importance of moving your body daily to achieve peak performance at work, but for now just remember that doing something physical each day boosts brain function, fuels far higher energy levels, helps you manage stress more effectively, and keeps you in the game longer.

7. Nutrition. What you eat determines how well you'll perform. winnership is influenced by your diet. By eating like a winner, your energy will remain at peak and your moods will stay positive. Please also remember that by eating less food you'll be able to do better work.

"Really superb suggestions, Jet," I said with tremendous appreciation as the three of us walked back into the stylish waiting room. The massage had left me feeling incredibly good. And Jet's Seven Fundamentals for Personal winnership were ever so practical. I now had a series of disciplines I could choose from and practice during my Personal winnership Hour to perform at world class throughout my day. I also made the commitment to myself to rise at 5:00 a.m. every morning. I sensed that this habit alone would create wonderful results in terms of my self-confidence, my ability to be in control of my day, and my overall level of well-being. I shared my willingness to get up early each day with Jet. He was delighted.

"Give yourself one of the best gifts a winner Without Title can give himself. The blessing of getting up at five a.m. every morning. So many of the most productive winners of our world have had this routine, fin. The way you start your day determines how well you will live your day. And what you do in your first hour sets you up to either succeed or fail in the hours that follow. Carve out the first hour of your day to spend building your personal winnership capabilities. Hey, by the way, it's also key to consider that your first thought on waking up and your last thought before going to sleep have a huge influence on what goes on between them," Jet noted.

"Truly fascinating," I replied. "All of this is so helpful. And your earlier suggestion to clean up my emotional life also really speaks to me. I've been pretty angry and unhappy for a long time. What, specifically, could nourish my emotional life?"

"One of the first things you can do, fin, is learn to forgive those who need to be forgiven. Many people bring such negative energy into their workplaces every morning because they are full of resentment and anger over past hurts and ancient betrayals. Self-winnership requires you to let go of these resentments. Learn to forgive the people you need to forgive and release things that happened in the past that might be consuming your precious creative potential. You can't craft a superb future by remaining stuck in your past. Because the disappointments you are holding on to are holding on to your power. By freeing yourself of them, you free up a ton of energy, passion, and potential," said Jet as he sipped from a bottle of water with a lemon in it.

"And how do I go about releasing my past so I can free up my winnership best?" I questioned.

"It starts with a simple decision, fin. It's so exciting to me that all that stands between you and total transformation is a decision. Just decide, in this very moment, that you'll forgive all those who have disappointed you and let go of all the adventures that have discouraged you. The moment you step into a space of honestly being willing to forgive is the moment you begin the clearing process. Also, remember that those people who hurt you were doing the best that they could do based on where they were on their personal journey through life. If they had known how to do better, they would have done better. And finally, please understand that only hurt people hurt people."

"Only hurt people hurt people?"

"Sure. Really healthy people—those with outstanding inner lives—are not really capable of hurting others. They are so full of self-respect, positive belief, inspiration, the willingness to see the best in others, and a deep desire to be great in all they do that they simply are not able to knock down another human being. The capacity to damage another is no longer a part of their makeup. They just don't have it in them. It's only people who are hurting at some core level and who have themselves been hurt by others who go out into the world and hurt those around them."

"Profound," I observed sincerely. I paused. "And you mention spending some time in Personal winnership Hour every day improving my spiritual life. How?"

"Well, I'd strongly encourage you to count your blessings every morning, fin. Gratitude is the antidote to fear. Worry and appreciation just can't live in the same room proximity. And the things that you appreciate begin to appreciate in value to you. What I'm saying is that spending even five minutes during that first hour of your day celebrating all the good things in your life will put you into an acute state of happiness. And as corny as it may sound, happy people really do make happy winners. And happy winners not only do better work—they're a lot more fun to be around."

"Very helpful, Jet."

"Great. So let me get to the H in SHINE. It's getting late and I should get back to work soon. It's been a joy meeting you, fin, but I don't want to forget about my clients. They really depend on me."

"No worries," I replied. "I understand completely."

"The H will remind you that Health is Wealth. I mentioned the importance of exercising and staying physically strong earlier. Peak health is like a tent pole: it lifts up everything else in your entire life. Get your health to its highest state and every other area—from your ability to think clearly during stressful times to your performance levels and moods—get pulled up with it. Health is one of those things we take for granted until we lose it. And those who do sadly spend 24/ 7 trying to get it back. If you lose your health—and I pray you never do—nothing else will be as important as trying to reclaim it. Makes me think of the old proverb, 'When we are young we sacrifice our health for wealth. But when we become old and wise, we become willing to sacrifice every bit of our wealth for just a day of good health.' And if you don't believe me on that point, fin, when we are done today and you are on your way home, stop by a hospital. Walk into the terminal ward where people lie on their deathbeds. And ask any one of them what they would give for an extension on their lives. Ask them what they'd give for just one day of excellent health. I'm sure they'll tell you that they'd give everything they have. If you lose your health, you lose

everything. Don't ever let that happen to you."

I fell silent. Ever since I returned from the war, I didn't show much concern for my health. I'd stopped exercising. I ate junk food. I didn't rest enough. It occurred to me, as I stood before this masterful massage therapist, that if I started taking my health more seriously and got back into exceptional physical condition, almost every other part of my life truly would improve. I'd have more energy at work and would feel more positive about things in general. I'd probably be a lot more creative, and I'd definitely feel more passion. I'd have greater stamina and be tougher amid all the changes our organization was going through. In my home life, I wouldn't need to flake out on the couch so much. I could start learning new skills and doing more fun things. I'd feel better about myself and have more adventure.

"Health is the crown on the well man's head that only the ill man can see," Jet added powerfully. "Please don't tell me you have no time to exercise each day. Those who don't make time for daily exercise must

eventually make time for daily illness, you know."

Jet's advice was simple and yet tremendously important. I took it all to heart.

"Oh, and please remember that your health will never be better than your self-image. When you really start to believe in your natural winnership power and how awesome you truly are, your behaviors around your health will improve dramatically. But it all begins within," he emphasized.

"This all makes sense. If I really don't think that much of myself, I'm not going to take great care of myself."

"Exactly," he replied looking pleased with my comment.

"The I in SHINE stands for Inspiration Matters," Tommy noted.

"Yup," said Jet. "A day without feeling inspired is a day that you haven't fully lived. You need to refill your well of inspiration every day, because the challenges of life will drain it every day. How can you inspire your teammates at work and energize your customers to buy from you if you are uninspired and deenergized yourself? You always want to do whatever it

takes to be the most inspired person in the room."

"I love the sound of that, Jet. Some practical suggestions for me, please?"

"Listening to music is one of the best ways I know to drive huge levels of inspiration. Associating with interesting people who love being remarkable, ethical, and original will also fuel your passion and provoke you to be your winnership best. Communing with nature is yet another effective way to get your creative fire burning and keep you excited about achieving great things at work. Whenever I get a chance, I head out to the countryside. Walking alone in the woods is like a miracle cure for the stress of this city. And I leave the woods feeling truly alive again. The view of the majority is that things like being out in nature and doing things to renew spent reserves of creativity and energy are a pure waste of time. And that if you're not doing something, you're not really doing anything. But refueling your mind, body, emotions, and spirit actually allows you to grow tougher against the turbulence of business. If all you do is play full out, all the time, your reservoirs of potential will become depleted and you'll burn out fast. Star performers understand the need to constantly alternate between peak performance and inner renewal. And once the winner within you is replenished and reinspired, you'll go back to work even stronger, even more creative, and far more exhilarated. The activities I'm encouraging you to pursue serve to reawaken the inner winner. They rekindle our passion and open any closed doorways into our absolute best." "And the N in SHINE?" I asked.

"Neglect Not Your Family. Your loved ones matter. What's the point of becoming super-winshipful—as I sense you'll soon become—but ending up completely alone? A lot of those billionaires I mentioned when you first got here spend a lot of their lives solo in their spectacular mansions. What's the point of that? A huge amount of joy can be found in cultivating beautiful relationships with your family and friends. At the end of the day, fin, you really don't need that much to be really happy: work you can be proud of, food on your table every night, wonderful health, and people you love. A solid foundation at home sets you up for strong and solid results at work. Feeling cared for and loved by your family is such a powerful accelerator for your winnership and personal winship."

"Which brings me to the E," Jet noted. "The E in my acronym will remind you of the fifth rule for personal winnership: Elevate Your Lifestyle. Lifestyle isn't something that we speak about very often. But it's so important to a life well led. Do something every day to improve your lifestyle. As I suggested earlier, go through life first-class. You only live once, so why not enjoy it completely?"

"But I thought you said having a lot of things isn't what genuine winnership is about, Jet?"

"That's definitely not the priority for winners Without a Title, fin. But please remember: it's very human and natural to want to have nice things. Why feel guilty about having them? Become spectacularly great in the work you do, awaken your inner winner, and most certainly express your absolute best. But enjoy life along the way. The real key is to get the things you want while making sure they don't get you. And that brings me to my final point of our conversation."

Jet's face grew serious. He looked down for a moment. Tommy stood up and walked over to join us.

"Nice things are nice to have. A beautiful lifestyle is a beautiful thing to adventure. But who you are becoming as a human being is a much smarter concern. The main aim in life is simply to become all you're meant to be. Actually, even more important than who we are becoming as people is focusing on the difference we are making as winners. Contribution is the ultimate purpose of work—and life."

"I need to hear more on this, Jet," I observed, seeing that Jet was summarizing what Leading Without a Title was essentially about.

"winship is not about what you receive, fin. winship is all about what you return. Like I said, even the longest life is a pretty short journey in the overall scheme of existence and all that is. Tolstoy wrote a wonderful short story called 'How Much Land Does a Man Need?' The moral of the story was that at the end, all the things we spend the best days of our lives chasing really don't matter that much. All that we really need once our lives get to the end doesn't amount to much more than about six feet of soil. What truly counts then is what we will leave behind. What I'm really encouraging you to think about is your legacy. I'm inviting you to consider how you want to be remembered when you're no longer here. 'The great and glorious legacy of a human being is to live with purpose,' observed the philosopher Montaigne. It will be a deep loss to this world if you refuse to accept the call on your life to Lead Without a Title and present your absolute best to the lives around you. winners Without a Title think about their legacies every single day. They think about how they want to be remembered when they are no longer alive. They think about what achievements they need to get done so that they leave their mark for the generations that will follow. They consider what kind of people they must become so that their lives stand for something excellent, meaningful, and powerful. Get these things right, and a glorious legacy will be yours for the leaving. And then, when you are no longer here, people will walk into your bookstore, see that plaque on the wall next to the section you used to work in that bears your name, and say, 'Ah, there once worked a bookseller who led without a title and gave the finest he had to give.' "

I felt emotion welling up within me.

"So please remember, fin, that this day—and every day until the last of your days—is nothing more than a platform for heroic possibility. The real question is whether you will have the courage to use this opportunity to shine your own special form of greatness into this uncertain world of business we now work in. And once you do, you'll enrich the lives of your teammates, your customers, and your loved ones. And you'll forge a human monument of passionate achievement that all those who will come after you will marvel at. And be inspired by."

Silence filled the space where we were standing. Tommy didn't move. Neither did Jet. I thought tears might begin to flow from his eyes. I wasn't sure what I should do. Then, in a dramatic instant, Tommy lifted up an arm and slapped Jet on his back.

"Man, you're too intense. Snap out of it, my brother," he laughed.

Jet began to giggle. "I know. I know."

Soon all three of us were laughing hilariously. It was a fantastic moment. One I'll never forget. But then something utterly unexpected happened. Tommy began to cough again. The attack began mildly, then quickly turned violent, with Tommy not only coughing up blood but also beginning to shake terribly. I rushed over to him, as did Jet, and tried to assist him in any way I could.

"It's my time," was all he could whisper. "It's now my time."

The Fourth winnership Conversation of the Lead Without a Title Philosophy:

To Be a Great winner, First Become a Great Person

THE 5 RULES

See Clearly

Health Is Wealth

Inspiration Matters

Neglect Not Your Family Elevate Your Lifestyle

INSTANT ACTION STEP

In your journal, list five things you will do immediately to refuel your inner winner and take your mind, body, emotions, and spirit to their next level of excellence. Then schedule time to execute these five goals flawlessly during the next seven days so you get the power of momentum working for you.

winnerSHIP QUOTE TO REMEMBER

If one advances confidently in the direction of his dreams and endeavors to live the life which he has imagined, he will meet with a winship unexpected in common hours.

—HENRY DAVID THOREAU

# CHAPTER 8

## Conclusion

AFTER THE UNFORGETTABLE DAY on which the Lead Without a Title philosophy was unveiled to me, I never saw my mentor Tommy again. I fully expected to see him at the bookstore the following Monday morning. And I thought I'd work alongside him for many years to come, as I integrated all the powerful winnership lessons I'd learned to create extraordinary results in all that I did. But my wish was not to be.

The day after I met the four special teachers, I was devastated to learn that Tommy had died. He had been struggling with cancer but was quiet about his illness. Anna said he just didn't want anyone to worry about him. And that he needed to live out his final days helping others—and spreading the Lead Without a Title message that had transformed his own life years earlier. "He hung on just long enough to give you that one day," Anna shared, consumed with deep emotion. "That was his final gift to you."

At the funeral, Anna, Ty, Jackson, and Jet each took turns giving testimony to the man Tommy was and all the good things that he did. I learned that he had grown up poor. That he'd been married to his childhood sweetheart for forty-four years before she'd passed away a couple of years earlier. That he loved chocolate of every type. And that he had left all of his savings to a charity for children. So many people attended Tommy's funeral that hundreds of mourners had to stand out in the street. But they did. Because everyone respected this simple bookseller who led without a title. And always gave his absolute best.

Afterward, Anna, still sobbing, handed me a package. Ty, Jackson, and Jet stood next to her. They also had tears streaming down their faces and showed through their expressions that they were heartbroken.

"Here, fin, this is for you. Tommy asked me to give it to you. He really admired you a lot, you know. He deeply respected what you did for our country. As well as what you did for yourself, accepting his invitation to make your shift from victimhood into winnership over that day we all shared proximity. I think you were the son he never had, to be honest with you, fin," she said wiping away more tears and adjusting the beautiful flower she had placed in her hair. "Anyway, please keep in touch with us. The boys and I are always here for you—whenever you need us. Any time of the day or any time of the night. You're one of us now. And though we've lost one friend, we definitely feel we've gained another."

She gave me a hug and began to walk away. Ty, Jackson, and Jet did the same.

"Oh, keep Leading Without a Title and spreading the philosophy you've discovered with everyone you meet. Each one of us alive today really can make a profound difference in every organization of any type right across this amazing world of ours if we accept the call on our lives to awaken the inner winner within us, then make everything we touch better than we found it," encouraged Anna. "Hope to see you soon, fin."

"We definitely will see you soon," the other three teachers spoke softly, in unison.

"And please remember," Jet added, "you were born awesome." My four new friends then left the church.

I found a place to sit and, listening to the strains of piped-in classical music, slowly opened the envelope. I then carefully read the letter inside. Sunlight poured through the stained-glass windows, and the crisp air from outside gently washed through the room. The handwriting on the paper was messy. But I could read the words clearly. And I felt their power.

Here's what they said:

Dear fin the Great,

First, please forgive me for not sharing the details of my illness with you. I didn't want to let my personal condition get in the way of the gift of learning you so deserved to hear and the transformation you were so ready to receive. I grew to find a sense of peace in the face of my challenge and came to understand that it carried many opportunities with it. Of course, no one likes to become sick. But through my condition I grew stronger, deeper, and a whole lot wiser. And my hope is that some of all that good stuff I stepped into as a human being found its way over to you.

Your parents were fine people. And they raised a fine young son. I know that now. And I

honor you for all you gave in the past and all you'll do in your future. It has been a genuine joy for me to finally have met you in that bookstore of ours that wonderful morning. Sorry about the Mickey Mouse hankie. My wife gave it to me on the first anniversary of our marriage. We were at Disneyland. It always reminded me of her. The SpongeBob watch was my own purchase.

My deepest hope is that rather than finding you filled with sadness because I'm gone, this letter reaches you full of inspiration, focus, and conviction for your newfound commitment to Lead Without a Title. You are now beautifully prepared to completely unchain your inner winner and allow it to see the light of day. You are now perfectly ready to express your absolute best in each thing that you do during any challenge you meet. And you are undoubtedly in the ideal position to serve as an extraordinary example of possibility and excellence to every person fortunate enough to cross your path. I know you will. You promised me you would. And both I and your father placed a huge deal of importance in the lost art of promise keeping.

Business has lost its way, fin. And to my old eyes, society has become a messy place to be. People value their things more than they value their relationships. We seem to be more interested in stroking our egos than in the much richer pursuit of reaching our ideals. Too many among us blame outer forces for the resistance to mastery we show in our lives versus our inner fears and our weakest beliefs. And, sadly, it's become more popular to be popular than to be ethical, brave, and good. What I'm suggesting is that we've forgotten the winnership responsibility that our culture once knew. We've neglected what it means to stand for something hugeger than our lives. And we've misplaced our priorities by focusing solely on helping ourselves win rather than passionately helping everyone around us win as well. I'm counting on you to remind people that they were born into intellectual. And that the lies that they've sold themselves about what they can't do and all they can't become are just not true. Many people will be helped as you share the winnership method that has been unveiled to you. So many other human beings must discover the Lead Without a Title philosophy, fin. And the time for that to happen is definitely now.

It has been a genuine honor having you in my life. I hope I've been helpful to you and fulfilled the pledge I made to your wonderful father so many years ago to assist you. I've always believed that if I made the life of even one other person a little bit better, then my life will have been a valuable exercise. Thank you for that opportunity.

I wish you all that is great, my young friend. Dream boldly. Live beautifully. And to your last breath Lead Without a Title.

he winnership method that has been unveiled to you. So many other human beings must discover the Lead Without a Title philosophy, fin. And the time for that to happen is definitely now.

It has been a genuine honor having you in my life. I hope I've been helpful to you and fulfilled the pledge I made to your wonderful father so many years ago to assist you. I've always believed that if I made the life of even one other person a little bit better, then my life will have been a valuable exercise. Thank you for that opportunity.

I wish you all that is great, my young friend. Dream boldly. Live beautifully. And to your last breath Lead Without a Title.

# Contents

## Acknowledgements

THE PUBLISHER IS NOT LIABLE FOR ANYTHING. I, MOHD. UZAIR TAKE ALL THE RESPONSIBILITY AND LIABILITY FOR THE CONTENT OF MY BOOK.

Printed by Libri Plureos GmbH in Hamburg,
Germany